STANDING UP FOR HUMANITY

STANDING UP FOR HUMANITY

Thoughts on the World Economy, the Politics of World Peace, and the Role of Religion

JOHN HUDDLESTON

Bahá'í Publishing Trust

Bahá'í House, 6 Canning Road
New Delhi-110001, India

First Edition : 1999 (January)

ISBN : 81-86953-43-4

Approved for publication by
The National Spiritual Assembly of the Baha'is of India

Laser typeset by Laser Print Craft, Delhi-110051
Rakmo Press Pvt. Ltd., C-95, Okhla Ind. Area, Phase-l,
New Delhi - 110 020, Phone : 6810424, 6814886, 6816282

CONTENTS

Religion and the Spiritual Dimension

NOTE ON PUBLICATION OF THESE ARTICLES ELSEWHERE

Article   **Publication**

1. Bahá'í Studies Notebook, Volume III, 1984
2. Herald of the South, April 1987
   Glory Magazine, Volume XII, number 3
3. Journal of Bahá'í Studies. Volume III, number 3
7. Towards the Most Great Justice, edited by Charies Lerche, Bahá'í Publishing Trust (UK), 1996
10. Finance and Development, March 1995
12. The Bahá'í Faith and Marxism: Proceedings, ABS Conference, 1986
13. Herald of the South, January-March, 1992
20. Herald of the South, June and April, 1986
21. Dialogue Magazine, Volume II. No 2/3, 1988
22. Transitions to a Global Society, edited by Suheil Bushrui, Iraj Ayman, and Ervin Laslo, One World, 1993.
23. Towards the 21st Century: Crisis and Renewal, Association of Bahá'í Studies (Japan) Proceedings, 1995

INTRODUCTION

This book is a follow up to a trip to India under-taken by my wife, Rouhi, and myself in the last quarter of 1995 at the invitation of the National Spiritual Assembly of the Bahá'ís of India. During that trip we visited some 15 cities in different regions of the country and gave 65 public talks on current events from the Bahá'í perspective and took part in some 66 media interviews and similar events. Ramnik Shah, Secretary of the National Spiritual Assembly asked that some of the talks be made available in book form. Accordingly, nine talks given on that trip, covering most of the main topics that were discussed, are included in this publication, of which 5 were repeats of presentations that had been given earlier in other countries. In addition, the book contains 11 other talks on related subjects given over the years elsewhere in Asia, Africa, the Americas, and Europe, together with 7 published and unpublished articles. In broad terms, they all address various aspects of the process of humanity becoming one, and are grouped under three general headings: the economy, peace and religion. I wish to express particular gratitude to Ramnik Shah and to my wife for all their encouragement and support during the long period of pulling together this book. Without such encouragement it certainly would not have seen the light of day!

Mclean, Virginia,
January, 1999

DEDICATION

This book is a small token of thanks for all the kindness we have received from the wonderful Bahá'ís of India, the largest Bahá'í Community in the world and great leaders in standing up for humanity.

THE ECONOMY OF A GLOBAL SOCIETY

THE ECONOMY OF A WORLD COMMONWEALTH

A presentation at the 7th Annual Conference of the Association for Bahá'í Studies, Ottawa, Canada, 1982

On September 3, 1912, 'Abdu'l-Bahá addressed a socialist group in Montreal. That address constitutes one of the principal sources of information on the Bahá'í approach to economics[1]. This subject and others dealing with a future Bahá'í society are not often reviewed because most of our efforts are directed to more immediate matters such as teaching, personal growth, and development of institutions. Nevertheless, periodic reviews of the long-term objectives of the Faith are necessary so that the outside world can be presented with a fully-rounded "Bahá'í option" and present struggles can be put in perspective.

Before beginning a discussion of the Bahá'í approach to economics, I should like to make two general observations. First, the teachings of the Bahá'í Faith constitute a comprehensive system for human society, and economics is only one aspect of that system. The teachings are for the whole world and are intended to apply for a thousand years. Consequently, what we have is a body of broad principles which may apply to a whole range of social situations and to the evolution of those situations over a considerable period of time. Second, though Bahá'í economic teachings include many "technical devices", their main feature is a change in values. These values are associated with such concepts as the spiritual evolution of mankind and the physical existence being a time for development of spiritual qualities needed for the spiritual afterlife. Such values include the idea of the brotherhood of mankind, justice, honesty, truthfulness, work as prayer, and service as the highest form of worship.

This view that values are at the heart of economics is hardly new, though sometimes easy to forget in a period when the emphasis in current economic discussion is on econometrics and mathematical equations. A noted example of past interest in values is the study ***Religion and the Rise of Capitalism*** by the eminent British economic historian, A.H. Tawney. More recently, there has been a growing interest in the part played by religion and spiritual values in the process of economic development, as noted for example in the report of the Brandt Commission, which said that there will be no action

> "Without global consensus on the moral plane....ideas must be accepted sincerely by governments and especially by individuals....requires intensive process of education....without which there will be no true economic development and above all no justice, freedom and peace."[2]

In the last year or two, at least two distinguished economic journals, ***International Development Review*** and ***World Development,*** have devoted complete issues to the subject of religion and development. In the World Bank there is now a voluntary informal group which comes together each week to discuss spiritual values and development.

The following discussion attempts to highlight distinctive features of Bahá'í economic teachings by reviewing them in terms of three broad subject areas:

—Organization and structure of the economy
—Distribution of wealth
—Goods and services

It must be stressed that the comments made in this review are intended as a stimulus to further thought rather than as an attempt at a definitive statement.

Organization and Structure

The general picture which emerges from the Bahá'í writings concerning the organization and structure of the Bahá'í economy is that it would be unified on a world scale but decentralized, diversified, and flexible. Shoghi Effendi wrote:

> "The worldwide law of Bahá'u'lláh repudiates excessive centralization on one hand and disclaims all attempts at uniformity on the other. Its watchword is unity in diversity....."[3]

The Bahá'í texts refer to a world government with legislative, judicial, and executive branches. The economic functions envisioned for the world government as outlined below suggest that the executive branch would have departments of finance, trade, development and conservation, and a central bank. One of the main economic functions of the world government would be to unify the world economy. The internationalization of trade and commerce, already a strong movement of great benefit to nearly all, even under today's imperfect conditions, would be taken to its logical conclusion. All tariffs, quotas and other barriers to free trade would be removed. In the long run, the idea of a world economy surely also implies the free movement of peoples, although this is not specifically stated. A single world currency would be established, weights and measures would be internationally standardized. There would be a world-wide system of education, which, inter alia, would increase the economic capability and flexibility of the population, as would a universal auxiliary language, a unified legal system, and a world-wide system of communications. During the transition to a more unified world economy it would, no doubt, be necessary for the world government to provide assistance to national and local economies so that they could adjust with a minimum of hardship and disruption.

Creation of a united world economy as envisaged in the Bahá'í Writings would mean considerably more than the removal of national barriers to trade and commerce, important as this would be. It would also mean coordination and long range planning on a world scale. It would be the function of the world government to flatten trade cycles, to develop the resources of the world for the benefit of all, to work for the narrowing of the differences which now separate the rich from the poor nations, to ensure the conservation of scarce resources for the use of future generations, and to protect the world's environment

> "The economic resource of the world will be organized, the sources of raw materials will be tapped and fully utilized, its markets will be coordinated and developed, and the distribution of its products will be equitably regulated."[4]

At a time when the world is experiencing the worst recession since the Second World War [this talk was given in 1982], it is perhaps of special interest to consider how Bahá'í economic principles would affect the trade cycle. 'Abdu'l-Bahá referred to the need for local communities to stock surpluses in good years for use in years of shortage. On a world scale, this practice would tend to reduce fluctuations in supply and demand and therefore in prices. Free trade and the elimination of monopoly power (including that now exercised by the State, corporations and unions) would remove many of the inefficiencies which contribute to trade cycle fluctuations. The cycle would also tend to flatten out as a higher proportion of the economy is devoted to services and essential goods and as greater social cohesion in a Bahá'í society makes for a greater willingness to accept fair sharing of the temporary costs of economic fluctuations, including lower salaries and wages to avoid unemployment.

National and local governments would undoubtedly set certain guidelines and goals, within the overall world plan, for the development of their economies. They would also be responsible for the collection of government revenues, some of which would be allocated to the world government according to the overall economic plan. Such revenues would include income and property taxes as well as royalties from the development of minerals and other treasure found within their jurisdiction and over which they would have full control. Thus the community rather than private individuals and would benefit most from available natural resources. Local communities would also run storehouses and would take pride in providing a full range of high quality social services, such as hospitals, health centres, homes for the elderly and orphans, schools, universities, and research centers. It would also be expected that there would be strong support for creativity in the arts. It is not unreasonable to assume that in addition local communities would provide comprehensive public transportation systems and so do away with the immense waste which comes from excessive reliance on private transportation. In short, the imbalance in capitalist society between what John Kenneth Galbraith has identified as private affluence and public squalor would be corrected[5].

There seems little doubt that in a Bahá'í economy some types of industrial and commercial enterprises would also be operated by government bodies, for example the world government might be responsible for a trunk network of world communication systems. Local or national governments might control other enterprises which proved to be most efficient under single management because of their nature or because of their vital importance to the economy.

Nonetheless, the Bahá'í Writings, laying down principles for a wide range of differing conditions both in time and place, seem to support considerable diversity in the management and ownership of industrial and commercial enterprises. Accordingly, I assume that most of the economy would be in the hands of non-governmental bodies. The whole spirit of Bahá'í society suggests that such bodies would often be organized on a cooperative basis[6]. In recent years there has been a certain amount of disillusionment with cooperatives because many schemes tried over the last hundred years or so have not achieved their goals. Yet even in today's imperfect conditions, the cooperative approach can work and can eliminate many of the problems which plague modern economies such as extremes of wealth and poverty, strikes, boring jobs, and poor quality workmanship. One example of a successful cooperative system is that in the small town of Mondragon in the Basque province of Spain[7].

The cooperative is only one approach. It is also assumed that there would be great scope in the economy for the individual enterpreneur, because in a free society there must be room for an individual to follow his own bent if he wishes. Moreover, there are certain types of occupation in which the individual is the most efficient economic unit. In addition, it is historically true that the individual entrepreneur has played a very important role in bringing desirable innovations and in finding places where there is a real need for additional services. To thrive, an economy needs the stimulus of such individuals. In a Bahá'í society entrepreneurs who hire employees would be obliged to run their business on a profit-sharing basis. The local community government would supervise such schemes to ensure a fair distribution and not an empty formula as has so often happened in the past. 'Abdu'l-Bahá has written:

> "Therefore, laws and regulations should be established which would permit the workmen to receive from the factory owner their wages and a share...of the profits.[8]

The goal of a Bahá'í society is to bring together all mankind in unity. Problems and grievances, in the economic sphere as elsewhere, would be settled not through confrontation but through a system of participatory communal consultation operating in conformity with the laws of Bahá'u'lláh. Accordingly, there would be no place for factions such as political parties and pressure groups or for lockouts, strikes, owners' associations, and trade unions.

An important feature of economic organization in a Bahá'í society would be the prevailing social attitudes of those involved. Mention has already been made of cooperation. Another important attitude would be that toward work. Bahá'u'lláh stated that work is worship and that the highest form of worship is work in the service of others. The logical outcome of this attitude is that articulated by 'Abdu'l-Bahá: All should take the utmost pride in their work, however humble it may seem. An enlightened society would not be content to exploit such attitudes but would make it easier for men and women to take pride in their work by giving them responsibility and meaningful, interesting tasks. In other words, it might be expected that there would be a reversal of the modern conveyor belt factory, the horror of which was so effectively portrayed by Charlie Chaplin in the movie **Modern Times.**

Bahá'í Writings do not appear to refer to the size of enterprises except indirectly as in the comment of 'Abdu'l-Bahá about monopolistic trusts:

> "No more trusts will remain in the future. The question of trusts will be wiped out entirely."[9]

It would therefore seem reasonable to assume that there will be a wide range of size from the one-man business to vast world enterprises. Non-governmental multinational companies which can serve a useful role in spreading new ideas and technology would be more easily supervised when there is a world government. The views of the London-based **Economist** are of interest in relation to the future of the large corporation. The magazine argues that the law of economy of scale, which has justified the growth of large corporations, has also resulted in many instances in which corporations have become as rigid and inefficient as any government bureaucracy, and it foresees a trend for corporations to be reduced to a coordinating role, buying most specialized technological services from sophisticated, highly-motivated, small-scale enterprises.[10]

Before leaving the subject of economic structure and organization, mention should be made of price and interest. In a Bahá'í economy, a fair interest would be paid on loaned capital, and a fair price would be paid for goods and services. Bahá'u'lláh said that

> "it is allowable, lawful and pure to charge interest on money...but this matter must be

conducted with moderation and justice."[11]

A fair or just price would presumably take into account both the cost of production and the needs of the buyer, and accordingly would essentially follow the law of supply and demand. Rational planning in a society free of today's neurotic fears would normally ensure that supply and demand keep in balance and that, consequently, the economy would not be disrupted by erratic or violent fluctuations in prices. Should extraordinary or unforeseen circumstances arise which might cause drastic changes in price, undoubtedly the government would intervene temporarily to help social and economic adjustment. The cost element which comes from exploitation of monopolistic or semimonopolistic power would be absent.

Distribution of Wealth

Since the purpose of any economy is to provide the goods and services required by the community, the question of distribution is of the utmost significance. Bahá'í texts stress that complete equality is neither possible nor desirable.

> "Equality is a chimera! It is entirely impracticable. Even if equality could be achieved it could not continue; and if its existence were possible, the whole order of the world would be destroyed."[12]

How much equality there is should be governed by two broad principles. One is the principle of reward and punishment which Bahá'u'lláh said is an essential prerequisite for an orderly society:

> "The trainer of the world is justice, for it consists of two pillars: reward and retribution."[13]

This would imply material reward for those who work hard and contribute to the public welfare and conversely, economic penalties for those who are indolent. Thus Bahá'u'lláh condemned begging and recommended that every able-bodied adult work in a useful profession or trade:

> "Waste not your time in idleness and indolence, and occupy yourselves with that which will profit yourselves and others beside yourself."[14]

Equity would clearly indicate that this principle applies to the rich as well as to the poor. Thus a Bahá'í society would have no place for the drone, whether poor or rich. Fair reward for work would seem to imply also a major change in the structure of wages and salaries. It is inconceivable that in a Bahá'í society there would be a continuation of the present extreme, nonsensical differences which exist between those who, for instance, do the dirtiest and most dangerous tasks for society and those who are able to exploit their position and power to extract greatly inflated payments for their services.

Another aspect of the "reward and punishment" principle is the Bahá'í injunction against gambling which is an attempt to gain wealth without working for it. The term "gambling" in the Bahá'í context presumably does not include the taking of reasonable risk in investment of spare capital which can be socially useful especially in financing desirable innovations. Typically, it is assumed to mean the risking of basic family necessities against long odds for no socially useful purpose, as for instance, betting on the outcome of a sporting event.

These points lead to the second Bahá'í principle bearing on the question of distribution of resources— namely, the abolition of extremes of wealth and poverty. As noted earlier, this principle would apply when dealing with national or regional communities which vary greatly in terms of resources and wealth. One of the main economic functions of the world government would be to reduce the differences in average per capita wealth now existing between such groups.[15] This principle would also apply to differences between individuals within a community. On the one hand, society has a responsibility to ensure that none of its members ever lacks the basic material necessities of life. Thus Bahá'u'lláh wrote:

> "Know ye that the poor are the trust of God in your midst."[16]

On the other hand, gross accumulation of wealth causes corruption and marginally less and less incentive to work. 'Abdu'l-Bahá said:

> "It is important to limit riches, as it is also of importance to limit poverty. Either extreme is not good."[17]

There are many ways in which a Bahá'í society would tend to work against the accumulation of excessive wealth. Perhaps one of the most important would be the encouragement of voluntary giving—an idea consonant with the very core of a spiritually advanced civilization in which voluntary action in the social interest would be a stronger force than the instruction and law of government. In such a social environment, the rich would find more satisfaction and joy from giving selflessly for the benefit of their fellow citizens than in accumulating wealth indefinitely to live in useless luxury. 'Abdu'l-Bahá has said:

> "The time will come in the near future when humanity will become so much more sensitive than at present that the man of

great wealth will not enjoy his luxury, in
comparison with the deplorable poverty
about him. He will be forced, for his own
happiness, to expend his wealth to procure
better conditions for the community in which
he lives."[18]

Such ideas are not dreams. Even today, when
there is so much fear, insecurity, and obsession with
material possessions, many find that their greatest
satisfaction in life is giving. The Bahá'í community
itself now relies entirely for its collective activities on
the voluntary giving of its members, many of whom
give at great personal sacrifice.

Another device to prevent the accumulation of
excessive wealth would be the requirement that each
individual prepare a personal will. Bahá'u'lláh
provides guidelines in the **Kitáb-i-Aqdas** [The Book
of Laws] for the drawing up of wills encouraging men
and women to distribute their wealth at death to a
much wider circle and much more evenly than is the
current practice in most societies, especially those
emphasizing primogeniture. These guidelines suggest,
for instance, that provision should be made in a will
for one's teacher, as well as for one's children, spouse,
parents, and siblings. In the absence of a will or any
of these classes, the share which would have gone to
them would be given to the public treasury.[19] This law
is of considerable significance because inherited
wealth is frequently a greater cause of economic
inequality than differences in earned income.

A third important device for eliminating extremes
of wealth would be a progressive income tax system.
The system would include negative taxes to assist
those whose income might be less than their essential
needs. Today many nations claim to have progressive
tax systems, but reality is often very different, for

many of those paying taxes see them as an unjust imposition to pay for ends which they regard as useless or undesirable. The result is massive tax avoidance, legal loopholes, and the support of a large part of public activity through other tax systems which are regressive.[20] In a spiritually mature society, those who pay large taxes would realize that they are fortunate and honored to be able to contribute more than the average to the ends desired by the community.

Yet another principle of relevance in this context is that pertaining to the equality of men and women which implies equal pay for equal work and the opening up to women of a much wide range of occupations on a world-wide scale. In view of the fact that in the United States, but increasingly in other countries as well, poverty tends to be associated with families headed by single women, the Bahá'í emphasis on strengthening marriage unity may also make significant contribution to the abolition of poverty.

In addition to voluntary giving, personal wills, progressive taxes, and the teachings on marriage and equality of men and women, there are a great many other factors which would tend to eliminate extremes of wealth in a Bahá'í society—for example, a fair system of wages and prices, profit sharing, cooperative sharing, communal ownership of natural resources, and provision of high quality community services, including a compulsory education system.[21]

A section on the distribution of wealth cannot be complete without reference to size and growth rate of population which is generally recognized to be a factor of vital importance in helping or hindering efforts to raise and maintain a reasonable standard of living for national communities. The Bahá'í texts do not make direct reference to population policy. There is, however, a whole range of Bahá'í teachings with long term bearing on the issue, such as the fundamental commitment to the abolition of extremes of wealth and poverty, universal compulsory education, the equality of men and women, and a heightened sense of social responsibility. The importance of such factors in curbing the growth of population was recognized in the World Population Plan of Action adopted by the 1974 United Nations World Population Conference in Bucharest. That document included the following clause:

> "...agreed that birth rates are moderated through reduced infant and child mortality; women's full sharing in the development process; more equitable distribution of income, land, social services, and amenities; wide educational opportunities for the young of both sexes; and the establishment of an appropriate lower limit for marriage."

Goods and Services

A third very important aspect of a Bahá'í economy would be the values and priorities determining the production of goods and services. Of special significance in this context is the fundamental Bahá'í concept that man is not merely an animal endowed with exceptional intelligence but is, rather, a spiritual being who finds fulfillment and happiness in the growth of knowledge of God and in the application of that knowledge to life. 'Abdu'l-Bahá said,

> "Man is, in reality, a spiritual being, and only when he lives in the spirit is he truly happy."[22]

This statement suggests that in a Bahá'í society there would be a more balanced view of material things. Accordingly, one can assume that a Bahá'í economy would be directed mainly toward the production of essentials.

It is not surprising, therefore, to find that the Bahá'í Writings indicate agriculture will play a leading role in a future world economy.[23] Agriculture will produce all food and materials for basic needs such as clothing and shelter and when properly managed will harmonize with nature much more easily than industry. It is foreseen that it would be possible to develop and grow on the land on a renewable basis the materials which could be used as substitutes for plastics and other industrial synthetics which now use so much oil and other limited natural resources in their manufacture.

In a modern, scientifically-oriented society, the old problems of poverty and ignorance often associated with agricultural economies would be eliminated, and full advantage could be taken of the basic improvement in health, both physical and spiritual, which comes from close contact with the rhythm and reality of nature. The leading role of agriculture in a Bahá'í economy suggests that there will be a greater emphasis than at present on the small community rather than on the huge metropolis. This would seem to be ~in keeping with the trend in industrial techonology which is moving away from mass employment factories and toward automated plants and small specialized workshops with highly skilled staff. For many, work in agriculture might be part-time in combination with other jobs or the pursuit of further education.

In this connection it is interesting to note that in the last few years the World Bank has put increasing emphasis on agricultural and rural development (30 precent of lending is now in these sectors) with a view to increasing food production and discouraging massive emigration from the countryside. This emigration has resulted in huge numbers of unskilled unemployed in the slums of many Third World cities.

The values of a Bahá'í society also suggest that the highest priority would be given to education, arts and sciences, and social and public services. They also suggest a much greater appreciation of nature and a greater willingness to pay for the protection of the environment. However, there would be much less expenditure on nonessential goods and services, especially luxuries. It is not unreasonable to assume that the advertising industry as we know it today in capitalist society, with its vulgar emphasis on cultivating ever-changing fashions and exaggerated materialistic dreams, would be quite different in a Bahá'í economy.

In view of the Bahá'í teachings on alcohol and drugs as harmful except when required for medicinal purposes, it can be assumed too that in a Bahá'í economy the resources now devoted to these products would be conserved for other ends. Similarly the Bahá'í teachings discouraging smoking would suggest a much reduced tobacco industry. Though Bahá'ís are not required to be vegetarians, it is interesting to note the following statement attributed to 'Abdu'l-Bahá in the light of present concern that it is inefficient to devote a large proportion of agricultural land to the production of meat:

> "The food of the future will be fruit and grains. The time will come when meat will no longer be eaten. Medical science is only in its infancy, yet it has shown that our natural food is that which grows out of the ground."[24]

The establishment of a permanent peace under the aegis of a world government would also release for more rewarding use the vast wealth which is now expended on "defense". The nations of the world today

[1982] expend about 6 percent of the world's annual production on military affairs.[25] This sum is six times the current United Nations target for international assistance for poor countries.

Finally, a word should be said on the quality of goods and services. The principle that work is worship and that the highest form of worship is service would restore an individual's pride in what he or she produces, which, in turn, would clearly have a considerable impact on quality. Such a tendency would be greatly strengthened by the encouragement of the highest standards of honesty, truthfulness, reliability, and faithfulness, which come when there is a revitalization of religion and society grows more spiritual. There can be little doubt too that there would be a reassessment of the need for low quality throwaway consumer goods and a complete abandonment of that highly wasteful practice of capitalist society—deliberate, planned obsolescence.[26]

Historical Perspectives

The Bahá'í Faith arose at a time when the economy of the world was undergoing immense change. The 19th century Industrial Revolution in the West created the possibility for the first time that all the peoples of the world might one day escape form the struggle merely to survive. Associated improvements in communications rapidly made the world potentially one economy in a way that had never been true before.

These developments stimulated major changes in economic views. Adam Smith, Cobden, Bright, and their school overthrew the narrow nationalist themes of mercantilism and argued that the road to prosperity was through free trade and the creation of a unified world economy. In 1846, only two years after the declaration of the Báb, there occurred the greatest single triumph of the free trade school: the abolition

in England of the Corn Laws which had been the most
significant barrier to the free importation of food. The
laissez faire capitalist system which then prevailed
had the great virtue of being dynamic, but it also
entailed a great deal of waste, for instance, periods
of high unemployment, and the excessive emphasis
on private enterprise often resulted in the neglect of
essential and desirable public services.[27] Furthermore,
in practice efficiencies of the free market mechanism
were often reduced because of the development of
monopoly and oligopoly.

Karl Marx and other socialists reacted against the
brutal extremes of wealth and poverty which resulted
from the pure capitalism of the free trade school and
advocated state ownership and control of the main
elements of the economy in the name of social justice.
This reaction also took place at the time when the
Bahá'í faith was evolving: Marx published the
Communist Manifesto in 1848 and the first volume
of **Das Kapital** in 1867. In practice the socialist
system, though it has brought a greater degree of
economic and social equality than existed before, also
has had major flaws such as rigidity, inefficient
pricing systems, and worst of all a weight on the
human spirit: declining incentive to work and much
greater restrictions on the freedom of the individual
than anticipated.

If, to use Hegelian terminology, the capitalist and
socialist themes are respectively a thesis and an
antithesis, then it might be argued that the Bahá'í
approach to economics is the synthesis, because it
combines the idea of one world economy and a free
market with a systematic series of approaches to the
need for the abolition of extremes of wealth and
poverty and the need for the establishment of social
justice—these latter goals to be achieved, however,
with flexibility and with emphasis on development of

the human spirit. It might be added, parenthetically, that the Bahá'í approach to economics also has an echo of the 18th century French physiocrats who emphasized the central economic role of agriculture.

Since the 19th century there has been a convergence of the capitalist and socialist themes towards the Bahá'í view. Thus some of the worst aspects of capitalism have been ameliorated as a result of the introduction of the welfare state by Bismarck, Beveridge and others and the Keynesian policy of countercyclical action by the state. The worst aspects of the communist state have been and are being reduced by greater decentralization, limited market economics, more international trade, and recognition that more freedom of thought is a necessary feature of an advanced economy [This of course was written several years before the collapse of the Soviet Union]. Most nations have accepted the need for cooperation on a world scale in economic matters and for that purpose have established the International Monetary Fund (which incidentally has introduced the Special Drawing Right, an embryonic world currency), the World Bank, the General Agreement on Trade and Tariffs (GATT) and the United Nations Conference on Trade and Development (UNCTAD). Though recession and politics have recently led to some doubts about free trade and development assistance, there can be no question of the world's clock being turned back to the 19th century.

In conclusion, it is suggested that Bahá'í texts provide a framework at both the micro and macro levels for a comprehensive economic philosophy which gives a long-term response to the main economic issues of the time: poverty, unemployment, inflation, conservation, environmental protection, and quality of goods and services. The significance of this response is becoming increasingly clear as the economies of the nations of the world become more interdependent, and a need emerges for a new system of economics incorporating new values and a global perspective.

NOTES

1. Two other key sources are Bahá'u'lláh's *Kitáb-i-Aqdas* (The Book of Laws), and Shoghi Effendi's essay, "The Unfoldment of World Civilization" in *The World Order of Bahá'u'lláh*, 2nd ed., Wilmette: Bahá'í Publishing Trust, 1974, pp. 202-206.
2. *North-South, A Program of Survival*, The Report of the Independent Commission on International Development Issues, MIT Press, 1980, p.268
3. Shoghi Effendi, *The World Order of Bahá'u'lláh*, 2nd ed., 1974, pp.41-42
4. Ibid., p.204
5. John Kenneth Galbraith, *The Affluent Society,* Boston: Houghton Mifflin, 1958, chapter 18, "The Theory of Social Balance".
6. The modern cooperative movement was started in Rochdale, England, in 1844, the same year as the Báb's Declaration.
7. The first cooperative in Mondragon was established in 1956 mainly as the result of the dedication and work of a local priest. Some twenty years later the town had 82 cooperatives engaged in manufacturing, agriculture, banking, and social services, and employed 14,000 people out of a population of 30,000. A typical cooperative is run by an assembly of all the workers who each have one vote. The assembly appoints a supervisory board which meets monthly and appoints in turn, the senior managers. Each group of 200 workers is represented on a social council which channels ideas and suggestions between management and workers on such matters as working norms and conditions. Generally, a cooperative in Mondragon will put 45 percent of its profits into reserve and investment, 10 percent will be used for community education and welfare projects, and 45 percent will be paid to workers in proportion to earnings. Earnings differentials do not exceed 3: 1. Thus the wage index for an unskilled worker is 1, for a foreman 1.6, for middle range executives 2, and for top management 2.5 to 3. This means that many executives earn only a fraction of what they might elsewhere. Nevertheless, few leave because

there is a strong sense of idealism and loyalty to the community and an appreciation of the dynamism and scope for innovation given in the cooperatives. The high rate of investment makes for up to date equipment and therefore a strong competitive position. It also makes it possible for cooperatives to expand and provide employment for others. If a worker's job should become redundant, the cooperatives will pay for him to be retrained for another job. As might be expected, there is a long waiting list of those wanting to join the cooperatives. Normally, a new employee has one year of probation and then is permitted to buy one share in the enterprise which is usually paid for with a low interest loan from the cooperative. When an employee leaves the cooperative he is paid the current market value of his share. Out of self-interest, workers themselves enforce a clearly defined disciplinary code against selfish behaviour. Strikes are extremely rare and in 1974 when a small group of workers at one cooperative did go on strike, the workers' general assembly voted overwhelmingly for their dismissal. (based on an article which appeared in *The Economist,* December, 1976).

8. 'Abdu'l-Bahá, *Some Answered Questions,* 4th ed., Wilmette: Bahá'í Publishing Trust, 1981, p.274.
9. J. Esselmont, *Bahá'u'lláh and the New Era,* 2nd ed., Wilmette: Bahá'í Publishing Trust, 1970, p.144.
10. *The Economist,* December 25, 1976, and April 17, 1982.
11. *Bahá'u'lláh and the New Era,* p.144.
12. Ibid., p.148.
13. 'Abdu'l-Bahá and Bahá'u'lláh, *Bahá'í World Faith,* 3rd ed., Wilmette: Bahá'í Publishing Trust 1956, p.195.
14. Ibid., p.195.
15. The *World Bank Atlas of Gross National Product, Population and Growth Rates* gives the following estimates of per capita incomes in 1980:

Less than $360	32 countries, islands and territories
$360-829	33 countries, islands and territories
$830-3,539	48 countries, islands and territories
$3,540-8,269	24 countries, islands and territories
$8,270 & above	27 countries, islands and territories
Total	164

These figures excluded Communist countries and a few islands in the Pacific.
16. Shoghi Effendi, *The Promised Day is Come,* 2nd ed., Wilmette: Bahá'í Publishing Trust, 1961, p.22
17. *Bahá'u'lláh and the New Era,* p.141.

18. *Star of the West*, vol. 8, no.1, March 21, 1917, pp.4-5.

19. *The Book of Laws* states that in the absence of a will the children should inherit approximately 43 percent of the estate, the widowed spouse 15 percent, parents 24 percent, siblings 14 percent and the teacher 4 percent.

20. Personal income taxes vary greatly from country to country in relation to other taxes. For instance the 1981 OECD report on revenue statistics in 23 member countries shows income tax yields as a percent of total tax revenue ranging from 12 percent (Greece) to 50 percent (Denmark).

21. It is said that because of an emphasis on education there has been much greater progress in eliminating poverty over several generations among the Bahá'ís of Irán than among other groups in that country.

22. 'Abdu'l-Bahá, Paris Talks, 11th ed, London : Bahá'í Publishing Trust, 1969, p.72.

23. Today [1982] about 60 percent of the population of developing countries is in agriculture-related pursuits. The proportion is much less in the industrial countries and is as low as 3 percent in the United States.

24. *Bahá'u'lláh and the New Era*, p.102.

25. *World Military Expenditures and Arms Transfers, 1966-1975*, United States Arms Control and disarmament Agency, 1977.

26. George Bernard Shaw pointed out a long time ago that electric light bulbs were deliberately made to have a shorter life than was techincally possible or socially economic in order to create a bigger demand and, therefore, more profit for the manufacturer. Seventy years later little has changed.

27. See again *The Affluent Society*, by John Kenneth Galbraith.

DEVELOPMENT : THE SPIRITUAL DIMENSION

A presentation at the Asian Bahá'í Youth Conference, New Delhi, India, 1985

The word, 'development', brings to mind national planning ministries and international development banks, such as the World Bank and the Asian Development Bank. In other words, it is very much associated with economic development and with use of public rather than private resources. There is also a general perception that development is something that has emerged only in the 40 years or so since the end of the Second World War.

A little reflection shows that these impressions are all very narrow. Development covers the whole spectrum of human progress and it has been a feature of human activity since the beginning of civilization. Looking back over the last 6,000 years, one can see periods of material progress resulting from good government and technological advances -for instance times of prosperity when strong princes established peace over wide areas and thereby encouraged the expansion of commerce, agriculture, industry and learning.

If we look a little more deeply, it can be seen that human progress has been largely associated with the periodic emergence of great world religions: Hinduism, Buddhism, Zoroastrianism, Judaism, Christanity and Islám. The founders of these religions inspired large numbers of people to live by advance ethical teachings and, as a result, the level of civilization was raised.

Though the advance of civilization can be seen in the perspective of a world view over 6,000 years, there was perhaps little consciousness of progress until about 200 years ago. This is because the long-term trend was obscured by periodic but traumatic events of a negative character such as the coming of an autumn and winter in each religion, when a hollow shell of superstition and ritual would be the only reminder of the spirit of the brilliant spring and summer; the fall of empires; war and pestilence; and the experience for most of a life which Thomas Hobbes, the English philosopher, called nasty, brutish and short. Thus for most peoples, history was an endless series of repetitive cycles with little or no awareness of development or progress.

There were two developments in man's experience which occurred in the 18th and 19th centuries which made popular the theme of progress and advancement of civilization: the political revolutions in England, North America and France, and the industrial revolution which began in the same regions of the world.

The political revolutions caught the imagination of millions with their ideas of equality before the law, greater freedoms for the individual, and representative government accountable to the people— in Abraham Lincoln's glorious phrase, 'government of the people, by the people, and for the people!' Some of the greatest achievements of the time were the abolition of serfdom and slavery in large areas of the globe and later the coming of national independence for many peoples who had been previously subjected by colonizing powers.

The industrial revolution brought with it vastly more efficient means of production which, for the first time, made it possible for all of mankind, not just a minority as before, to escape the grinding burden of the day-today struggle just to survive, and for all to be able to have sufficient amounts of the material necessities of life: food, shelter and clothing.

The industrial revolution also brought new means of communications—the railway engine, the steamship, the telegraph and, later, the automobile, airplane, telephone, and satellite which, again for the first time in history, linked together the various regions of the world on a continuous basis and, in effect, made the world one.

These earth-shaking events led to further developments of immense importance. Though the industrial revolution brought greater wealth, the distribution of that wealth was very uneven and millions continued to live in the most deplorable conditions. In protest against such conditions, there emerged a socialist movement which echoed the original universal teachings of all religions that society has the moral obligation to help the less fortunate and to reduce extremes of wealth and poverty. Socialist ideas on state intervention to ameliorate the condition of the underprivileged led to state planning for economic development, with one of the earliest and most comprehensive examples being the system of five year plans initiated in Soviet Russia during the 1920s.

The industrial revolution also immensely increased the power of weapons which, in turn, made war far more destructive than ever before. The experience of two world wars frightened even the mightiest nations into agreeing for the first time to the establishment of permanent international organizations (first the League of Nations, then the United Nations) which were intended to be instruments for maintaining international peace and eliminating conflicts between nations.

The new institutions were supported by a range

of subsidiary specialized and regional agencies for cooperation between nations on various economic, social and cultural matters. Among these agencies were several, of which the World Bank is perhaps the most well known, with the mission of promoting economic development, first in the countries severely damaged during the wars and then in those countries which had not progressed far with industrialization.

During the 1960s there was an effort to put this mission on a long-term footing when the United Nations adopted a goal that the materially wealthier countries should contribute one per cent of their gross national product to the economic development of the less prosperous countries. To put this goal in perspective, it might be noted that at that time six per cent of the world's gross product was spent on military activities.

It is clear that, as a result of these events, there have been great advances in the level of civilization in terms of more responsible and less oppressive governments in a number of countries around the world; international co-operation which has benefited many; a great increase in material wealth; and moves towards more equitable distribution of resources.

Much that has been achieved can be attributed to a social conscience among those taking the initiative— a spiritual dimension derived from the principles of the great religions of the past.

Nevertheless these advances have been far less than had been hoped for and there is a distinct sense today that the rate of advancement has slowed down. Indeed there are many who feel that the tide of progress has started to recede. It is easy to see why there should be such a feeling.

Despite international institutions the threat to world peace is still very great. Representative, accountable government is still confined to a minority of countries (1985) and even in those countries where it is established, it is often corrupt, short-sighted and not fully committed to the well-being of all citizens. There remain immense disparities in the distribution of material resources, both within countries and between countries, and the vast majority of the world's population still lives in material poverty. Even in those countries which have thrived materially there has been a tremendous cost in terms of unemployment, pollution of the environment, and the breakdown of social order and ethical values.

Many leaders of thought are coming to the view that though there are still some dedicated people who have a strong spiritual commitment to improving society, generally they are fighting a losing battle against short-sightedness, cynicism and greed on the part of the majority. What is needed on a world scale is a new vision, a sense of purpose and ethical values, all of which are essential for progress, perhaps even for survival.

Thus the 1979 Brandt Commission on International Development Issues in its report to the world's leaders said there would be no action: 'Unless there is a global consensus on the moral plane. . . ideas must be accepted sincerely by governments and especially by individuals. . .it requires an intensive process of education without which there will be no true economic development and, above all, no justice, freedom and peace.'

Others realize that religion has a key role to play in this process. Thus Arnold Toynbee, the distinguished English historian, wrote: 'Conflict will be carried to a suicidal extremity unless man experiences the miracle of conversion. . .The unity of mankind. . .can be achieved only as an incidental result of acting on a belief in the unity of God and by seeing this unitary terrestrial society as a promise of

God's Commonwealth'. In February, 1980, the prestigious Society for International Development devoted a whole issue of its quarterly magazine to an examination of the role of religion in development.

There are at least two reasons why religion is considered to be of critical importance in relation to development. The first is that the universal teachings which are common to all great religions are the source of the values which are both the measure of development and one of the chief means for its achievement. Some of these values are:

- A belief in the brotherhood of man, with all that this implies in terms of goodwill and concern for the welfare of others; kindness, charity, service and cooperation.
- A sense of self-respect and personal responsibility because man is recognized to be at the highest level of creation, with all that this implies in terms of attitudes to honesty, truthfulness, intellectual integrity and work.
- A sense of humility before God which encompasses a whole range of values including understanding of the unity of creation and the inter-connections of our environment, a respect for all forms of life, and appreciation of physical things combined with a sense of detachment because they are known to be ephemeral when compared with the life of the spirit.

The second reason for the importance of religion in development is that history has shown that it alone has the power to inspire people of all backgrounds to strive for the highest ethical standards and to maintain these standards over extended periods of time.

The challenge to the religions of the world is to provide that renewal of the spiritual dimension which is so clearly needed for man's further progress, indeed perhaps for his very survival. There has been some response but it is clear that the leaders of established religions are, to a greater or lesser degree, severely hampered in such an enterprise because of corruptions of their own original teachings, disunity within their own ranks and antagonism towards others— in short, by the loss of the spiritual dynamism which they are being called upon to inspire in others.

In searching for a solution, more and more people are coming to recognize that the main hope lies with the Bahá'í Faith. Though its adherents are at present relatively small in numbers, just a few million, it does have thousands of local communities which are established in just about every country of the world, where men and women equally (a crucial aspect in view of the exceptionally important economic role of women in many countries) have open and universal participation in the conduct of their affairs. This gives it an essential facility for knowing how people of all backgrounds think about different matters and for inspiring action at the grass roots level in every type of culture.

The fact that the Bahá'í community is now relatively small in numbers is not a handicap because Bahá'í teachings on, for instance, equal reverence for the Founders of all the great religions, the balance between science and religion, protection and appreciation of the cultures of minorities, encouragement of the family, the equality of men and women, the need to abolish extremes of wealth and poverty, loyalty to government, and abstention from partisan politics, give it the potential to attract the allegiance of large numbers from any background at any time. This is already beginning to happen in several countries.

The Bahá'í community itself recognizes the leading

role it is destined to play in responding to the
challenge of our times. There are at least four different
aspects to that response.

It is spreading knowledge of its principles and
teachings to all strata of society with the hope that,
as a result, many more will either adopt them or
otherwise be persuaded to contribute more to the
development of our world society.

It has a steady worldwide program for all members
of the community to have practical experience in
organizing their affairs according to spiritual values
and universal participation, with the objective of being
more effective in the development process and of
providing an alternative model for the peoples of the
world as obsolete, old-style institutions collapse
around them.

It gives support and encouragement to other
progressive movements which are also working to
achieve a just world society. There is a particular effort
to support the United Nations and to encourage it to
operate according to the highest ethical standards in
the interest of all mankind.

It is providing a wide variety of services which
contribute to the spiritual and material progress of all
Bahá'ís and non-Bahá'ís alike.

On this last point concerning services (pertaining
to specific economic and social development projects),
there are schemes organized and managed by
institutions where Bahá'ís might have some influence
either as individuals in their professional capacity or
collectively as a recognized group with interest in
development.

Bahá'ís do a number of things to try and
strengthen the spiritual dimension of these projects
so that there is personal development for all who are
involved. They try to ensure, for example, that projects
are developed in close and continued consultation

with those who are the intended beneficiaries and that their views are given decisive weight.

The intended beneficiaries are given a large interest in the governing corporation including, possibly, a cooperative structure, profit sharing, or workers' participation in management.

The greatest care is given to safety both for employees and those living in the vicinity and to the protection of the physical environment and the social fabric of the community.

Benefits are spread as widely as practicable in the community to maximize support and minimize dissension. There should be no discrimination in any way on grounds of religion, class, sex or race.

There is preference for projects which have a direct impact on spiritual development-education, for example— or are concerned with providing basic material necessities rather than luxury items. There is an avoidance of projects whch produce goods or services which are harmful to society such as alcohol or tobacco or gambling facilities.

Bahá'ís, as individuals and collectively as a community, have been involved in providing development services since the Faith began, but this activity has been given much sharper focus and impetus following the establishment in 1983 of a new Office of Social and Economic Development at the Bahá'í World Center in Haifa, Israel. The purpose of this office is to promote and co-ordinate Bahá'í development activities throughtout the world. As a result, a multitude of new services are already being provided and many more are planned.

Bahá'ís often borrow practical ideas on development from other progressive groups and, in turn, Bahá'í projects can be useful models for others, both in terms of methodology and purpose. As they develop, they offer the opportunity for expansion through co-operation with other institutions in the field.

This exciting process has already begun. For instance, several Bahá'í projects are now partially funded by the Canadian International Development Agency (CIDA). Contacts are now being made with other institutions. Such partnerships have potential for immense service to mankind because they combine the strengths of the Bahá'í community— its clear sense of purpose, spiritual values, and worldwide contacts at the local community level— with the financial resources and technical experience of the professional aid institutions.

The Bahá'í response to the challenges of the modern world is exhilarating, whether it be broadcasting its principles to all strata of society, building up a new system of institutions based on spiritual principles, co-operating with and encouraging other progressive movements, or providing a growing range of economic and social services for all. Not for Bahá'ís a sense of despair at the state of the world; on the contrary a sense of purpose, promise and joy.

TOWARDS A WORLD ECONOMY

**A presentation at the Conference of the
Association for Bahá'í Studies (Europe),
Lausanne, Switzerland, 1988**

Most of us take some interest in looking into the
crystal ball of the future-even the most unworldly
spare a thought about the source of their next meal.
But as individuals our perspective is generally short
term: the next few days, or weeks, or months, or
maybe a year or two—rarely a decade, and certainly
not a century or millennium. This short-term
perspective is reinforced by the political process when
considering public affairs, particularly in democracies,
where the prime interest is often on the next election.
When public affairs are narrowed to the economy, the
focus is the same. Capital and labor alike worry if the
next year or two will see the economy crash. Financial
markets focus on the next quarterly report of
companies quoted on the stock market; others worry
about currency exchange movements over the next six
months, and so forth. The point is reinforced by Lord
Keyne's famous remark: in the long run we are all
dead.

Clearly, the short term is important, but it should
not be allowed to block out long-term perspectives,
for these can be of vital importance for both our
generation and the next. First, experience shows that
any society which tries to resist the underlying forces
of history will create much pain and anguish for itself

e.g. the resistance to democracy and national self-determination by the *ancien* regimes of Europe prior to the Great War. To avoid this mistake, we have to find out what are the long-term trends. Second, if there are major long-range factors that will have a harmful effect on society, it is often necessary to begin taking corrective action well in advance e.g. with regard to the environment and conservation of resources. Similarly, we can sometimes miss singular opportunities to benefit humanity if we do not see that opportunity in advance. Examples of such missed opportunities have included 1919, when a lasting peace might have been established, and 1974, when the oil crisis might have been used to end once and for all profligacy in our use of non-renewable energy resources.

There is, of course, a minority that does have a relatively long-term perspective: social and economic planners, environmentalists, futurologists, etc. But to a greater or lesser extent each of these groups has a narrow vision related to their particular interest, and it is usually focused on the advance of technology and its side effects. There is very little about the pulsating life of society as a whole. The one major exception is religion, which has always had as one of its main concerns the broad long-term trends in society.

Now, of course, the very term *religion* makes many of us nervous: it is all too often associated with superstition, division, and irrelevant issues. Though such fears are often justified, it is not rational to jump to the conclusion that religious principles and experience are best ignored. A balanced view of history surely has to acknowledge the great advances society has made as a result of the teachings and examples of the Buddha, Jesus, and Muhammad, for instance. In our own day, a growing number of peoples from an immense diversity of backgrounds all around the world are coming to recognize that the newest of the world's religions, the Bahá'í Faith, has something of great value for society. Here, there are no barriers of superstition: the emphasis is on the partnership of science and religion in seeking the truth, and there is little ritual. Here, there is no division: all religions are recognized as essentially one in their teachings of universal truths, and the Founders of all the great religions are revered equally with the Founder of the Bahá'í Faith, Bahá'u'lláh. Here, there are no irrelevant issues. The Bahá'í Faith is about the vision of a new, ever-advancing civilization based on the oneness of humanity, and it represents a practical, comprehensive, step-by-step plan for the achievement of that vision.

This brings me to the theme of this conference, "The Economy and Society: What are the Prospects after the Present Crisis?" The Bahá'í Faith has quite a lot to say about the economy in that vision of the future. Two of the most important themes, which are closely interlinked, are (i) that the economies of the world will become one global economy serving the material, intellectual, and spiritual needs of all humanity; and (ii) that the underlying force driving the economy will be spiritual or, in secular terms, ethical. The purpose of this presentation is to discuss briefly what evidence there is that this is happening, and second, what this means in terms of present and future policy.

From the beginning of civilization right up until recent times agriculture has completely dominated the vast majority of the economies of the world. Agriculture could normally meet local needs for food, clothing, and shelter, and consequently communities were largely self-subsisting. There was, therefore, little incentive to have contact with other communities, and in practice the vast majority of people rarely travelled more than twenty or thirty miles from where they were born. This tendency to isolationism was reinforced by inefficient and slow systems of transport, by language barriers, and ,by sheer risk of travel over long distances even when peace was enforced over a wide area and for considerable periods of time by mighty empires such as those of Rome and China. No wonder that high interests were charged for loans to finance overseas trade. What trade there was outside the average locality was generally in commodities that were light and compact in relation to value, for example, preservatives and precious gems, or that were vital and not immediately available, for example, metals, timber, or hemp. The modern concept of importing goods because they might be cheaper than those produced locally barely existed. On the great land mass of Euroasia, where the bulk of the world's population lived, there was a thin network of communications— a spiderweb in Europe, others in the Middle East, India, and China, and so on-that were joined together at times by such fragile links as the silk road between China and Europe. Whole continents-the Americas, Australasia/Oceania sub-Sahel Africa-were for the most part totally isolated from the rest of the world.

This general picture of the economies of the world over several thousand years began to change with the Renaissance and the rise of Europe. Over a period of three centuries (from the fifteenth to eighteenth), Europe established contact with North and South America, India, south east Asia, Australasia, and sub-Sahel Africa. These contacts were vastly strengthened in the nineteenth century by the improved systems of communication of the Industrial Revolution, systems which were fast, had increased capacity for bulk cargo and for cargo that hitherto would have deteriorated en route: the fast sailship, the steamship, the refrigerator ship, the telegraph. The Industrial Revolution also brought a vast increase in the volume and the variety of goods and services, first in Europe and North America, then in parts of Asia, and there was pressure to sell these goods to the rest of the world in return for a growing range of agricultural products, as well as for raw materials needed for industry. New trading posts were established and expanded; mass migration from Europe colonized sparsely populated lands in America, Australasia, and Africa. Lands were joined together in vast globe-encircling empires, and passage on the high seas became safe with the dominance of the British navy— Pax Britannica. Capital was exported from Europe to develop the new lands and conquered countries alike, helped by an increasingly sophisticated financial system based on a common currency, the gold-backed pound.

Old mercantilist theories, which encouraged states to export for gold rather than for imports and which therefore created artificial barriers to international trade, were replaced by the free-trade theories of Adam Smith, who promoted the view that all benefited when nations, as well as individuals, specialized in those activities where they were most efficient— the theory of comparative advantage. Great Britain, with the richest economy in the world, within the space of three or four decades, adopted free trade and despite increasing problems towards the end of the century, particularly in agriculture, maintained that policy for decades. Most of the other great trading nations followed the lead of Great Britain in varying degrees.

It was also recognized that the new world trade system would be strengthened and thereby give benefit to all, if there was technical cooperation among nations. As a result, the world's first international public service agencies were established—the

International Telegraph Union (1865), the Universal Postal Union (1874), the International Institute of Agriculture (1905), the International Office of Public Health (1909), etc. Not to be forgotten was the emergence of a network of transnational private organizations promoting the idea that national economies were becoming interdependent— such organizations as the Workers International and the International Chamber of Commerce. As a result of these mutually supporting developments, world trade in the nineteenth century expanded in real terms at unprecedented rate—nearly 5 percent per annum.

And then a disaster, which for a time seemed to put the process into reverse: the greatest war in the history of the world to date not only killed and maimed millions but also destroyed states, ruined others, created huge debt burdens, and undermined established patterns of trade. After the fighting stopped, valiant attempts to restore the old international economic order failed. Industrial countries suffered from persistent unemployment; the financial markets indulged in wild speculation; currencies were unstable; new nations disrupted trade with barriers to protect their industry and agriculture. The Great Depression of the thirties led to a major shrinkage in the economies of the world and in international trade in particular as each nation unilaterally tried to improve its own economic situation at the expense of the others. A second war even more destructive than the first was a logical consequence.

After six years of war, a peace of sorts was reestablished, and as had happened after the previous conflict, there was a great public yearning to make a better world. In the context of this discussion, there was general agreement that greater integration of the national economies of the world would be mutually beneficial and that the process should be encouraged by cooperation among national governments. The core arrangement was to be the establishment of two new international agencies: an International Trade Organization (ITO) and an International Monetary Fund (IMF), which respectively would sponsor removal of physical barriers to trade such as tariffs and quotas, and monetary barriers such as manipulation of currency exchange rates and restrictions on use of currencies. The ITO proved too controversial, and it was replaced by a much weaker General Agreement on Trade and Tariffs (GATT). Though weaker, the GATT has nevertheless proved a useful instrument for encouraging the growth of international trade. Over four decades, it has been used to negotiate some eight rounds of reductions in trade barriers, and as a result, tariffs on industrial goods of the richer nations have been reduced from an average of forty percent *ad valorem* to about five percent.

The IMF has also had its successes. Most of the important trading nations have removed restrictions on use of currencies, and agreement was reached on the establishment of a new international reserve— the Special Drawing Right— which can be seen as an embryo world currency, a major monetary device for reducing risk in international trade. The problems associated with establishing stable exchange rates and flattening the world trade cycle so as to avoid recessions on the one hand and inflation on the other have drawn attention to the need for cooperation among nations with regard to both monetary and fiscal policy. Discussions of these issues now take place annually at meetings of finance ministers at the IMF and among the heads of governments of the major trading nations at regular summit meetings.

Broad cooperation to remove barriers to trade at the world level has been supplemented by regional and bilateral arrangements. Undoubtedly, the most spectacular of the regional arrangements was the 1957 formation of the European Community, which now [1988] embraces twelve countries that have taken a multitude of steps to remove mutual barriers to trade, capital movement, and migration. Of particular interest are arrangements to provide transitional assistance to regions hurt by changing patterns of trade that occur when national barriers are removed. With regard to bilateral arrangements to expand international economics activity, it is perhaps sufficient to mention two recent and significant arrangements: that between the United States and Canada and that between Australia and New Zealand.

The result has been that world trade since the end of the Second World War has expanded in real terms at a rate of six percent per annum, even faster than in the nineteenth century. Of course, not all of this success can be attributed to government action. The drive to remove barriers to integration of the world's economies on the part of national governments has been greatly strengthened by a series of interconnected technical, economic, and political developments. One of the most visible has been the vast improvement in communication systems since the end of the Second World War, e.g. the jet airliner and the application of electronics in such devices as the artificial earth satellite, radio, television, telephone, and computer. At the same time, English has, in effect, become the language of international commerce. One consequence of communications technology is that financial markets in North America, Europe, and East Asia for currencies, commodities, and corporate shares are increasingly affecting each other, and in some cases it is not an exaggertion to speak of a global market open twenty-four hours a day, 365 days a year. Consumer products such as soft drinks, cigarettes, automobiles, television, radio, and records are becoming standardized around the world. The red and white Coca-Cola sign epitomizes the world market. Vastly more significant is the unified world market in oil and associated products. Yet another development has been the enormous growth in tourism, first within nations, then between nations, and now between continents. In turn, these developments have led to a growing number of transnational and global corporations that increasingly have a world rather than national view. The attraction of the international consumer market has made it increasingly difficult for governments to pursue policies that isolate their peoples from the rest of the world: the most obvious case being the gradual integration into the world trade system of the socialist group of nations, which for decades essentially functioned as a separate economy. As in so many areas of life, national governments are losing sovereignty and will only regain it through mutual cooperation.

So far the discussion of the trend towards a world economy has focused on one dimension: the integration of national economies into one system. But there are at least two other important dimensions to this process. The first of these is some acknowledgement that the economies of the world are divided by extremes of wealth and poverty and that it is in the interest of all that poverty should be elimated and further, that distribution of wealth should be more equitable. The great religions of the world, promoting the idea of humanity being one family, have always shown concern for the poor and encouraged charity. However, it was not until the Industrial Revolution brought the real prospect that a decent material standard of living could be provided for all humanity (if the economy were properly organized) that the drive for a more equitable society began in earnest. The gap between the potential and the actual was perceived to be too outrageous to be left to the slow corrective action of the market and trickle-down theories. Accordingly, a multitude of activist approaches to the problem came into being: trade unions, cooperatives, socialism, profit sharing, the welfare state, etc. Attention was focused on such issues as guaranteed minimum incomes and provision of adequate health care, housing, education, and safety regulations in the workplace. Some approaches involved progressive taxation, state ownership of the "commanding heights of the economy"[1] and state planning. Rich vested interests and laissez-faire ideologues resisted the latter idea in particular; but in the long run much was achieved, and there can be no question that the internal distribution of resources in what are known as First and Second World countries is much more equitable now than it was a hundred years ago and perhaps ever was. This judgement is also, no doubt, true of many Third World countries as well.

Initially, the move towards a more equitable society was essentially confined to arrangements within each nation, but since the Second World War growing attention has been given to the need for greater equity among nations. The founders of the United Nations (UN) recognized that one of the major flaws with the preceding League of Nations had been lack of sufficient attention to the underlying causes of war: whole nations in poverty and widespread violation of basic human rights. One result was a development unprecedented in the history of civilization: agreement for the volunatry transfer of resources and technical assistance from wealthy countries to poor countries, partly bilateral with strings attached, partly multilateral on a more detached basis.

The first major event in this process was the Marshall Aid Program of the United States to help European nations ravaged by the Second World War to rebuild their economies. More long term were new or expanded international organizations for managing multilateral transfer of assistance to the world's least economically developed nations, such as the World Bank, the World Health Organization (WHO), the Food and Agriculture Organization (FAO), the UN Development Program (UNDP), the UN Children's Emergency Fund (UNICEF), and the UN Educational, Scientific and Cultural Organization (UNESCO). In addition, there were a multitude of regional organizations including the Organization for Economic and Cultural Development (OECD). In the last three decades, the UN has set agreed targets for international aid for rich countries, expressed in percentages of gross national product (currently, 1988, 0.7 percent). Furthermore, a special effort has been made to give less developed nations opportunities to expand their overseas trade with the establishment of the United Nations Conference on Trade and Development (UNCTAD) and such arrangements as the Lome Convention of the European Community. One of the potentially most significant of recent developments is the cooperative project of several international organizations to work for the elimination of illiteracy by the year 2000.

The third dimension to the evolving global economy is the growing acknowledgement that in physical terms the economy is an integeral part of the natural environment and that there will be enormous costs for all if this fact is ignored. Throughout history there have been instances of major damage to the world's ecological system as a result of humanity's economic activity, but the issue has become increasingly important since the Industrial Revolution. There were pioneer actions to control the problem in the nineteenth century and the first half of the twentieth century, but it has only been in the last few decades that humanity has started to wake up to the great dangers involved. One aspect of the problem is pollution or poisoning of air, water, and land, and possibly even climatic change, with all the massive long-term consequences that implies. The other is exhaustion or destruction of limited or fragile resources: fertile soils, clean water, forests, minerals, fish stock, and species of animal and plant wildlife. The sources of the problems are wide and include such aspects of the economy as industry, energy systems, transportation, agriculture population growth, military activities, destruction of traditional culture, and wasteful and excessive materialism. As with the poverty issue, vested interests have resisted practical action to protect the environment, and many were persuaded at first that it meant anti-growth and anti-development.

As with the poverty issue, the main initial thrust to protect the environment was also within national communities, but increasingly it is recognized that environmental problems do not stop at national boundaries. In consequence, there have been a series of international agreements on the issue, starting with the establishment of the UN Environmental Program, regional agreements such as those covering the Baltic and Mediterranean Seas and the great European river systems, and culminating with the Montreal conventions with regard to action to protect the earth's ozone layer. It is of interest that one of the most influential events in persuading nations to be more frugal in their use of energy was the massive increase in world oil prices in the 1970s as a result of the activities of the Organization of Petroleum Exporting

Countries (OPEC). A recent, potentially significant development is a proposal to retire international Third World debt in return for domestic conservation measures— an idea now [1988] being considered by the Congress of the United States. Another is the suggestion of the World Wildlife Fund that particular attention be paid to seven 'megadiverse' countries (Brazil, Columbia, Mexico, Zaire, Madagascar, Indonesia, and Australia) that between them contain fifty-four percent of all known living species on earth.

This short recital of some of the highlights in the evolution of the economies of the world surely gives evidence that there is an overriding trend towards their integration into one global system and that this has been paralleled by growing spiritual imperatives with regard to the need first to integrate all peoples into the economy so as to abolish the division caused by extremes of wealth and poverty, and second to integrate them into the global ecological system. I would suggest it is of vital importance that we, individually and collectively, accept these historical trends and act to smooth their further evolution rather than attempt to oppose them.

In particular, this should be the mental attitude we have as we tackle important economic issues on the world agenda. That agenda includes issues pertaining to all three dimensions of the world economy that have been mentioned in this discussion.

Among the issues concerning further integration of national economies into a real world economy are:

1. Extension of the effort to reduce trade barriers to include the agricultural and service sectors, and strengthening of means for enforcing the terms of liberal trade arrangements;

2. Stabilization of currency relationships so as to reduce monetary risks in international commerce, with the ultimate goal of a unified currency system

managed by a world authority;

3. Greater coordination of national monetary and fiscal policies so as to reduce the risk of world recession, on the one hand, and world inflation, on the other;

4. Development of international law for the regulation of transnational and global corporations so as to prevent possible abuse of monopoly, exploitation of employees in different countries, avoidance of fair taxation, and environmental regulations, etc.

Among the issues concerning further reduction of extremes of wealth and poverty are:

5. Should the real goal be true equality of opportunity rather than direct greater equality of wealth regardless of effort?

6. How best to ensure that reduction in poverty continues while pursuing policies to make the economy more efficient through such means as reducing the public sector, decentralization, deregulation and increased competition, lower and less progressive taxation (all policies that are being pursued in varying degrees in socialist as well as capitalist countries). Experience so far suggests that, in the short run at least, such policies are *increasing* the number who are impoverished.

7. Can the problem be solved by changing the welfare state so that it is more targeted to benefit the poor, by greater emphasis on training, by encouraging dispersal of wealth through taxation of inheritance according to the recipient rather than the donor, greater use of profit sharing, and by elimination of racial and sexual discrimination in employment?

8. How best can we convert the phenomenon of an aging, static population in rich countries into an asset rather than liability?

9. What is the optimal model for an educational system, a key input and output of any economy? What

should be the mix of sciences, arts, and ethics? What proportion of the population should have the opportunity to receive secondary and tertiary education? What role should the teacher have in society?

10. What to do about the international trade in drugs that destroys the lives of millions and vastly increases the power of criminals, and yet at the same time represents for many poor countries one of the main sources of foreign currency necessary to buy vital imports?

11. What to do about the economic consequences of the arms race and the international arms trade? What is euphemistically called "defense" consumes or wastes some six percent of the world's gross annual product [1988], but, at the same time, provides employment for large numbers of people.

12. How to make international aid more effective and attractive to donor countries? This question raises such issues as:

—Involvement of aid recipients at the grassroots level in the choice, planning, and management of their projects so that they have a real sense of ownership;

—Greater involvement of women;

—Elimination of corruption in aid programs, both in donor and in recipient countries;

—The problem of continued rapid population growth in Third World countries, which aggravates food shortages, slows down efforts to reduce per capita poverty, and presents a major threat to the world's environment;

—Revival of the rural sector so as to improve the food supply and reduce the growth of the slum megapolis;

—Ensuring that IMF programs to stabilize economies do not hurt the poor;

—Finding ways to relieve the international debt of

the poorest countries without discouraging future international investment in these countries.

Among the issues concerning the reconciliation of a growing world economy with the need to protect and strengthen the natural environment are:

17. What is the most efficient and least risky approach to the energy problem: nuclear power, fossil fuels (oil, coal, gas), hydroelectric power, renewable power resources (wind, sea, sun), greater efficiency in the use of power, or a switch in the mix of goods and services in the output of the economy so that the need for power is reduced?

18. How to make natural agriculture and traditional cultures as efficient as the environmentally damaging modern system based on monoculture and chemical fertilizers;

19. How to manage the oceans, forests, soils, and rivers for the maximum long-term benefit of all;

20. Is the Western consumer society with its present emphasis on massive use of resources to produce extravagant, disposable goods a practical or desirable model for a development strategy intended to abolish international poverty?

In considering these questions, it becomes apparent that the issue is not just a matter of moving in accordance with the tides of history. Underlying any approach to the economic agenda are some deeper philosophical questions, including at least two concerning our perceptions of what it means to be a human being.

First, we have to decide if humans are merely superior animals with interests that are essentially materialistic, or if they are distinguished from the animals by a spiritual side to their nature that yearns for the transcendental, as is the theme of religion.

Second, we have to decide if humanity is a collection of groups contending for dominance in one world, or if it is one family—another theme of religion.

The very act of asking these questions, I would suggest, is what is important. This is because once asked the practical evidence in each case points all in one direction.

With regard to human nature, it is, of course, fashionable to have a pessimistic view: humanity is essentially self-centered, greedy, selfish, and violent. This point of view is no doubt justified by some of the major collective experiences of this century: two world wars and the Holocaust of the European Jews. But a moment's reflection is surely enough to show that this view is one sided and not in accordance with either individual experience or the collective experience of history. Human beings do have a spiritual side to their nature, as shown in noble actions, and an instinct for the transcendental that even the most powerful of militantly atheistic regimes have been unable to crush in seven decades of dictatorial rule.

Similarly, the forces of history make it clear that groups struggling for dominance today are dangerous to all, including themselves, and that their goals are unattainable and irrelevant. To advance, indeed, to survive, we have to act as one family—to be true to the findings of biology, which show that our physical differences are minute compared with our physical commonality.

If we do indeed perceive human beings to have a spiritual side to their nature and humanity to be one family, there are, it seems to me, some clear guidelines on how to deal with the economic agenda of the next decade or so.

Thus, if we are in essence spiritual beings, then the end product of an economy should be those goods and services that help each man, woman, and child develop their full physical, mental, and spiritual potential. This surely means an economy that puts emphasis on basic physical needs-quality food, clothing, shelter, health care, and exercise facilities— and on cultivation of the mind and spirit education in the arts, sciences, and ethics, skills in crafts and native culture, appreciation of nature. It suggests reduced emphasis, if not outright voluntary abolition, of those goods, services, and practices that are essentially harmful and degrading to the body, mind and spirit: excessive luxury, conspicuous waste, throw-away goods, and other practices that are damaging to the global ecology—junk foods, alcohol, tobacco, and other drugs. In very broad terms, this all means a long-term shift in economic activity from production of goods to production of services-a process already started: the post-industrial age.

If we are one family, then in economics, as in politics and social affairs, the spirit of management should be cooperative and mutually supportive. Competition and striving for excellence is indeed to be encouraged, but with the purpose of maximizing service to humanity, rather than mere self-advancement. Labor and capital markets should provide a more rational system of reward based on this theme of real service to the community. In particular, if we are one family, the poverty of even one human being is intolerable to the rest, and the elimination of poverty throughout the world will be of the highest priority and will justify sacrifice by all those fortunate enough not to be in poverty. The cessation of war between nations (which must be a logical consequence of adoption of the idea of the oneness of the human family) would alone release large resources for the relief of poverty.

To summarize, the opportunities for the advancement of humanity presented by the evolving world economy are immense—greater even than those that occurred with the introduction of agriculture and with the coming of the Industrial Revolution. But to exploit those opportunities, the right decisions have to be taken, and that will to a large extent depend on the system of values that we follow.

Postcript

This presentation was made at a conference on the theme "Economie et Societe: quelles perspectives au-dela des crises actuelles" held in Lausanne, Switzerland in October 1988. The Association for Bahá'í Studies for francophone Europe, which sponsored the conference, had invited a wide range of participants including some who might well have had a typical Western European perspective of extreme scepticism with regard to religion. Accordingly, the approach taken was to minimize direct reference to the Bahá'í Faith both in terms of quotations and solutions. As will be noted, the emphasis was on raising fairly conventional questions rather than answers and on suggesting that when seen together such questions inevitably lead back to fundamental spiritual principles.

However, in a published paper, it is perhaps appropriate to make some more direct comment on the Bahá'í approach to economics. In the Bahá'í Writings, economics is not treated as a separate subject as such but rather as an aspect of the human condition at both the level of the individual and of the community, and, therefore, references with economic significance form a part of a seamless whole. Nevertheless, there are some key passages in the Writings and in statements of the Universal House of Justice and its associated institutions that are particularly relevant to the discussion in this presentation. With regard to the Bahá'í view of the evolution of a global economy, there are two passages in *The World Order of Bahá'u'lláh* by Shoghi

Effendi[2] in sections headed respectively: "The Goal of a New World Order" and "The Unfoldment of World Civilization":

> Some form of a world super-state must needs be evolved, in whose favor all the nations of the world will have willingly ceded. . .certain rights to impose taxation. . .A world community in which all economic barriers will have been permanently demolished and the interdependence of Capital and Labor definitely recognized. . .a single code of international law. . .(40-41)
>
> . . .a world legislature, whose members will, as the trustees of the whole of mankind, ultimately control the entire resources of all the component nations. . .A mechanism of world inter-communication will be devised. . . A world language will either be invented or chosen from among the existing languages. . . A world script. . .a uniform and universal system of currency, of weights and measures, will simplify and facilitate intercourse and understanding among the nations and races of mankind. . .The economic resources of the world will be organized, its sources of raw materials will be tapped and fully utilized, its markets will be coordinated and developed, and the distribution of its products will be equitably regulated.
>
> . . .economic barriers and restrictions will be completely abolished, and the inordinate distinction between classes will be obliterated. Destitution on the one hand, and gross accumulation of ownership on the other, will disappear. The enormous energy dissipated and wasted on war, whether economic or political, will be consecrated to

such ends as will extend the range of human inventions and technical development, to the increase of the productivity of mankind, to the extermination of disease, to the extension of scientific research, to the raising of the standard of physical health, to the sharpening and refinement of the human brain, to the exploitation of the unused and unsuspected resources of the planet, to the prolongation of human life, and to the furtherance of any other agency that can stimulate the intellectual, the moral, and spiritual life of the entire human race. (pp. 203-4)

With regard to economic and social development, the key document is: ***The Bahá'í Mandate for Development***[3] issued by the Universal House of Justice in 1983. A useful supplement is a report issued by the Bahá'í World Centre in 1985 summarizing information on Bahá'í development projects around the world at that time.[4] The Bahá'í approach to environmental issues has been officially summarized by the Bahá'í International Community Office at the United Nations in ***A Statement on the Environment***[5], which was prepared for the World Commission on Environment and Development, and by the Research Department of the Bahá'í World Centre in a compilation headed ***Conserving our Natural Resources***.[6]

As for commentaries by individual Bahá'ís, perhaps the most comprehensive summary of Bahá'í economic teachings is to be found in "Economics and the Bahá'í Teachings: An Overview" (Gregory C. Dahl, ***World Order*** Magazine, Fall 1975), which includes a wide range of references to the Bahá'í Writings. Very useful also is a compilation from the Bahá'í Writings entitled, A Bahá'í Perspective of Economics of the

Future, by Badi Shams (New Delhi: Bahá'í Publishing Trust, 1989). A broad picture of Bahá'í economic goals is given in the first article of this book: "The Economy of a World Commonwealth"[7]. These articles include some discussion of transitional arrangements to regime of world free trade. A comprehensive review of the Bahá'í approach to development is given in **Social and Economic Development: A Bahá'í Approach** by Holly Hanson Vick (Oxford: George Ronald, 1989).

NOTES

1. This was a common phrase of the fifties and was particularly used in the election manifestos of the British Labour Party of that time.
2. Rev. ed., Wilmette: Bahá'í Publishing trust, 1974.
3. *Bahá'í News,* January, 1984.
4. *Bahá'í News,* March and April, 1986.
5. *Bahá'í News,* November, 1988.
6. Reprinted in *Bahá'í News,* January, 1990
7. A short version was first published in *World Order* Magazine, Summer, 1975, and the longer version in *Bahá'í Studies Notebook,* vol. III, nos. 3 and 4, February, 1984.

ECONOMIC PERSPECTIVES OF THE GREAT RELIGIONS

**A presentation at the "Other Economic Summit",
Houston, Texas, U.S.A., 1990**

I should like to congratulate the organizers for having included 'religious perspectives' on the agenda of this conference. I doubt that our friends attending the G7 summit will be discussing such a subject. Nevertheless, if I may say so without seeming ungracious, it does seem that an objective outsider might be puzzled to find this subject slotted for a non plenary session on the afternoon of the third day of this three day conference. After all the conference is really about 'values' and religion, for all its faults, has historically been a most powerful force affecting the value systems of ordinary people. Perhaps the next time logic will dictate a more central place on the agenda!

I have been invited to make a brief presentation of the Bahá'í perspective on economics. As the Bahá'í Faith is the newest of the great world religions and is not particularly well known despite frequent mention in the news during the last decade because of the community's persecution in Irán, it might be useful for me to start with a few words of background information. The Bahá'í Faith was founded in nineteenth century Irán by Bahá'u'lláh (a title meaning the Glory of God in Arabic) who lived from 1817 to 1892. Since then the Faith has spread around the

world and is credited by the Encyclopedia Britannica
with having adherents in more countries and lands
than any other religion except Christianity. World wide
there are (1990) about 5 million Bahá'ís.

The Bahá'í view is that man is essentially a
spiritual being, not merely a super intelligent animal
who consumes things. The purpose of life is to develop
ourselves to our full potential and in particular to
develop the qualities of the spirit: those qualities
which make us noble. We are given guidance in this
task by the Messengers of God, those inspired and
insightful Founders of the world's great religions.

Bahá'ís see their Faith as being both a renewal of
religion and a new religion. It is a renewal in the sense
that it teaches the same universal principles about life
that have been taught in the past by all the great
religions. Thus Bahá'ís see all religions as essentially
one and therefore revere equally the Founders of all
religions—a viewpoint which can create a profound
sense of the unity of humanity. The Bahá'í purpose
is to give renewed energy to the flame of inspiration
which has become suffocated by corruption and
superstition as religious organizations have grown old.

The Bahá'í Faith is seen as a new religion in the
sense that it recognizes that each religion adapts
universal principles to the practical circumstances of
its age. Thus in this age of the "global village" the Faith
puts emphasis on that aspect of the universal
principle of love which pertains to conscious striving
to abolish prejudice against those who are different,
and to cultivate an appreciation of the enriching
beauty of the diversity of humanity. The purpose of
the Bahá'í Faith is to bring about the unity of all
humanity on the basis of diversity. Such unity is
viewed as necessary both in order to simply survive
as well as to maximize the opportunity for the creation
of an "ever advancing civilization".

How does this all relate to economics? The program notes point out that "the majority of all religious doctrines do come to a common conclusion that an economic system be a part of a moral order which is based on the unity of the people and brings them together. Social justice becomes a basic source of economic efficiency." Most recently in a remarkable book **For the Common Good,** Herman Daly and John Cobb have identified four basic characteristics of the religious viewpoint which have an important bearing on economic thought.[1]

From a Bahá'í perspective there are perhaps three broad aspects of religious thought that are significant in this context and which embrace and broaden the characteristics mentioned in the agenda notes and by Messrs Daly and Cobb. The first is a sense of detachment when relating to the material world which is seen as only one part of the life of the spirit. By detachment I do not mean asceticism or indifference to what is going on in the world but rather a balance —the golden rule. With such a view, material possessions are not an obsession and this clearly has bearing on selfishness, greed, violence, etc...We have the models of a Jesus and a Buddha. The second characteristic is a sense of harmony with nature and the universe-all the creation of God. We recognize our status in this God-given environment and this gives a sense of responsibility and trusteeship, humility, a concern for the future, and interconnectedness. Well known examples of awe and reverence for nature inspired by religion include the culture of Native Americans and Australian Aborigines, St. Francis of Assisi, and the way of life of the Hindus and Jains of India. The third characteristic common to all great religions is a sense of universal solidarity and care for the welfare of all our fellow human beings.

Of course, religious organizations as they have

aged and become corrupt have often strayed from these fundamental and universal themes of life. Churches, far from being detached, have become obsessed with the collection of material wealth. There have been dangerous trends towards anthropocentrism and an arrogance we were warned against by the Greek philosophers. Too often religious institutions have upheld the rich oppressors and diverted the poor with Marx's 'opium of the people'. The truly spiritual person cuts through this undergrowth of corruption to find the original and pure spring of religion.

Let me now briefly turn to the specifics of the Bahá'í Faith—the Faith in its role as a new religion with the mission of uniting humanity and establishing a universal peace based on justice. This mission is more than exhortation; it is supported by a practical program of teachings for both the individual and the community which are mutually supportive. The program is based on solid foundations: changing people and institutions from the inside, and in a step by step process. An example of a step in the latter process is the critical stage of abolishing war between nations (the Lesser Peace) which it is promised will be achieved by the end of this century.

There is no chapter in Bahá'í writings labeled 'economics' but there are a large number of teachings which have economic relevance and which when brought together give a reasonably detailed picture of the economy of the Bahá'í model of a World Commonwealth. To contrast the Bahá'í model with the conventional model of consumer capitalism, it is perhaps useful for me to say a few words about three subjects which are of basic importance for any economy: goods and services, distribution of those goods and services; and economic organization.

It seems very clear that with regard to types of

goods and services there would be a sorting into several priorities. One priority would be to make sure that all humanity would be provided with the basic material necessities with regard to food, clothing, shelter and medical care. Without such necessities people are potentially handicapped in working to reach their full potential, physically, intellectually and spiritually.

A second priority of equal importance would be to deliver to all humanity a range of services which will nurture intellectual and spiritual development: literacy and education, including support for both local languages and an auxiliary universal language, participatory institutions, sport and outdoor activities, a beautiful and harmonious environment, and the arts. Because material resources are comparatively limited, present Bahá'í programs for economic and social development are largely concentrated on activities pertaining to this second group of priorities. These activities are often characterized by innovativeness and a high benefit to cost ratio, such as training of village tutors in India and radio stations managed by and for the benefit of indigenous rural communities in Africa and the Americas. The emphasis is on goods and services of a high quality. This characteristic is associated with pride in local culture and a belief that service is the highest form of worship.

On the other hand, it is clear that goods and services that are harmful to the human spirit would be strongly discouraged e.g. alcohol and other drugs, tobacco, prostitution, excessive luxury and ugliness, throw away goods and wasteful services which are so extremely individualistic as to be anti-social. This does not imply Puritanism. Bahá'ís enjoy the good things of life but within a code of social responsibility and an awareness of the dangers of attachment.

Two other aspects of the Bahá'í view of goods and services should be mentioned. First, it is foreseen that humanity will ultimately become vegetarian and move away from a meat diet with all its inefficiency and spiritual coarseness. Second, it is clear that agriculture would play a central role in a Bahá'í economy. This has major implications for sustainable production of basic goods and for the development of spiritual sensitivity as a result of being in daily contact with the cycle of nature. The vision, of course, is not one of a return to bucolic ignorance and poverty but of harmony between science and nature.

It is important to stress that Bahá'ís believe that these priorities and characteristics would arise more from the choice of spiritually motivated individuals than government decree. There is an obvious point of connection between this vision and important present day economic and social trends: a shift from goods to services, greater decentralization as a result of the computer and other advanced communication technology, and concern for a healthy lifestyle.

With regard to our second subject, the question of distribution of goods and services, there is, as so often in religion, a creative paradox or tension. On the one hand is the basic universal principle of reward and punishment, a natural, spiritual, law which guides man along the path of his own best interest. In economics this means reward for those who strive to contribute to the general welfare and with holding of reward for those that do not. Every person is expected to have a useful occupation, and begging and gambling are forbidden. The approach applies equally to the rich drone as well as the welfare cheat!

On the other hand, modifying this principle, is the specific Bahá'í teaching deploring extremes of wealth (which corrupts) and poverty (which handicaps in perhaps a more obvious way). To achieve this goal there is much reliance on individuals becoming increasingly mature spiritually and, as a consequence, voluntarily giving of wealth for the benefit of the community, as well as practicing equity in passing on wealth from generation to generation. In addition there is provision, as necessary, for community action to redistribute wealth more fairly through such methods as progressive taxation and management of the world's natural resources for the benefit of all (ie. as distinct from the present practice of allocating natural resources to those who happen to be born in the right place at the right time). To minimize the emergence of extreme differences in the first place, Bahá'í teachings put great emphasis on education and literacy, equality of men and women, upholding the family, and various features of a Bahá'í approach to economic organizations.

This brings me to our third subject, the organization of a model Bahá'í economy. Here again there is a creative paradox. On the one hand is an emphasis on individual initiative and responsibility and clearly a major role is intended for the entrepreneur. On the other hand, there is at least equal emphasis on the individual as a member of a global community and on the spiritual and the material value of cooperation. In the broadest sense the latter theme entails the establishment of a democratically elected and spiritually inspired federal world government to manage a global economy, initiating such activities as fair distribution of natural resources, a single world currency, and unified systems of commercial law, and weights and measures. It also involves local communities providing socials services, including storage of basic commodities to protect against fluctuations in supply and demand, as well as privately and publicly organized cooperatives. The style of operation in all enterprises, public and private, would put emphasis on consultation and on properly supervised profit sharing rather than on confrontation between manager/owner and worker/employee. The community would intervene to prevent monopoly and oligopoly and the associated inefficient and unfair manipulation of prices.

In this very brief overview of the Bahá'í perspective on economics I have placed most emphasis on values and spirit rather than formal economic models because, as in all aspects of human society, it is the former which determined how things will really be. Yes, the Bahá'í economy will undoubtedly make use of such concepts as scarcity, division of labor, prices based on a balance between supply and demand, etc., but the net result is a system which is very different from conventional consumer capitalism. At the same time it bears no resemblance to the Marxist model. Its strength lies in the logic which follows from seeing humanity not as a species devoted to consuming things but rather as one whose unique and highest aspect is its spiritual dimension.

NOTES

1. Published by Beacon Press, Boston, 1989
2. The long term shift from goods to services may have bearing on flattening out the trade cycle.

SOCIALISM

A draft article for the Bahá'í Encyclopedia, 1990

Socialism is a philosophy and political movement of the industrial age which has spread around the world but which is essentially western in origin. Its central thesis is the need for state intervention in the economy to ensure a reduction in extremes of wealth and poverty. Both elements of the thesis have long roots in the past. The idea of state intervention in the economy goes back to the beginning of civilization and has embraced a wide variety of purposes including, as in the case of subsidized bread for the citizens of Rome, occasional concern for the welfare of the poor. The idea that society as a whole should care about the material welfare of the poor is clearly associated with the concept of the brotherhood of mankind and charity propagated by all the great religions. An early example of a political movement advocating greater economic equality were the Levellers during the English Commonwealth of the seventeenth century.

The socialist movement came to life with the industrial revolution because the latter (a) vastly increased man's ability to produce wealth and thereby for the first time made the abolition of poverty a feasible goal; and (b) resulted in the concentration of large numbers of workers in factories and industrial towns, a development which made it easier to organize mass support for socialist goals. Thus, though socialism is concerned for the poor in general, it has a tradition of special concern for and support from the industrial working class. Outrage at the sharp contrast between the new wealth of the factory owners and other capitalists on the one hand and the appalling living conditions of the industrial workers, on the other prompted a change of perspective from religious compassion for the unfortunate to demand for greater economic equity on the basis that wealth was essentially created by the labor of the worker. Inevitably, the socialist movement has always had close ties with the trade union and the cooperative movements.

In broad terms, there have been three elements to the socialist idea of state intervention in the economy on behalf of the poor. The most distinctive has been that society i.e. the state, should own the main instruments for production of wealth (the commanding heights): manufacturing, finance and distribution. The second element, which has in practice often been given a higher priority because the benefits for poor people can be made more immediate and because of practical considerations, has been a network of measures collectively known as the welfare state. The welfare state involves measures to ensure (i) minimum income especially during the times of vulnerability, e.g. insurance for unemployment, sickness and injury, old age, etc; (ii) safe and reasonable working conditions; (iii) adequate housing and health care; as well as (iv) universal free or low cost education. The cost of state welfare as well as the other activities of the state should be largely paid out of taxes which are progressive, i.e. based on ability to pay. The third element of the socialist program is to develop a general plan for the economy to make sure that it produces and distributes the desired goods and services at the right prices and that unemployment is minimized. Though the welfare state and state planning of an economy are both features of the socialist program which have been just as important as nationalization of the "commanding heights" of the economy, they are practices which have been adopted to greater or lesser degree by other political parties and therefore, in the popular view, they are not considered especially socialistic.

Because the poor have always been the majority it would be natural for the socialist movement to be strongly democratic, on the assumption that the poor, recognizing that socialism is in their interest, would vote for socialist governments. This has been often the case, but there has always been a tendency for part of the socialist movement to be impatient with democracy because its procedures slow down the process of eliminating the injustice of extreme poverty. Sometimes the poor are slow to realize where their best interest lies; sometimes the state is not democratic anyway. Such circumstances, some socialists have argued, justify use of force and revolution. Since its beginning the socialist movement has been divided on this fundamental issue: achieving economic justice through democracy and law or through revolution and violence. (The main revolutionary wing of the socialist movement has been Marxism: please see separate article). Socialists have been united, at least in theory, in not being seduced by the temptations of nationalism. On the whole, the socialist movement has been more world minded than most other political movements, arguing that the untrammelled sovereignty of the national state is not in the best interest of the poor of the world who have more in common with each other than with the oppressive classes of their own nations.

The socialist movement had its beginnings in the three leading countries of nineteenth century Western Europe: France, where it was prompted by the principles of the 1789 Revolution; Germany with its traditions of state regulation of the economy; and England where the industrial revolution started. In the first six or seven decades of the nineteenth century the movement was small and insignificant and totally overshadowed on the political left by liberal and radical movements struggling to win political democracy. However, with the expansion of industry which created a growing industrial working class and volatile trade cycles which frequently caused massive unemployment, the socialist movement gradually began to win popular support and by 1914 socialist parties were in existence in virtually every independent state. In 1912, the German socialist party, which was the strongest in the world, won 35 percent of the vote in that year's national elections and became the largest party in parliament. Two years earlier, the first national labor/socialist government came to power in Australia. In addition, the influence of the movement was a significant contributing factor in the passing of laws in several countries which represented the beginnng of the welfare state.

The turmoil resulting from the Great War (1914-1918) created the opportunity for perhaps the greatest single triumph of the socialist movement: the Russian revolution of 1917 and the establishment of a permanent socialist government in one of the largest states of the world. Elsewhere, labor/socialist parties came to power at various times in several countries but always as a partner in a coalition rather than as the sole party of government. This trend helped to create a more moderate image for the socialist movement while limiting the range of socialist policies that could be implemented. The high tide of socialism came in the decade or two after the Second World War. Virtually all Eastern Europe became socialist through force of Russian arms. After decades of civil war the Communits party achieved power in China in 1949.

Soon the revolutionary wing of socialism ruled about one third of the world's population and was winning support in other parts of the world, notably in Third World countries struggling to achieve independence from the great colonial empires. The democratic wing of the movement had its moments of triumph during this period also, most notably in the United Kingdom, where a model welfare state was established, as well as in Scandinavia, Western Europe, and Australasia.

By the nineteenth seventies, however, the confidence and prestige of the socialist movement had begun to wilt. This was partly due to disillusionment with the record of communist governments where harsh dictatorships and abuse of individual human rights more than cancelled out achievments in making for a more economically equitable society. More generally it was argued both in the East and the West that state ownership of enterprises and other state interventions in the economy tended to cause inefficiencies and rigidities and that a competitive market economy would be more democratic, productive, and responsive to the wishes of most of the population. Even the welfare state which was generally popular was reviewed critically with a view to making it more effective, especially with regard to those functions such as unemployment benefits which it was believed created dependency and sapped individual initiative. Everywhere the tide of socialism seemed to be in retreat.

In response to these developments the movement is beginning (1990) to change its strategy for achieving the goal of greater economic equality and the abolition of poverty. The emphasis is increasingly on such strategies as equality of opportunity, especially in education and with regard to inherited wealth, rather than imposed equality regardless of merit: on encouraging competition in the provision of goods and services, on dismantling monopoly power whether private or public, on open government, on protection of the environment, etc.

Any statement about a Bahá'í perspective on the socialist movement should start with acknowledgement that there is virtually no direct references in the Bahá'í Writings except for the comments of Shoghi Effendi with regard to certain aspects of Communism, the revolutionary wing of the movement discussed in the article on Marxism. Unfortunately, there is not even a full record of 'Abdu'l-Bahá's address given to the Socialist Society of Montreal in 1912. Nevertheless, it is possible to make some general and specific comment on the socialist movement from the perspective of Bahá'í principles. Thus, there is an obvious sympathy with the socialist concern for the poor because a fundamental Bahá'í principle is to eliminate extremes of wealth and poverty. Furthermore, it is clear that this will require intervention by the community in the operation of the economy. The idea of the welfare state is generally in line with Bahá'í teachings on universal compulsory education, progressive taxation and community responsibility for looking after orphans, the sick and the aged.

Strategic economic planning by the state in broad terms is also a policy akin to some Bahá'í teachings such as the goal of ensuring that the natural resources of the world are used for the benefit of all and that every community establish a store house to provide for emergency needs. With regard to the third main element in socialist policy: state ownership of the commanding heights of the economy, the more pragmatic approach of the socialist movement in recent years is clearly closer to the Bahá'í position than the tradition approach of the old left wing of the movement. Though undoubtedly there would be a role in a Bahá'í commonwealth for community enterprises, there would also be a major role for cooperatives and for individual entrepreneurs, though it should be noted that the latter would be obliged to share their profits with employees, and that such profit sharing schemes would be supervised for fairness by the community.

From a Bahá'í perspective, the main deficiency in socialist philosophy to date has been an over reliance on the power of the state to achieve its goal and an unestimation of the importance of individual motivation and initiative. At heart this arises from the different perspectives of progressive movements, one of which is essentially secular and one which has a spiritual or religious foundation. In the Bahá'í view, there are several key elements in the religious perspective which are vital for the struggle to achieve a just economy. One is the sense of detachment from material goods and services which is associated with a larger view of life than the simple physical existence. Such detachment greatly modifies the motive of greed which is one of the main causes of persistant economic inequality. A second religious perspective is a sense of the brotherhood of mankind: a sense which can be so strong that it will not permit the truly religious person to rest while his or her fellow human beings are deprived of the necessities of life and hampered thereby from achieving their full potential. A third and closely related religious motivation is belief in personal responsibility for our actions and development. Poverty, no matter where it is in the world, is not someone else's problem, it is ours.

MARXISM

A draft article for the Bahá'í Encyclopedia, 1990

Marxism is the name given to political, social, and economic ideas developed by Karl Marx (1818-1883) in association with Frederick Engels (1820-1895). It has been the single most powerful influence in the world socialist movement (please see preceding article on Socialism). It is a term which is often used interchangeably with Communism, although it should be recognized on the one hand that Marxism is a philosophy which extends beyond politics and economics into such fields a sociology and history, and on the other hand, that communism has been a term applied to several pre-Marxist political groups. Karl Marx developed his ideas in response to the writings of the early French socialists which he dismissed as sentimental and impractical. His aim was to make socialism seem highly scientific and an inevitable development of history, an approach which would strengthen the confidence of the socialist movement and undermine the resolution of its opponents. Three of the most well known works spelling out the Marxist thesis are *The Manifesto of the Communist Party* (1848) and *Capital,* Volume 1 (1867) both by Karl Marx and *Anti-Duhring: Socialism Utopian and Scientific* (1878), by Frederick Engels. The main structure of the Marxist philosophy is a follows:

History is about man's struggle to free himself from the bondage of nature so that he can rise to his full mental and physical potential. One of man's inventions to achieve this goal has been the division of labor which, by having each concentrate on doing what he is best at, increases the efficiency of society as a whole and thereby creates wealth over and above that which is necessary just to survive. However, the division of labor leads inevitably to inequality and then to exploitation of the weaker by the most powerful. History becomes a series of struggles between the exploiters and the exploited (the majority), each struggle ending with the exploited, driven by desperation, overthrowing their oppressors and thus fulfilling Marx's theory of dialectical materialism. According to this theory, there is a dialectical process whereby the struggle between the oppressor (representing a thesis) is eventually overthrown by the oppressed (anti-thesis) and as a result a new force emerges (syn-thesis). Marx identified several main stages in history in accordance with this theme: primitive society; slave-based society; feudalism; and capitalism. He contended, though, that the outcome of the struggle between the capitalist and the worker would be different from the pattern of the past and would not lead to a further round of exploitation, because once the worker was victorious all property would be communal and there would not be a new exploiter class.[1]

The capitalist system bore within itself the seeds of its own destruction because its main driving force, competition, forced the capitalist to beat down the wages of the workers to the point where, in order to survive, they would be obliged to counter-attack and defeat him.[2] Competition also led to the elimination of the weaker capitalists over time so that in the end there would be just a few powerful capitalists left wielding monopoly power against the rest of society, which would have sunk into the ranks of the working class.

These underlying laws of society, Marx argued, have been obscured by superficial ideas such as religion, which distracts attention from the misery of the poor in this world by promises of happiness in the next; nationalism, which divides the working classes of the world so that the oppressors can more easily hold them down; and the concept of the great leader, who in fact is only a tool of the ruling class. All culture is a reflection of class interest, and therefore morality is relative, not absolute. It is the duty of the enlightened person to tear aside these superficial veils and to demonstrate to the workers what is the reality of their exploitation and encourage them to take action in their own interest. Though capitalism will fall of its own accord, the pain involved for all concerned will be reduced if action is taken to speed up the course of history.

The workers should form their own party to fight for their own interest alone. Such a "socialist" party could make temporary alliances with reforming parties of other classes for tactical advantage in a particular situation, but should never compromise on the ultimate goal of overthrowing the capitalist system by whatever means is available, democratic or revolutionary. A socialist party should not support reform of the capitalist system because that would only serve to delay its final demise. Violence is unfortunate but is justified by the end result. A successful revolution might initially leave pockets of resistance made up of disgruntled former property owners. Therefore it might be necessary to have a transitional period during which there would be a worker's dictatorship, as earlier advocated by the French revolutionaries, Babeuf and Blanqui, to protect the socialist system of state ownership of all productive property, before the ultimate goal of communism would be established. In the state of communism all goods and services produced would be free for those who need them, and all would voluntarily contribute to the general wealth of the community according to his or her ability.

It was clear that Karl Marx believed that industrialization was a vital prerequisite of socialism. When asked if socialism could be built in an agriculture or feudal country such as Russia, he said yes because he did not want to discourage his followers in such countries, but he added the caveat that this would only happen after socialism had been established first in some industrial capitalist countries.

In fact, the first socialist state was established in Russia (1917-1918) and this was to have a profound effect on the evolution of Marxism. If, for instance, Marxism had been first successful in Germany, as many expected because for long the German socialist (Marxist) party was the most powerful in the world, then its evolution would likely have been more benign. One key development was a 1903 decision of the Russian socialist party, at the insistence of Lenin (1870-1924), that it would not be a mass democratic party but rather a small elite group of professional revolutionaries, which would be organized on a cell system with top down management and appointment. This decision reflected security needs when operating against the Czar's authoritarian government and secret police, as well as perhaps recognition that for a long time the party's main supporters, the industrial workers, would be a small minority of the nation's population and therefore not likely to win by democratic means.

Lenin's group, the Bolsheviks (the majority) drove out the Mensheviks (the minority) who there upon formed their own Marxist socialist party. Under Lenin's leadership, the Bolsheviks, following Marxist theory, were pragmatic in their tactics concerning seizure and maintenance of power. For instance, during the Civil War (1918-1922), that followed the Revolution of 1917, the state took over all productive enterprises under a policy called "War Communism". However, in 1922 this gave way to a more moderate "New Economic Policy", which allowed small private businesses, when the former policy proved to be unpopular with the mass of the people.

The special stamp of the Russian party on Marxism was taken further by Lenin's successor as leader, Joseph Stalin (1879-1953) with his Five Year Plans for speedy industrialization of the country. This policy was partly on account of the Marxist theory that socialism required industrialization. It also partly reflected security considerations—the need for a large arms industry—in the face of a world of hostile capitalist nations. The main cost of the Five Year Plans had to be borne by agriculture, by far the biggest sector of the economy, and this was to be achieved by forced collectivization and nationalization of the land. The peasantry objected strongly to this policy and this was the beginning of one of Marxism's greatest failures: its inability for decades to be able to motivate agricultural workers to be productive and efficient. Opposition to the Five Year Plans prompted Stalin to repressive measures on an unprecedented scale, not only against the peasantry but also against a high proportion of the Bolsheviks who had sacrficed so much to win the Revolution. Repression went hand in hand with a personality cult to make Stalin the great and infallible leader. Stalinism was heir to both Czarist autocracy and a dynamic of violent revolution which compels it to "eat its own children".

Though Marxism was to be dominated for decades by the policies and practices of Lenin and Stalin, this domination was by no means monolithic and over time other variants were to emerge, most notably, Trotskyism, Maoism, Titoism, and Euro-Communism.

Leo Trotsky (1879-1940) one of the principal leaders of the 1917 Revolution broke with Stalin because he believed that socialism would only succeed if there was active stimulation of revolution all around the world. Stalin argued for establishing a strong base in one country first: "Socialism in one country". Trotsky was driven into exile and was eventually assassinated in Mexico by Stalin's agents. Nevertheless his ideas lingered on for several decades in many parts of the world.

After the Russian Revolution of 1917, the second greatest triumph of Marxism was the Chinese Revolution of 1949 led by Mao Zedong (1893-1976). China in 1949 was even less industrialized than Russia in 1917, and the revolution had been won largely as a result of a long lasting guerilla war waged by a peasant army operating, as Mao said, in its natural environment, the countryside, like a fish in the sea. The Chinese Revolution was seen as a model by many radicals in colonial countries who were leading the fight for political and economic independence. Mao argued that a revolution must be continous or permanent so as to prevent the party from becoming a rigid and elitist bureaucracy—a characteristic of Chinese society for more than 2,000 years. Thus, the resulting Cultural Revolution (1966-1976) was aimed at the party bureacracy as well as traditional culture and values such as Confucianism.

Whereas in the East, Marxism evolved in the direction of centralized authoritarianism, in the West there was a tendency towards decentralization and democracy. In Yugoslavia, the one European country where a Communist government achieved power independently and not from the dominance of the Russian Red Army, Marshall Tito (1892-1980) and his successors pioneered a form of Communism which gave a much greater degree of autonomy to localities and individual industrial plants. As Western European countries prospered after the Second World War, the appeal of revolution, never very strong, withered away, and most of the Communist parties in this region had by the nineteen seventies announced a willingness to work within the democratic framework a policy with roots in the nineteenth century German socialist party (which was generally Marxist in its outlook) as well as the inter-war writings of the Italian Marxist leader, Antonio Gramci (1897-1937).

As the winds of change blew eastwards: demands for "socialism with a human face" were heard in Hungary, Czechoslovakia, East Germany and Poland. By the nineteen eighties, the liberal interpretation of Marxism had reached into the very heartlands of China and Russia. In China, land was leased to the agricultural workers with a resulting rapid increase in the production of food and the general standard of living. In Russia, a new leader, Mikhail Gorbachev, pushed for a policy of restructuring of the economy (perestroika)—decentralization and market pricing—and for greater political freedom (glasnost). In both countries there was a willingness to abandon support of violent revolutions elsewhere in favour of policies of cooperation with democratic capitalism. The new Soviet leaders put emphasis on working within United Nations to achieve peaceful resolution of conflicts, to protect the natural environment, and to manage the world economy for the benefit of all.

For decades the Marxist movement enjoyed immense prestige among intellectuals, students and the poor, because it seemed to promise the just society as well as a more efficient economic system. The Party itself, was for long full of confidence, because of a belief that the workers' communist state was an historial certainty, as captured by Nikita Krushchev's (1894-1971) boast that 'we will bury you'.[3] The movement's influence reached a peak in the nineteen sixties and seventies as Marxist parties came to power, or seemed on the verge of doing so, in East Asia, Africa, the Caribbean and Latin America.

Despite such apparent success there were signs for many years that all was not well: deep ideological splits eg. between the Soviet Union and China, as well as increasingly obvious failures of the centralized command system in managing a complex economy and in delivering consumer goods. Nevertheless, the total collapse of the system in Eastern Europe and the Soviet Union in a three year period (1989-1991) was an event that was almost universally unexpected. The reforms of Mikhail Gorbachev, courageous and often visionary as they were, proved to be too little and too late. For millions who had live under Marxism it was no longer associated with justice and equality, but rather with the police state, waste, inefficiency, corruption and nepotism. The collapse of the system in Eastern Europe and the Soviet Union was accompanied by a similar, though perhaps less dramatic, process in other parts of the world, with the result that by the beginning of 1992 there were only a few Marxist governments still in power: in China, North Korea, Cuba, Vietnam, Laos and Cambodia.

Clearly the theory and practices of Marxism have had important features which are deplorable from a Bahá'í point of view. The most fundamental is the undue weight given to materialism and the absence of a spiritual dimension. While Bahá'ís will agree that material considerations have played a large part in the shaping of history and that decadent religion has indeed been the "opium of the people", it is believed that fundamentally history is about the spiritual evolution of man and that true religion is the channel for this evolution. It can well be argued that absence of a spiritual dimension would explain the complete failure of Marxism to fulfill its ambition to create a change in the outlook of the citizens of Russia—the much heralded "Soviet man".[4] The materialistic perspective can easily be linked to some of the aspects of Marxism which are now generally deplored: thus the arguments that the end justifies the means and that ethics are only a narrow reflection of class interest, have encouraged division of society along class lines, widespread violence, dictatorship and denial of basic human rights, cynicism, the personality cult, etc.

"The chief idols in the desecrated temple of mankind are none other than the triple gods of Nationalism, Racialism, and Communism, at whose alters governments and peoples, whether democratic or totalitarian, at peace or at war, of the East or of the West, Christian or Islamic, are, in various forms and in different degrees, now worshipping. Their high priests are the politicians and the worldly-wise, the so-called sages of the age; their sacrifice, the flesh and blood of the slaughtered multitudes; their incantations outworn shibboleths and insidious and irreverent formulas; their incense, the smoke of anguish that ascends from the lacerated hearts of the bereaved, the maimed and the homeless."[5] Shoghi Effendi.

The turmoil of the present time is not conducive to a balanced assessment of the successes of Marxism in, for instance, reducing poverty and raising standards of health and education. Nevertheless it seems safe to opine that history will not judge such achievements to have been worth the tremendous suffering that was involved, for instance in numerous wars of aggression and revolution (Korea, Indo China, Africa and Central America) as well as in such horrendous events as Stalin's Great Terror (1936-

1939), Mao's Cultural Revolution (1966-1976) and the Cambodian killing fields (1975-1976).

Having noted all this, it is surely only fair to add that there are also some aspects of Marxism that are in accordance with the Bahá'í viewpoint. First, there is moral indignation against an unjust economic system which results in extremes of wealth and poverty, and a shared determination that a more just system must be established. Bahá'ís may admire the many Marxists, including Karl Marx himself, who have made great personal sacrifices in order to further the cause of justice. Second, there is a shared recognition of the importance of the age we live in, that humanity is passing into a new stage in its evolution, and that though this is inevitable because of the forces of history, it is the duty of all to assist with the process so as to reduce the pain of transition. Third, Bahá'ís could also applaud the generally global vision of the Marxist movement and its ultimate recognition that a fundamental goal of man is to develop himself to his full potential.

NOTES

1. There would still be a right to private PERSONAL property.
2. Marx argued that labor is the source of, and determinant of, real value in a good or service. A material thing has no value unless it has been worked on by man, modified in structure, or transported, etc. Marx defined labor as the average amount required to make a socially needed product. He recognised that the amount would change as the tools used improved. The vast wealth of the capitalist gives him a leverage over his employees whereby he is able to force them to accept wages which are no more than sufficient to keep them efficient and productive workers. The difference between these wages and the amount he is able to sell their product for, which Marx called the "surplus value", he keeps for himself.
3. A phrase meaning that the Soviet economy would overtake that of the West, not a military threat, as some believed.

4. One interesting aspect of this failure from a Bahá'í perspective is attitude to "service" which for a Bahá'í is the highest form of worship. The Marxist-socialist ethic would clearly imply a high value on public service yet in practice service in Marxist states is almost always extraordinarily slow, uncaring, even surly, and of a low quality. This may be because of lack of personal responsibility in a highly centralized command system; it may also be a lingering association of service with the perceived demeaning servant-master relationship of the past.

5. *The Promised Day is Come,* pp.117-118.

PRINCIPLES OF ECONOMIC JUSTICE

Presentation at the Third International Dialogue on Transition to a Global Society, Llandegg, Switzerland, 1992

Webster's Dictionary defines economics as "a social science concerned chiefly with description and analysis of the production, distribution and consumption of goods and services". Such a definition covers a large range of activities such as labor, management, technology, ownership, trade, banking and finance, government regulation and taxation, and innovation, as well as the key concept of efficiency, which is to produce the most wealth with the least resources. Many other activities could be included in an exhaustive list, and in fact it is probable that most social and political activity has some bearing, great or small, on the functioning of an economy. It is likely, therefore, that most aspects of the general concept of justice also relate to the narrower idea of 'economic justice'. However, in what follows, the discussion is restricted to three key principles of justice which are generally acknowledged to be directly and significantly relevant to economics.

The first of these principles, which is perhaps the most universally recognized in nearly all cultures, past and present, is the right of every person to earn and create wealth for his or her own benefit, by the production of goods and services which are useful, or otherwise desirable, for the producer or for others.

Implicit in this principle is an understanding that it
excludes activity which causes obvious direct harm
to others. This principle seems to bear a close
relationship to the most basic drive of all life, which
is to survive, and it is advocated by all the great
religions of the world, most notably in the Mosaic
teaching concerning just deserts, reward for good
behavior and punishment for bad behavior, i.e. the
encouragement, *inter alia,* of hard work, enterprise
and service. There are a number of sub-themes to this
principle. One is honesty in business dealings,
another universal religious teaching, which is
especially evident in the philosophy and practice of
Zoroastrianism. Honesty strengthens the idea that
reward for enterprise is merited. A second sub-theme
is an emphasis on the value of education, as in
Confucian teachings. This results in the acquisition
of greater skills with which to create wealth. A related
idea is found in Adam Smith's principle that efficiency
is promoted when an individual or nation concentrates
on economic activities which he, or she does best;
what a few years ago Michael Porter called 'competitive
advantage'. The beginnings of such an idea can be
found in Hinduism, in the philosophy of Plato, and
in the feudal system of medieval Europe, where in
differing ways, there is the advocacy of specialization
in occupation, though, of course, each of these
systems omits the complementary vital factor of
freedom of choice. Efficiency is economically just,
because it means making the best use of resources
available to create wealth, which in turn will typically
mean lower prices that will benefit society as a whole.
Conversely, waste is unjust because it reduces the
general well-being.

   The right to create wealth, the first principle of
economic justice, is an aspect of 'freedom', and it has
as a normal consequence a tendency to result in

differences in levels of wealth, often including extreme riches for some, and extreme poverty for others. This has prompted the emergence of a modifying second principle of economic justice, which is that extremes of wealth and poverty are not conducive to the peace and well-being of society.

Such extremes are morally abhorrent because it is believed that the wealthy, by holding on to surpluses and living in comparative luxury, are depriving the poor of basic necessities, and that poverty could be alleviated or even abolished if wealth were more evenly distributed. This concept is parallel with the economic law of marginal utility, which suggests that an additional unit of wealth for a poor person would create more happiness than the happiness foregone by a rich person surrendering the same unit of wealth. Another aspect of this principle of economic justice is that extreme wealth (relative to that of others in a society), will tend to divert government from pursuit of the general interest in favor of the special interest of those who have the most resources to influence or bribe it. To summarize; social peace and harmony demands, in the wider context of justice, that freedom, though desirable, should be limited, to some degree, so as to enhance the level of equality.

Some cultures try to hinder the development of extremes of wealth and poverty by teaching the wealthy that they have a moral responsibility to give help to their extended family or tribe. Sometimes such cultural constraints are comparatively effective, as in several East Asian countries. On the other hand, such a culture can have a negative result under modern conditions. For example, government employees, raised with such values, often use their offices to obtain illegal benefits for their families at the expense of society as a whole. In any case, concern for the extended family is usually not sufficiently systematic to significantly reduce the incidence of poverty, and religions have almost always taught the need for a second remedy, namely voluntary giving by the rich, charity for the poor, a teaching which is underpinned by the basic theme of love, brotherhood, and social solidarity. In some cases religious teachings go further and, for instance, require limits on interest rates for loans and, as in Islám, a general tax with proceeds being used for the benefit of the poor. Again such measures, in practice, have been generally an amelioration, rather than a root and branch solution, and in most societies throughout history, extremes of luxury and desperate need continue to exist, side by side. Until modern times this was generally accepted as an inevitable condition of life: "The poor are always with us".

Attitudes changed dramatically with the coming of the industrial revolution in the nineteenth century, because it appeared to promise, for the first time in history, that enough wealth could be created to abolish poverty, if there were a fairer distribution. As a result, numerous movements sprang up which offered various ways to achieve such a just distribution: socialism, trade unions, syndicalism, and the cooperative movement, to name some of the more important. Within these movements, a major distinction arose between those who believed that greater equality should be achieved through law and the democratic process, on the one hand[1], and those who, on the other hand, believed that extremes of wealth and poverty were so morally offensive that they justified extreme measures, such as revolution. Democracy, the latter would argue, does not exist in many countries and in any case, where it does, it takes too long and results in weak half-measures. In practice the revolutionary option (typically the

Communist system) often was close to straightforward robbery by those whose motivations were less than pure, and the result was the substitution of one economic injustice for another.

As the improved communications associated with the industrial revolution made for a more closely integrated global society, the original concern to reduce extremes of wealth and poverty *within* nations was broadened to include the goal of reducing the per capita wealth gap *between* nations, and, to help achieve that goal, advocacy of voluntary transfers of wealth to the poor nations, bilaterally, or, preferably, multilaterally through international organizations such as the World Bank.

The third principle of economic justice, which is now generally acknowledged, is the need for an economy to be in harmony with nature, i.e. to be 'sustainable'. This is basically another modifier or constraint of the first principle, though for a time there were many who feared that it would become a constraint of the second principles as well, i.e. it would be used as an argument to slow down the struggle to eliminate poverty. This third principle is also relatively new; in its fully developed form it is essentially a product of the second half of the twentieth century, when a horrifying picture began to emerge of the side effects on the environment of widespread industrialization. However, it is evident that this concept of economic justice does have deep historical roots. Disastrous damage to the environment caused by human economic activities is, after all, not new; what is extraordinary about present day depredations is their speed of occurrence, complexity and geographic extent. There are early signs of warnings about this issue in the teachings of Hinduism and Buddhism, with their respect for all life and relative detachment from material wealth. This

third principle of economic justice is about requiring
wealth to be created with minimum pollution and
immediate health hazard. In the longer perspective,
it is about wealth creation and, more long term,
without robbing future generations of their birthright
to the scarce resources of the planet. There is also
present, I believe, a more profound underlying
religious perspective, namely that humankind is the
custodian of the earth, and is responsible for
protecting nature for its own sake, simply because it
is all a creation of God.

The prevailing wisdom has been that the three
basic principles of economic justice outlined above
pull in different directions, and that the art of creating
a just economic system is to find the optimum balance
between them. In modern times, the economy of the
world has been dominated by two fiercely competing
systems which, the respective proponents argue, are
based on this optimum balance: capitalism, which
gives greatest value to the first principle, and
socialism, which gives the most value to the second.

In the last decade, there has been world-wide
disenchantment with the socialist approach, a sharp
reversal of view from that prevailing some thirty or
forty years ago. The most dramatic manifestation of
this disenchantment was, of course, the collapse of
the Communist regimes of the Soviet bloc, but no less
remarkable has been the gradual retreat from the
welfare state in modern industrial economies, changes
of direction in the economic policy of Communist
China, and the widespread conversion of third world
economies to a free market system. Socialism has
been a great disappointment, it is generally believed,
because its formula for equality, which involved
varying degrees of state ownership of enterprises, free
social services, and heavy regulation and taxation
created immense inefficiencies and a 'dependency'

culture. With minimum market discipline, there was little incentive for enterprises to keep down costs; goods and services were often of poor quality and unattractive to consumers; and there was little encouragement of financial reward for hard work, initiative and innovation. A common saying in Communist Europe was 'They pretend to pay us, and we pretend to work'. The result, too often, was equality in poverty and environmental disaster rather than equality in prosperity.

The collapse of the socialist approach to economic justice has apparently left the field to a triumphant consumer capitalist system. But this system has generally shown inadequacy in responding to the second and third principles of economic justice which have been identified. Indeed, it was its failure on the second point, the elimination of the extremes of wealth and poverty, which provoked the rise of socialism in the first place. It may create more wealth and the types of goods and services that many want, but it also causes greater extremes[2], and its record with regard to harmony with nature is frequently not much better than that of the Communist system. Side effects of the system are crime, drugs and a breakdown of social cohesion and community spirit.

In recent years, there has been a significant effort to reform both systems with a view to eliminating these deficiences. For instance, socialists are now focusing more on equality of 'opportunity', e.g. provision of first class education for all and removal of special privileges, rather than on equality of 'results'; whilst advocates of capitalism are arguing for a more consistent attack on the privileges of monopoly in all its manifestations, so as to make for a more democratic and merit-based market, and for the development of social safety nets which are targeted to assistance of those in genuine need, instead of the socialist concept of a universalist welfare state.

These discussions have been useful, but it seems doubtful that they will result in a full answer to the problem of finding the optimum balance between our three principles of economic justice. This is, I suggest, because there is missing a unifying sense of the ultimate purpose of an economy, indeed of life itself, and a value system needed to achieve that goal. It is true that Karl Marx and Adam Smith, for example, have each in their different ways written of such ultimate objectives as social refinement and the advance of civilization, and in recent years the UN Index of International Development has attempted to measure the general physical and intellectual well-being of all humanity. However, such concepts have not been part of the common understanding of either socialism or capitalism in recent decades. Rather, the prevailing emphasis has been on a straightforward materialistic philosophy of maximizing production and consumption as the real objectives of society: a crude perversion of the Utilitarian principle of the greatest happiness of the greatest number.

The related values that have become associated with such goals have been, in the case of socialism, a dependency culture, with demand for the support of all, regardless of effort at self help, and a contempt for the idea of serving others, an idea associated with past demeaning relationships between masters and servants[3]. In the case of capitalism, the predominant ethos is increasingly one of greed and a ruthless willingness to cut corners and evade the law, especially with regard to taxation, whenever opportunity arises. The view that 'the end justifies the means' seems just as prevalent as it has been amongst Marxists. I suggest that such goals and value systems are not going to be the basis for a system of economic justice.

Where, then, to turn in these circumstances? A reasonable approach, I would venture, is to look for a system which has its roots, in terms of purpose and values, in humanity's religious experience, which, as observed earlier, is the main source for the three basic principles of economic justice. This is not surprising, as one of the main purposes of religion itself is to give guidance on how to make the most of our physical lives, with an authority above, and independent of, personal prejudice and political convenience. Though there may be differing emphasis in the way teachings are presented in the current practices of the world's great religions, it is clear they all are agreed that the main purpose of life is to grow towards God, to develop our spiritual qualities, to become noble beings. From this can be derived a unifying purpose for a just economy, which is to provide the resources that will enable every individual on the planet to reach his or her full potential: physical, intellectual, and, above all, spiritual. Noble thought and action, the highest ethical values, are the means to achieve that purpose. In other words, there is a unity of purpose and means.

The problem is that the traditional religions have lost their power to inspire most of their adherents to strive for higher standards of behavior, and show little interest in uniting with other religions to provide guidance for a world which is becoming more integrated with every passing day. One exception is the Bahá'í Faith, which has both the energy and inspiration of a new Revelation, and has teachings which restate universal principles in terms of the needs of the modern age.

Given this perspective, I would like to briefly outline an alternative to socialism and capitalism, a third economic system which would be based on social and economic principles which are clearly presented in Bahá'í teachings. In discussing this third model, I propose to group my remarks around the activities and functions of three key players in any economic system: that is, the individual, the firm (or enterprise), and the community (or State).

It is generally acknowledged that culture and a value system at the personal level are vital factors in determining the success or failure of an economy. Thus, the Scandinavian countries, Switzerland, Japan, Korea, Taiwan have all achieved economic prosperity despite limited natural resources, whilst other countries with much greater natural resources, which furthermore have not been struck down by war or natural disaster, have remained poor. Economic success is an important consideration in this discussion because it usually facilitates a more balanced mix of the three key principles of economic justice: thus, the rich industrial countries generally make better provision for the poor, have a narrower range of extremes of wealth and poverty, and, as shown in recent World Bank reports, are able and willing to take greater measures to protect the environment than countries that are materially less well off.

The qualities at the personal level which are traditionally seen as conducive to a successful economy include a strong sense of personal responsibility for the material well-being of one's self and one's family, a commitment to hard work and finding a useful occupation, pride in what is produced, honesty, truthfulness, respect for the law, etc. Conversely, gambling, which explicitly involves trying to obtain something for nothing and risks family well-being on the basis of chance, is a habit that invites economic disaster. It is also generally recognized that a successful economy is often based on a high value being placed on education, both scientific and moral. In the Bahá'í view, the highly intimate role that the mother plays in nurturing her child, thereby prompting the values of the next generation, justifies priority being given to the education of girls, if circumstances force a choice. Perhaps less obvious, though this may be changing, is a need for commitment to the unity of the family[4] and to the equality of men and women. The latter principle is not only a direct question of economic justice[5], but, in addition, it is a key way to increase the size and quality of the workforce which is creating wealth.

The level of economic justice in a society is also affected by the values of the individual as a consumer as well as producer. One important value in this context is a willingness to save part of an income, as insurance against future unforeseen difficulties, to provide for the education of children as well as for old age, and to fund productive investment. A second is to have a balanced view of material consumption, being conscious of the desirability of providing for the necessities basic to physical well-being: food, clothing, shelter, and medical care, and then essentially using the remainder of the resources available for services which contribute to the ennoblement of the mind and spirit[6]. A third important value is to abhor waste, so as not to deprive others, and at the same time avoid unnecessary consumption of scarce natural resources. A fourth is to have a strong sense of community solidarity, and to be committed to the idea of voluntary giving of wealth for the benefit of the less well-off and other community needs. This strong sense of community responsibility should also have a bearing on individual decisions of how many children to have. Whilst children are one of the main purposes of marriage, their number should take account not only of the parents' capacity to provide adequately for them, but also the larger social concerns about the size of the global population in relation to the environment and quality of life. Finally, justice requires that everyone makes a will to ensure that assets left at the end of life are broadly distributed in the family, so as to avoid a situation in which some are unduly privileged or put in a position where they are discouraged from exerting themselves and developing themselves to their full potential. Continuation of extremes of wealth and poverty is as much a function of transfers of wealth between generations as it is of income during an individual's lifetime.

Most of the qualities desirable at the personal level to achieve a just economic system apply equally to the behavior of the business enterprise and to government. But there are additional elements in the behaviour of the business enterprise which would greatly facilitate achievement of a just economic system. Experience suggests that such factors, together with basic ethical principles, as discussed above, should receive special attention in the former Communist countries. This is because lack of experience of a free market system has led many to believe that economic success depends on ruthlessness and the law of the jungle.

Though some enterprises are 'not for profit', most do view profit, in return for services rendered to others, to be a key objective. Sometimes there are strong pressures, especially when management is separated from ownership, as happens typically when shares are bought and sold on the stock market, for the firm to see maximization of profits as its only objective. Experience indicates that such a narrow and selfish goal is unlikely to contribute to a fully rounded system of economic justice. What is essential is that a firm balance is legitimate concern for profit—its reward for its services— with an explicit commitment to the general well-being of society. This implies, at a minimum, that a business should be conducted with complete honesty and trustworthiness. Beyond that, such a commitment has additional special implication with regard to each main category of its relationships : with its customers, its employees, its suppliers and competitors, its community neighbors, the world community at large, and government.

In relation to its customers, an enterprise should be focused on providing goods and services which are to their benefit and contribute to the achievement of the overarching purpose of life which is the creation of a noble race of men. Providing goods and services which are harmful and pander to the lower aspect of human nature e.g. drugs, alcohol, pornography, etc.- undermine that purpose. Likewise, the firm should be aware of the environmental impact of its product, and should give high priority to eliminating any that is negative, e.g. with regard to manufacture, packaging, distribution, use, maintenance, and ultimate disposal.

This theme of concern for the welfare of humanity applies equally to relations with employees. One practice advocated in Bahá'í teachings, because of its obvious potential for promotion of two of the principles of economic justice, is sharing of profits with employees, as well as full and regular consultation with them on all aspects of corporation management. Such a partnership arrangement shares rewards and risks more equitably than orthodox relationships, which so often lead to disruptive conflict within the firm between 'them and us'. A promising variant of the profit sharing model is an arrangement whereby employee shares are financed with credit arranged by the firm, which allows for a relatively speedy and more effective sharing process, and provides employees with a security independent of the firm's possibly varying needs for labor. A firm should also be committed to the highest standards of safety in the workplace, and to equal treatment of all, regardless of race, religion, class, gender, etc.

In relation to suppliers and competitor organizations, an enterprise committed to a just economic system has an obligation not only to practice the general ethical principles mentioned earlier, but also to specifically shun such unfair practices as bribery, cross subsidization of prices, and other non-economic measures which are intended to drive other companies out of business or into submission. On the contrary, opportunities to cooperate should be pursued, as a matter of principle, so long as the intent and result is not a reduction in the level and quality of service to the public.

Finally, an enterprise has an obligation to the community at large, especially to its neighbors. An enterprise must be concerned about the impact of its activities on the community, and should be committed to significant voluntary giving to help with its development and well-being.

I should now like to turn briefly to the role of government, the collective instrument of the community, in relation to the goal of establishing a just economic system. In recent years, the general failure of socialism has created a near universal reaction against 'big' government, and many have adopted the view that it should be limited to certain basic functions that only the State can carry out. The most basic such function is the provision of physical security for life and property of all citizens against both external and internal threat, and administration of law and order. With regard to the economy, it is argued that the State's role should be limited to the dual functions of maintaining a 'level playing field' so that all enterprises have an opportunity to operate freely on an equal basis, and ensuring appropriate safety and environmental standards. The State should minimize its activity with regard to redistribution of wealth, and in management and ownership of enterprises producing non-government types of goods and services. Some have even suggested caps on the total size of the public sector, perhaps 25 to 40 percent of the gross domestic product, which compares with levels which today are in the region of 45 to 60 percent for a significant number of nations, rich and poor alike. In many ways, this has been a useful discussion and forces necessary intellectual discipline and analysis. However, in terms of economic justice such an approach can be a risky path unless it is complementary to a major effort to encourage just behavior at the levels of the individual and the enterprise, as previously discussed. It should be added in this context that there is no proof that the State is inherently inefficient as a manager of economic enterprises, and it may be that some means will be found in the future to overcome present weaknesses, just as, in the nineteenth century, reforms in Western countries increased the efficiency of State administration by reducing corruption and by recruiting for the civil service on the basis of merit rather than privilege or the spoils system.

The other general observation that should be made with regard to government and economic justice is that the economy is increasingly global, and inevitably that means government has to be global too, if anarchy is to be avoided e.g. the already widespread practice of corporations evading national taxes and regulations by maneuvering internationally. A weak confederal arrangement, as now exists in the shape of the United Nations, simply does not have the authority to carry out even the minimum functions which are necessary to establish a just political, social and economic system, at the global level as has been demonstrated repeatedly in response to military aggression against members, abolition of world poverty, and protection of the environment. This clearly indicates a need for a democratic federal world government.

In recent decades, there has been a great deal of hostile, and often irrational, rhetoric, especially in the USA, against the idea of a world federal government, on the grounds that it would inevitably be some sort of Orwellian dictatorship. This fear always seemed somewhat exaggerated, because the key players in establishing such a world federal government would have been the USA itself, along with other powerful democratic nations which have been its allies for many years, and they would surely have the power to ensure whatever safeguards against such a dictatorship that they consider necessary. In any case, such objections have been significantly weakened in the last few years by the rapid spread of democracy, both in terms of numbers of countries[7], and in terms of depth and strength[8]. In short, the majority of the national 'pillars' of a world federal government are themselves largely democratic and this, in itself, is an added guarantee that any world federal government would also be democratic.

What should be the structure and functions of a future democratic federal world government in terms of relevance to the question at hand? The Bahá'í view is that the structure should be built on maximum decentralization to national and local community levels[9], with the world level limiting its activities to those that can only be performed at that level, i.e. the concept of 'subsidiarity' now frequently discussed in connection with the European Community. As for functions, there appear to be two of special importance.

The first would be the protection and fostering of a genuine global economic system— a system which would facilitate the growth of global wealth, because it would serve to maximize the market for all enterprises. This is turn would create opportunity for efficiencies associated with economies of scale, whilst at the same time facilitating the more equal distribution of wealth, because poorer areas would have improved opportunity to exploit their competitive advantage of low costs. This function would include provision for the following measures, all clearly delineated in the authoritative texts of the Bahá'í Faith.

1. The maintenance of peace and international law and order, by means of a comprehensive international legal system, a World Court with compulsory powers of arbitration, and a world police force[10].

2. The abolition of all trade barriers[11].

3. The establishment of a single world currency, to eliminate the risk and costs of international transactions associated with constantly volatile market relationships between national currencies; as well as a standard global system of weights and measures[12].

4. The selection of an auxiliary world language[13].

The second broad function of the world federal government necessary to achieve a just economy would be provision of measures, supplementary to those already discussed, at the individual and enterprise levels, that would facilitate the abolition of extremes of wealth and poverty, and keep the world economy 'sustainable' over the long term. Some of these measures would be:

1. Administration of mineral and other limited natural resources of the world so that this common heritage is used for the benefit of all

humanity, and not just for a minority who happen to be at the right place at the right time— as has happened most obviously in our own time with regard to oil[14].

2. Establishment of a compulsory universal education system providing the highest quality instruction in the arts, sciences and ethics, including emphasis on the unity of humanity, so that all men and women would be properly equipped to work in a useful occupation[15].

3. Special attention to agriculture[16], because of its vital role in feeding humanity and in harmonizing society with nature. One related measure would be provision of facilities in all towns and villages for storage of surplus production, as a safeguard against years of shortage, as well as the stabilization of prices[17].

4. Application of a progressive tax system, which would ensure fair contributions to public needs according to ability to pay, whilst not being so burdensome that it weakens financial incentive to be productive. The greater the commitment to voluntary giving in the community, the lower the tax level can be. Low rates would also be facilitated by a system which is simple and clearly understood by all, and which, for instance, excludes loopholes that presently undermine the theoretically progressive structure of many national systems, giving privileges to some and creating resentment in others[18].

5. Provision of high quality social services for orphans, the aged, the sick, the handicapped, and others in need[19].

6. Supervision of the economy to prevent exploitation of the public in the case of monopoly, to safeguard the interest of all parties in profit

sharing arrangements, and to ensure sustainable use of the natural environment[20].

Conclusion

The Bahá'í economic model is not so much one of trade-offs, or compromises, between the three basic principles of economic justice, but rather a means for them to be merged into a single unified theme of justice. This is achieved by developing an ethical standard throughout society that puts emphasis on service to humanity as the highest form of worship, and which explicitly acknowledges that the purpose of life is to acquire the qualities of nobility. To be effective the model depends on voluntary action by individuals and enterprises, with the State giving supplementary support and overarching guidance to ensure achievement of the basic goals of economic justice. History shows that religion is by far the most powerful instrument for inspiring high ethical standards, because it speaks to the heart as well as the head of every man, woman and child. The Bahá'í Faith adds the vital nuance, in this time of global convergence, that it teaches, without reservation, equal reverence for all the Founders of the world's great religions, and appreciation for the diversity of culture, both essential in the task of unifying humanity on the basis of justice.

NOTES

1. The rise of democracy has been a major factor in the movement towards greater economic equality because it gave much more influence to the poor, usually the majority, in the affairs of a nation, than in earlier days of authoritarian government and privilege.
2. The frequently quoted "trickle down" phenomenon is often slow to develop, if at all.
3. One unfortunate manifestation of this attitude in socialist

countries is a culture of insolence towards customers and ordinary citizens on the part of anyone with even the least degree of authority or power.

4. Poverty, especially for children in western countries, is associated to a large extent with broken families—an injustice in itself where men escape responsibility for their actions.

5. That is, why should there be discrimination in the economy on the basis of gender?

6. It is of interest of note, in this context, that "Ábdu'l-Bahá is recorded as having said, "The time will come when meat will no longer be eaten". Cited in Julia M. Grundy, *Ten Days in the Light of 'Akká,* rev. ed., Wilmette, Bahá'í Publishing Trust, 1979, p.9.

7. For instance, in Latin America, South and Eastern Europe, Central and Eastern Asia, and Africa.

8. The end of the Cold War, and advances in communication systems have had the combined effect of making it increasingly difficult for "bad" governments to keep secret their human rights abuses, corruption and other criminal activities.

9. See 'Abdu'l-Bahá, talk at Church of the Ascension, Fifth Avenue and Tenth Street, New York, 2 June, 1912 (notes by Esther Foster), *The Promulgation of Universal Peace: Talks Delivered by 'Abdu'l-Bahá during His Visit to the United States and Canada in 1912,* comp. Howard MacNutt, 2nd ed., Wilmette: Bahá'í Publishing Trust, 1982, p.167.

10. See Shoghi Effendi, letter to "Fellow-believers in the Faith of Bahá'u'lláh", 28 November 1931, published as "The Goal of a New World Order", *The World Order of Bahá'u'lláh: Selected Letters,* 2nd rev. ed., Wilmette; Bahá'í Publishing Trust, 1974, pp.40-1.

11. See ibid., p.41.

12. See ibid, letter 'To the beloved of God and the handmaidens of the merciful throughout the West", 11 March 1936, published as "The Unfoldment of World Civilization", ibid., p.203.

13. See ibid.; also, Bahá'u'lláh, *Epistle to the Son of the Wolf,* trans. Shoghi Effendi, 1st pocket size ed., Wilmette: Bahá'í Publishing Trust, 1988, p.138.

14. See Shoghi Effendi, op. cit., p.204.

15. See the Universal House of Justice, statement "To the Peoples of the World", October 1985, published as *The Promise of World Peace,* rev. ed., London: Bahá'í Publishing Trust, 1992, p.14; also, Bahá'í International Community,

Office of Public Information, *The Prosperity of Humankind,* London: Bahá'í Publishing Trust, 1995, *Passim.*

16. See Bahá'u'lláh, *Lawh-i-Dunya* (Tablet of the World), Bahá'u'lláh, *Tablets of Bahá'u'lláh revealed after the Kitáb-i-Aqdas,* comp. Research Department of the Universal House of Justice, trans. Habib Taherzadeh with the assistance of a Committee at the Bahá'í World Centre, first US hardcover ed., Wilmette: Bahá'í Publishing Trust, 1993, p.90.

17. See 'Abdu'l-Bahá, *Foundations of World Unity,* comp. Horace Holley, rev. ed., Willmette: Bahá'í Publishing Trust, 1968, pp.39-41.

18. See ibid., p.40.

19. See ibid.

20. See 'Abdu'l-Bahá, *Some Answered Questions,* comp. and trans. Laura Clifford Barney, 1st pocket size ed., Wilmette: Bahá'í Publishing Trust, 1984, pp.274-5.

21. See Bahá'í International Community, Office of Public Information, op. cit., *passim.*

ELIMINATING EXTREMES OF WEALTH AND POVERTY

A press briefing note for the Second Bahá'í World Congress, New York, U.S.A., 1992

Eliminating extremes of wealth and poverty is a basic Bahá'í principle[1]. Such extremes are not conducive to the well being of either the particular groups affected or society as a whole. There are at least three important aspects to the application of the principle. The first is that it should be global; one of the main purposes of the Bahá'í community is the promotion of the unity of humanity. The second is that it is linked with another basic economic principle, the law of reward and punishment[2], which is common to all the great religions. This law promotes individual initiative and thus the growth in the amount of wealth available for distribution. Finally, the principle has to be understood in the context of the Bahá'í view of the purpose of life[3], which is for every human being to develop his or her potential to the full, especially our spiritual or noble qualities, and to assist in the development of an ever-advancing civilization. The Bahá'í teachings on eliminating extremes of wealth and poverty can be summarized in terms of the individual, the business and public administration.

At the individual level, Bahá'í teachings encourage both self reliance and care for others. There is a strong work ethic based on the theme that work, when in the service of others is the highest form of worship[4]. We should all have a useful occupation[5], and begging[6] and gambling[7] is forbidden. This is reinforced by a very high value being given to education[8] in both the arts and sciences as well as in character training. Two other Bahá'í concerns, namely teachings to uphold the family[9] and the equality of the sexes[10], serve the same purpose. If a choice has to be made, education for girls has a higher priority than for boys[11], because girls will be the mothers of the next generation. The relevance of such concerns is clear when it is considered that poverty in Western countries is often associated with single parent households, particularly those headed by a female, and that in many agrarian societies the economic role of women is equal to or even more important than that of men. With regard to distribution of wealth, there are two key teachings. The first is a model Will[12] which encourages wide distribution of wealth within the family when it is transferred between generations; it even makes provision for the teacher who, in the Bahá'í view merits a special status in society. The second is very strong encouragement of voluntary giving[13] for the benefit of the community.

The same themes of self-reliance and care for others apply to business. Individual initiative is highly encouraged. This is combined with a business ethic which promotes trust: honesty, truthfulness, reliability and faithfulness. At the same time, the businessman is to see his function as not simply making money but providing a service to the community. As service is the highest form of worship of God that service must be of the highest quality[14]. In practice, this means both a focus on those services which are conducive to the well-being of the body, mind and spirit, and an avoidance of those products which are harmful, e.g. alcohol[15] and tobacco[16]. The other side of the coin is a concern for sharing profits with employees CMS and voluntary giving, such as a willingness to provide help to the local community—the former provision to be supervised by the community to ensure fairness. Businesses, like any collective endeavor, should be managed on the basis of full consultation with those concerned. Trusts and monopoly situations would be strongly discouraged[18] and if absolutely necessary would be regulated to prevent unfair profit. On the basis of such standards, employee trade unions would be unnecessary[19], and lockouts and strikes would be strongly discouraged.

In the public sector, there is a clear link, in the Bahá'í perspective, between elimination of wealth and poverty and the establishment of a democratic world federal government[20] for overall supervision and planning of the economy. Such a federal system would follow the principle of subsidiarity[21] and give a significant role to the local community. A key economic function of the world federal body would be the creation of a single world economy based on such policies as free trade[22], a world currency[23], unified commercial law[24], a standard system of weights and measures[25], and a world communications network[26]. It would also involve a policy of ensuring that there is compulsory education for all children[27], including teaching of an auxiliary world language[28]. Creation of a true world economy is in the long run the most effective way of creating more wealth and reducing extremes of wealth between nations. The world government would also have the task of managing the world's mineral and other natural resources for the benefit of all humanity[29]. National and local communities in a society organized on Bahá'í principles would be responsible for managing a progressive income tax system with provision for negative tax in the case of the most poor[30], as well as royalties on use of mineral resources[31]. Local communities would provide a wide range of high quality social services such as colleges, hospitals, homes for orphans and for the incapable[32], etc.

As management of a sustainable economy in harmony with nature is necessary in order to avoid continuing poverty in the world, mention should also be made of important Bahá'í teachings conducive to this end. Some have already been discussed. For instance, an economy focused on the spiritual needs of all humanity beyond the basic material needs for food, clothing, shelter and medical care, would be service-oriented and therefore less demanding on scarce natural resources than the materialistic consumer society. This would be reinforced by encouragement of higher quality goods and services which would reduce waste. Other key teachings bearing on this question include responsible concern for the number of children in a family[33], and therefore population size; and encouragement, over time, of a switch to a vegetarian diet[34] which is not only likely to create a more healthy population (poor health is often associated with poverty), but more efficient use of agricultural resources than is possible with a meat-based diet. The key principle of "unity in diversity" protects not only the economic welfare of minority groups, but helps ensure different cultural solutions to agricultural problems which may be a critical means of protecting and maximizing the efficiency of an economy under greatly varying conditions.

Finally, a word should be said about social and economic development which after all has, as one of its most important goals, the elimination of poverty. At the present time, the Bahá'í world community has in hand some 700 projects[35] in such fields as education, health care, agriculture and radio communication. Common themes are an emphasis on self help, involvement of the user at all stages in the process, and a human scale.

NOTES

1. *Eliminating Extremes of Wealth*
   "We see among us men who are overburdened with riches on the one hand, and on the other those unfortunate ones who starve with nothing. . .This condition of affairs is wrong and must be remedied. . .The rich must give of their abundance. . .There must be special laws made dealing with these extremes of riches and want. . ."

   'Abdu'l-Bahá: *Wisdom of 'Abdu'l-Bahá*, p.140

2. *Reward and Punishment*
   "The trainer of the world is justice, for it is upheld by two pillars, reward and punishment. These two pillars are the source of life to the world."

   Bahá'u'lláh: *Bahá'í World Faith*, p.195

3. *Purpose of Life*
   "Noble have I created thee, yet thou hast abased thyself. Rise then unto that for which thou wast created."

   Bahá'u'lláh: *Hidden Words*, [Arabic], No.32

   "All men have been created to carry forward an ever advancing civilization."

   Bahá'u'lláh: *Gleanings*, p.214

4. *Service is Worship*
   "We have made this—your occupation—identical with the Worship of God."

   Bahá'u'lláh: *Bahá'í World Faith*, p.195

   "This is worship: to serve mankind and to administer to the needs of the people."

   'Abdu'l-Bahá: *Bahá'u'lláh and the New Era*, p.77

5. *Useful Occupation*
   "Waste not your time in idleness and indolence and occupy yourselves with that which will profit yourselves and others beside yourself."

   Bahá'u'lláh: *Bahá'í World Faith*, p.195

6. *Begging*
   "The most despised of men before God is he who sits and begs."

   Bahá'u'lláh: *Bahá'í World Faith*, p.195

7. *Gambling*
   "If a person gambles he will lose his money. . .it is quite clear therefore that. . .sorrows are the result of our own deeds."

   'Abdu'l-Bahá: *Paris Talks*, p.50

8. *Education*
"It is enjoined upon the father and the mother, as a duty, to strive with all effort to train the daughter and the son, to nurse them from the breast of knowledge and to rear them in the bosom of sciences and arts. Should they neglect this matter, they shall be held responsible and worthy of reproach in the presence of the stern Lord."
'Abdu'l-Bahá: Tablets Vol. III, pp.578-579

9. *Marriage and Family*
". . .a fortress for wellbeing and salvation."
Bahá'u'lláh: *Bahá'í Prayers,* Section 2, p.44

10. *Equality of the Sexes*
". . .He (Bahá'u'lláh) taught that men and women were equal in the sight of God and there is no distinction to be made between them."
'Abdu'l-Bahá: *Promise of Universal Peace,* p.169

11. *Education of Girls*
". . .furthermore the education of women is of greater importance than the education of men, for they are the mothers of the race and mothers rear the children."
'Abdu'l-Bahá: *Promise of Universal Peace,* p.169

12. *Model Will*
"When a person lies without leaving a will the value of the property shall be estimated and divided in certain stated proportions among seven classes of inheritors, namely children, wife or husband, father, mother, brothers, sisters, and teachers. . .Bahá'ís will naturally be influenced, in making their wills, by the model Bahá'u'lláh has laid down for the case of interstate estates which ensures distribution of the property among a considerable number of heirs."
with 'Abdu'l-Bahá's approval: *Bahá'u'lláh and the New Era,* pp.138-139

13. *Voluntary Giving*
"The time will come in the near future when humanity will become so much more sensitive than at present that the man of great wealth will not enjoy his luxury in comparison with the deplorable poverty about him. He will be forced, for his own happiness, to expend his wealth to procure better conditions for the community in which he lives."
'Abdu'l-Bahá: *Star of the West,* Vol. 8, No. 1 (March 21, 1917)

"And among the teachings of Bahá'u'lláh is voluntary sharing of one's property with others."
'Abdu'l-Bahá: *Foundations of World Unity,* p.30.

14. *High Quality Goods*
"The man who makes a piece of notepaper to the best of his ability, conscientiously, concentrating all his forces on perfecting it, is giving praise to God."
    'Abdu'l-Bahá: *Bahá'u'lláh and the New Era*, p.15

15. *Alcohol*
"The drinking of wine is. . .forbidden; for it is the cause of chronic diseases, weakenth the nerves and consumeth the mind."
    'Abdu'l-Bahá: *Advent of Divine Justice*, p.27

16. *Tobacco*
"There are other forbidden things. . .They are also abhorred, blamed and rejected of God, but their prohibition is not recorded in an absolute way. . .One of these last prohibitions is the smoking of tobacco, which is unclean, malodorous, disagreeable and vulgar and of which the gradual harmfulness is universally recognised".
    'Abdu'l-Bahá: *Bahá'í World Faith*, p.334.

17. *Profit Sharing*
"Therefore, laws and regulations should be established which would permit the workmen to receive from the factory owner their wages and a share. . .of the profits."
    'Abdu'l-Bahá: *Some Answered Question*, p.315

18. *Trusts and Monopolies*
"No more trusts will remain in the future. The question of trusts will be wiped out entirely."
    'Abdu'l-Bahá: *Foundations of World Unity*, p.43

19. *Trade Unions*
". . .the rights of the working people are to be strongly preserved. Also the rights of the capitalists are to be protected. When such a general plan is adopted by the will of both sides, should a strike occur, all the governments of the world should collectively resist it."
    'Abdu'l-Bahá: *Foundations of World Unity*, p.43

20. *World Federal Government*
"A world federal system, ruling the whole earth and exercising unchallengeable authority over its unimaginably vast resources. . .such is the goal toward which humanity, impelled by the unifying forces of life, is moving."
    Shoghi Effendi: *World Order of Bahá'u'lláh*, p.203

21. *Decentralization*
"The world wide law of Bahá'u'lláh. . .repudiates excessive centralization on the one hand, and disclaims all attempts at uniformity on the other. Its watchword is unity in diversity."
    Shoghi Effendi: *World Order of Bahá'u'lláh*, p.241

22. *Free Trade*
"Economic barriers and restrictions will be completely abolished."
> Shoghi Effendi: *World Order of Bahá'u'lláh,* p.204

23. *World Currency*
". . .a uniform and universal system of currency, of weights and measures, will simplify and facilitate intercourse. . . among the nations and races of mankind."
> Shoghi Effendi: *World Order of Bahá'u'lláh,* p.203

24. *Unified Law*
"This commonwealth must as far as we can visualize it, consist of a world legislature. . .(which) will enact such laws as shall be required to regulate the life, satisfy the needs and adjust the relationships of all races and peoples."
> Shoghi Effendi: *World Order of Bahá'u'lláh,* p.203
"A world community. . .in which a single code of international law. . ."
> Shoghi Effendi: *World Order of Bahá'u'lláh,* p.41

25. *Weights and Measures.* See note 23

26. *Communications*
"A mechanism of world inter communication will be devised, embracing the whole planet, freed from national hindrances and restrictions."
> Shoghi Effendi: *World Order of Bahá'u'lláh,* p.203

27. *Compulsory Eduction*
"The Bahá'í Faith. . .advocates compulsory education."
> Shoghi Effendi: *Bahá'í Education: A Compilation*

28. *Auxiliary World Language*
"A world language will either be invented or chosen from among the existing languages and will be taught in the schools of all the federated nations as an auxiliary to their mother tongue."
> Shoghi Effendi: *World Order of Bahá'u'lláh,* p.203

29. *Mineral resources*
"The economic resources of the world will be organized, its sources of raw materials will be tapped and fully utilized, its markets will be coordinated and developed, and the distribution of its products will be equitably regulated."
> Shoghi Effendi: *World Order of Bahá'u'lláh,* p.204

30. *Progressive Tax*
"One of the principal sources of revenue should be a graduated income tax. . .on the other hand, if a person. . . is unable to earn an income sufficient to meet his necessary expenses for the year, then what he lacks for the maintenance of himself and his family should be supplied

out of public funds."
                                    approved by 'Abdu'l-Bahá: *Bahá'u'lláh and the
                                                New Era,* p.149
"Each person in the community whose income is equal to
his individual producing capacity shall be exempt from
taxation. But if his income is greater than his needs he must
pay a tax until an adjustment is effected. That is to say, a
man's capacity for production and his needs will be
equalized and reconciled through taxation. If his production
exceeds he will pay no tax; if his necessities exceed his
production he shall receive an amount sufficient to equalize
or adjust. Therefore taxation will be proportionate to
capacity and production and there will be no poor in the
community."
                        'Abdu'l-Bahá: *Foundations of World Unity,* p.37
31. *Royalty on Mineral Resources*
"The third revenue, from the minerals, that is to say, every
mine prospected or discovered, a third thereof will go to this
vast storehouse. . .Fifth if any treasures shall be found on
the land they shall be devoted to this storehouse."
                        'Abdu'l-Bahá: *Foundations of World Unity,* p.39
32. *Social Services*
"Then the orphans will be looked after, all of whose expenses
will be taken care of. The cripples of the villages—all their
expenses will be looked after. The poor in the village—their
necessary expenses will be defrayed. And other members
who for valid reasons are incapacitated—the blind, the old,
the deaf—their comfort must be looked after. In the village
no one will remain in need or in want. All will live in the
utmost comfort and welfare. Yet no schism will assail the
general order of the body politic."
                        'Abdu'l-Bahá: *Foundations of World Unity,* p.40
"The Mashriqu'l-Adhkár has important accessories, which
are accounted of the basic foundations. These are; schools
for the orphan children, hospital and dispensary for the
poor, home for the incapable, college for the higher scientific
education, and hospice."
        'Abdu'l-Bahá: *Bahá'u'lláh and the New Era,* pp.173-174
33. *Population Growth*
There are no specific teachings on population and numbers
of children, and it is clear that one of the main purposes of
marriage is to produce children: "Marry O people, that from
you may appear he who will remember Me amongst My
servants". However, it is now generally recognized that the
best way to reduce population growth to a sustainable level,

is to provide for education, especially of women, and the skills which will raise peoples' ability to earn an income—precisely the teachings of the Bahá'í Faith.

34. *Vegetarian Diet*
"The food of the future will be fruits and grains. The time will come when meat will no longer be eaten. Medical science is only in its infancy, yet it has shown that our natural food is that which grows out of the ground."

'Abdu'l-Bahá: Bahá'u'lláh and the New Era, p.98

35. *Bahá'í Development Projects*
"Now 78 National Spiritual Assemblies and two Bahá'í Administrative Committees manage 703 projects, the vast majority of which are grassroots efforts operating with little or no outside support."

Bahá'í News, March, 1986, p.2

THE CHANGING ROLE OF THE INTERNATIONAL MONETARY FUND

A presentation at Dokko University, Osaka, Japan, 1994.

This article has been updated to take account of events since 1994, including the East Asian financial crisis of 1997.

Introduction

Today, of all the UN specialized agencies, the International Monetary Fund (IMF) is probably the most often in the media headlines. This is because it is frequently at centre stage with regard to developments in the international economy and its activities have an important impact on the lives of millions. Nevertheless, public knowledge of what the IMF is and how it functions is generally limited. The purpose of this presentation is, in a very modest way, to contribute to a correction of that situation. One of the most useful ways of achieving this goal is to review the historical evolution of the IMF since it was founded some 50 years ago, an approach for which I have a personal inclination because of an abiding interest in history as such. What I would like to do is review that history in terms of six broad periods. But before I do, perhaps I should briefly touch on some basic background issues: why it was created; its mission and functions; its membership; and its structure and organization.

Why the IMF was Created

During the Second World War, when the Allies were planning for the post war peace, there was concern to avoid mistakes that had been made after the First World War, and, in particular, the need to consider not only how to strengthen the main international organization (the League) and its ability to maintain peace, but also the question of how best to defuse the main causes of conflict and war in the first place. Two themes emerged from this concern. The first was protection of basic human rights, and from this theme came the Universal Declaration of Human Rights and related conventions and agreements. The second was the need to reduce poverty and to make for a prosperous global economic system.

There were two sub-themes to the economic question. The first was international cooperation to reconstruct the economies of nations that had been devastated by the war, an activity that later evolved into assistance in promoting the advancement of the economically less developed parts of the world. The second was the imperative need to avoid a repetition of the Great Depression that had immediately preceded the Second World War, and specifically "beggar my neighbor" international trade and financial policies such as massive increases in tariffs, restrictive quotas, competitive currency devaluations, multiple exchange rates, currency exchange restrictions, and so on. Because the economic issues were so important they were discussed as a separate issue from the general task of establishing the new United Nations, at a 1944 special conference held in the United States, at Bretton Woods in New Hampshire.

To meet the identified needs, three new international economic organizations were considered. The first was the International Bank for Reconstruction and Development, later known simply as the

World Bank, which was to channel capital to help reconstruct areas devastated by the war, and later to develop the non industrialized nations. The second was to be an International Trade Organization [ITO] which would promote free trade through the abolition of tariffs, quotas and other government imposed barriers to international trade. Such an institution proved to be too radical for the time and in 1948 it was decided to substitute a weaker General Agreement on Tariffs and Trade [GATT]. Nevertheless, in practice, GATT was much more successful than might have been expected, and in the next forty or so years it was instrumental in negotiating nine rounds of reductions in trade restrictions, the last of which culminated in the establishment of a new World Trade Organization which has much of the function and authority originally intended for the ITO. The third organization was the IMF which would complement the activities of the trade organizations by reducing barriers to trade on account of manipulation of relationships between national monetary systems.

Mission and Functions of the IMF
    The constitution of the IMF is the Articles of Agreement. Article I of that Agreement states that its mission is to "To promote international monetary cooperation" so as "to facilitate the expansion and balanced growth of international trade, and to contribute thereby to the promotion and maintenance of high levels of employment and real income and to the development of the productive resources of all members as primary objectives of economic policy". There were two main aspects to this mission:
    (i) Establishment of stable exchange rates between currencies on the basis of a new ***par value*** system, which represented a return to the nineteenth century gold standard, but with more conscious management

and flexibility. The system fixed the price of all currencies in relation to the US dollar which in turn was valued at $34 to an ounce of gold (Article IV), whilst making provision for occasional adjustments after full consultation.

(ii) Elimination of exchange restrictions on current account transactions (Article VIII). Restrictions on capital transactions were not addressed because at the time this was not perceived to be a major impediment to an efficient world economy.

To carry out this mission, the IMF was given functions at the international level that are similar to those of a central bank at the national level:

(i) Supervision: enforcement of the Articles of Agreement;

(ii) Lender of last resort: provision of financial loans from a revolving fund (hence the name of the organization), established under Article III, for short term use by members with balance of payments deficits with the purpose of giving them time to correct the situation without use of protectionism and beggar my neighbor practices;

(iii) Provision of Advice: with regard to policies on how best to correct balance of payments deficits, technical assistance on monetary and fiscal matters, etc.

(iv) Provision of Research and Information: collection and distribution of economic and financial data on member countries on a systematic basis, economic forecasts[1], policy research analysis, etc;

(v) Act as Permanent Forum for consultation on international monetary affairs.

Membership

When it opened for business in 1946, the IMF had some 46 member countries, mostly from the Americas and Western Europe, plus a few from Asia and Africa.

Its size was significantly less than that of the UN proper, mainly because of the absence of the Soviet bloc which decided not to join because they did not wish to reveal key data about their economies on the grounds that this would weaken their security. Over the next fifty years membership grew in two main surges: first the newly independent former colonies of the European empires, and then the former members of the Soviet bloc. Thus, by 1997 membership had grown to 181, only slightly less than that of the UN. By then the only important non members were North Korea, Cuba and Taiwan.

Structure and Organization

Quotas. A key element in the structure of the IMF is the "quota" or the subscription that each member nation pays to join the IMF, a sort of club membership fee which provides the revolving fund mentioned earlier. Individual quotas vary in size according to a broad formula that takes into account national income, imports, exports and reserves. In other words, big international trading economies such as the USA, Japan and Germany have much larger quotas[2] than smaller ones such as Seychelles or Antigua. A member pays 75 percent of its quota in its own currency and 25 percent in gold [originally] or in other currencies that are freely convertible ie usable by all nations. When the IMF came into existence in 1946, total quotas were the equivalent of US$7.6 billion. Since then, to meet the growing needs of the IMF, quotas have been periodically increased and today [1997] they are equal to about $200 billion[3]. Not all of these sums have been usable for lending purposes because they included subscriptions which were partly in unconvertible currencies [ie some of the contributions in members own currencies] which borrowing countries would not want to receive.

Borrowing and Voting. In terms of the operation of the organization the quotas are important in two ways. First, they determine the amount a member can borrow from the IMF. A large quota gives a larger borrowing entitlement than a small one, which is logical enough as the needs of a large trading nation are likely to be proportionately greater than those of a smaller one. Second, voting in the organization decision-making bodies is unequal, with each member's vote being weighted roughly in proportion to its quota. This is rationalised on the basis that voting should be determined according to contribution to the resources of the IMF, a realistic approach necessary to win the support of the wealthier countries which contribute the bulk of the financial resources of the organization. In this respect, of course, the IMF and the World Bank, which follows the same principle, are different from the UN General Assembly where every country has one vote, and in theory at least, Seychelles, for example, is the equal of the United States.

The Boards of Governors and Directors. The organization of the IMF has four basic components. The ruling body is the Board of Governors which consists of a Governor, supported by an Alternate from each member country (usually the Minister of Finance and Governor of the Central Bank, respectively). Naturally such a large body of important persons is somewhat unwieldy and as such it only meets once a year, generally in September [on a three year cycle, with two of the meetings being in Washington DC where the IMF has its headquarters, and one elsewhere on rotating basis]. In the last few decades, however, a series of crises have made it necessary to have an "Interim Committee" which meets twice every year. Representation on the Committee is similar to that on the Executive Board, the second level of the organization. Because the IMF has to make swift decisions on operational matters and there is a need for in depth discussion of policy issues, the founders agreed that the Board of Governors should delegate the day to day management of the IMF to an Executive Board, which would be on call more or less permanently at headquarters. The Executive Board originally had ·12 members but this has gradually increased to 24. Eight represent individual members countries[4] and 16 represent the other membership, organized into constituencies of broadly equal quota totals and by geographic region e.g. Latin Amercia, Africa, Asia etc. Both boards (Governors and Executive Directors) try to make decisions on the basis of consensus. When this is not possible they are generally on the basis of a simple majority, though for some important operational decisions the requirement is for a 70 percent affirmative vote, e.g. for a change in charges or interest payment rates, or, in the case of major policy issues, such as an amendment of the Articles or a general quota increase, an 85 percent affirmative vote. In the latter case, the USA has veto power because its vote exceeds 15 percent.

Management and Staff. The third component of the organization is the Managing Director who is elected by the Executive Board for five year terms. He has two main functions: to act as chair of the Executive Board and to be the Chief Executive Officer, or head of the staff which is the fourth component of the organization. Hitherto the Managing Director has always been a European, just as the President of the World Bank has always been from the USA, but this practice has been under increasing question and may well change in the near future. In 1946, the IMF had about 400 staff but since then, to meet expanding needs of a growing and diversified membership, the number has increased to about 2,500 drawn from some 125 members (1997). The goal is to recruit the most highly qualified staff [macro economists are the core of the staff], but within that criteria, as far as possible, to achieve also a nationality distribution based on quota ratios. Generally, both the IMF and its twin, the World Bank have avoided political appointments which have done so much to undermine the effectiveness and efficiency of other international organizations.

Phase I: The Decade of Transition, 1946-1955

When the IMF came into existence, most of the national economies of the world were in disarray as a result of the Second World War and were simply not strong enough to comply with IMF rules regarding removal of exchange restrictions, as required under Article VIII, and so there was widespread resort to Article XIV which allowed for their temporary suspension. A second difficulty was that the par value system, based on past currency relationships proved to be too demanding on many of the war ravaged nations and in consequence, in 1949 there were a series of major devaluations lead by the pound sterling which went down from US$4.00 to US$2.80.

During this time a large amount of financial assistance for Europe, as it struggled to recover from the war, was provided by the USA, the only strong economy of importance, on a bilateral basis, through the Marshall Plan. Comparatively little went through the Bretton Woods international institutions. Nevertheless, it was during this pencil that the IMF laid the foundations of operational methods followed in subsequent decades. First, it established the practice of sending staff consultation missions to each member on a routine basis, which did so much to make for close working relations with most ministries of finance and central banks. Second, it developed standard rules for use of IMF financial resources, including a normal banking principle of **conditionality** as a guarantee of security. Member countries needing to borrow an amount equal to 25 percent of their quota (the "gold" or "reserve" first tranche), ie to borrow back their real contribution, could do so with little in the way of conditions. However as the number of tranches needed increased, an indication of the seriousness of a countries balance of payments situation, the more rigorous would be the conditions. Conditionality, typically provided— for targets for a controlled devaluation of the currency, to make the economy more competitive, together with such supporting monetary actions as restrictions on credit and increases in interest rates[5]. The effects of conditionality could be quite painful in the short term, in terms of higher costs for imported consumer goods, on the one hand, and deflation and associated unemployment, on the other. Some argued that these effects were aggravated by the fact that conditions had to be met over a short period of time (12 to 18 months), as was true also of the loans repayment schedule (three to five years). The latter requirement was linked to the revolving nature of the IMF's resources and to the fact that loans had to be returned comparatively quickly in case they were needed to help other members that might in the meantime have encountered balance of payments difficulties[6].

Another important event during the latter part of this period was approval of membership for the former enemy nations, Japan, Germany, and Italy, all of whom were later to become major contributors and participants in the working of the IMF.

Phase II: Years of Expansion and the SDR, 1956-1970.

By the late fifties the economies of most countries devastated by the Second World War had recovered and, in consequence, several important members were able to implement the IMF requirements concerning removal of exchange restrictions under Article VIII, a precedent followed in subsequent years by the majority of other members[7].

Shortly afterwards there was a large influx in membership of newly independent states, including most of Africa, which more than doubled the size of the organization and to a degree modified its perspectives. In response to the changing membership, the IMF took three important actions. First, to meet the potential increased demand for financial resources it instituted procedures for periodic review of the overall size of quotas and made additional arrangements for supplementary stand by resources through the *General Agreement to Borrow* (GAB) from ten industrial countries[8]. Second, three new staff departments were added to provide fiscal and monetary technical assistance and training of govern officials in international monetary affairs and related subjects, all to meet the extraordinary needs of many of the new members that lacked much of the basic government and financial infrastructure of a modern state. Third, two new financial arrangements were instituted to facilitate lending to those new members whose exports were largely dependent on primary products, because the prices of such products are often subject to unusually degrees of volatility: the *Compensatory Financing Facility* and the *Buffer Stock Facility*[9].

Another important initiative of this phase of the evolution of the IMF was a response to concern that the growth in total international reserves was not keeping abreast of the needs of international trade and thereby acting as a break on its expansion and on the world economy as a whole. To meet this deficiency, the Articles of Agreement were amended in 1969 to permit the creation, under IMF auspices, of a new supplementary international reserve: the **Special Drawing Right** (SDR). The SDR was limited in how it could be used: it was essentially a bookkeeping device to be used between Central Banks only when a member had balance of payment needs. By contrast with normal currency, such as dollars or rupees, there are no SDR notes or coins for use by the general public. The initial (and so far only) distributions, in 1972 and 1981, were in proportion to quotas and in total (SDR21.4 billion) equalled about 20 percent of international reserves at that time. At first, one SDR equalled one US dollar, but later its value was based on a basket of the five leading internationally traded currencies, weighted according to their relative importance. This change made it the most stable international monetary unit, and for that reason it became a convenient measure of accounting in the international monetary area. The accounts of the IMF itself were converted from expression in US dollars to SDRs. Later, fears of global inflation prompted members to freeze plans for further SDR distributions. As a result, SDRs have not reached the level of importance in international monetary affairs and trade initially expected (they now are equal to less than two percent of international reserves). This has been particularly disappointing for those who advocated additional distributions of SDRs on the basis of need rather than quotas[10]. Nevertheless for all its limitations, the SDR can, with some justice, be seen as a first step, in the direction of a future world currency, and accordingly one of the successes of the IMF.

Phase III: The End of the Par Value System, 1971-1973

In the early 1970s the value of the US dollar in terms of other leading currencies came under increasing pressure. This was due to several factors. First, the growing strength of the other industrial economies, as they recovered from the Second World War, meant that their currencies were also stronger in relation to the dollar than was the case when the par value relationship had been fixed. Second, the huge cost of the war in Vietnam for the United States, which was being carried without any´ cut back in normal peacetime spending, following a political strategy of "guns and butter", put additional pressure on the dollar. Finally, the situation was further aggravated by the growing evolution of an overseas market in US dollars, the so called eurodollar market.

On August 15, 1971, the US government suspended gold payments for dollars; this prompted decisions by other important trading nations to free "float" their currencies in relation to others. Two years later (1973) the US government devalued the dollar by 10 percent. These events, of course, meant the end of the par value system, one of the key aspects of the original IMF mission, and for a time it seemed that the IMF might actually lose its raison d'etre. To respond to the crisis, member countries, recognizing the reality of modern market conditions, agreed to the Second Amendment of the Articles so as to legalize and systemize the new floating system. By the middle seventies the shock had passed and the market became accustomed to a formal regime of floating between the main currencies, with lesser currencies usually have a fixed relationship with the dollar, or the SDR or another major trading currency. Nevertheless, the new system does not provide real protection against volatile currency relationships and therefore adds to the cost of international trade. For this reason, in the long run it cannot be regarded as an optimum system.

Phase IV: The Oil Crises, 1973-1982

No sooner had the par value crisis started to subside than the world trading system was hit by a second major crisis. The huge increase in oil prices that resulted from the 1973 war in the Middle East was a particular burden for many poorer countries that depended on imported oil to keep their economies functioning. They were simply not able to pay the new prices and there was a real risk that their economies would break down with disasterous consequencs for their peoples, in many cases already living on the edge of survival. The international community responded by focussing much of the rescue operation through the IMF and World Bank, a vote of confidence despite the collapse of the par value system.

Four new financial arrangements were created at the IMF specifically to alleviate the crisis. The first was a new *Oil Facility* which would swiftly provide a significant amount of temporary financial assistance, on a concessional basis, to members unduly suffering from the increase in oil prices. The Facility (about $7 billion) was financed by IMF borrowing from 17 rich members countries, including several oil exporting nations "recycling" their new wealth. The second new arrangement was the *Trust Fund,* again for providing concessional loans, which was financed from profits from selling one sixth of the IMF's gold [contributed as quotas] in auctions after abolition of the official price of $35 per ounce. A further arrangement was a new *Subsidy Account,* Financed by voluntary contributions from members, which was to be used to subsidize interest charges on loans to poor countries. Finally, a new *Extended Fund Facility* was created to give medium term loans to countries so as to reduce the burden of early repayments. Under this program repayments were in stages over a 5-10 year period as compared with 3-5 years for the normal use of IMF resources[11].

The new measures worked reasonably well as shown by the fact that not a single national economy collapsed despite initial fears. Nevertheless, it was at this time, largely in reaction to the emerging North-South conflict, as expressed, for instance, in the South's "New World Order" resolutions in the UN General Assembly, that the wealthier countries started to organize their own G7 annual summits to consult on the international trading and monetary system, and thereby to partly bypass the global institutions such as the IMF in particular.

Phase V: The International Debt Crisis, 1982-1990

Just as the Oil Crisis was beginning to subside the world economy was hit by the international debt crisis of the 1980s. In the previous decade the oil exporting countries poured their enormous profits into the world banking system which in turn looked for opportunities to lend especially in Third World Countries where there seemed to be possibilities for high profits. In the process they became careless and often pushed loans, without the normal careful assessment of risk, on countries all too ready to accept. Inevitably many of these loans, especially those to the public sector, were badly used and increasingly could not be paid back, a situation made worse by high interest rates caused by inflation.

Once again the IMF and World Bank were given the mandate of taking the lead in correcting the situation which for a time seemed to be leading towards a collapse of the global financial system. The IMF response was to provide additional medium term financial assistance, but this time with more stringent conditionality. The vehicles for such assistance were two new programs: a **Structural Adjustment Facility** and an **Extended Structural Adjustment Facility.** As the titles of the new programs indicate, the intent was to encourage recipient countries to make fundamental reforms in their financial systems so that they could be strong and competitive in a free global system. The emphasis was not only on the usual prescriptions to devalue, tighten credit and raise interest rates but also (i) to deregulate the financial markets so that they functioned more efficiently, and (ii) to reduce public sector deficits, which had become a growing problem in many countries, including, specifically, the elimination of inefficient subsidies and slimming down of bloated and overpaid bureaucracies. At the same time, the IMF, responding in part to calls for even handedness, made efforts to strengthen its overall "surveillance" of the impact on the world economy of the practices of all members including creditor nations not subject to conditionality associated with borrowing.

An important consequence of the debt crisis was that it brought about some convergence of the activities of the IMF and World Bank, which hitherto had pursued their respective missions fairly independently, with the IMF focussed on short term balance of payments loans and the Bank on long term project development loans. On the one hand, the medium term nature of the new IMF loans brought them closer to those of the Bank and, on the otherhand, the Bank, recognising the overwhelming nature of the debt crisis, began to switch from individual project loans to broader sector loans (Structural Adjustment Programs), encouraging the same types of economic efficiencies as the IMF.

Hand in hand with these programs of medium

term conditional loans went a steady process of international meetings, within the general framework of the so called **Baker** (1985) and **Brady** (1989) initiatives[12], in which the two institutions played a major facilitating role, aimed at a rescheduling of all types of international debt, both public and private. In short, it was recognised that creditors, including most especially private sector banks, must bear some responsibility for the crisis, and therefore some of the cost.

Though the process was slow and painful and economic growth in many countries came to a halt for several years, it was evident, by the end of the decade, that the system had largely stabilised and many countries were in a much sounder and more efficient position than before from which to build steadily expanding economies.

Nevertheless, during this period there was an intensification of criticism of the IMF, particularly from the political left and from religious communities, on the grounds that its "conditions" (especially those relating to structural adjustment) tended to hurt the poorest sections of the population disproportionately, and more generally that there was not symmetry between debtor countries (generally the less well off) and creditor countries (generally the richer industrial countries) in bearing the burden of imbalances in balance of payments e.g. debtors were required to carry out deflationary policies to reduce imports but creditors were not required to inflate so as to attract more imports[13]. There were so called "IMF riots" in Cairo and Caracas and even criticism from other UN agencies such as UNICEF.

Individual staff members at the IMF and the World Bank were not indifferent to these criticisms, after all many had come to work for these institutions because they wished to contribute to the creation of a more human society. In both institutions small but active voluntary groups were formed to promote internal discussion of such issues as IMF/World Bank policies and how they related to poverty, excessive military expenditures, human rights and damage to the environment. Such activity could easily have been interpreted as criticism of Board and Management, perhaps even as disloyality, and therefore it was not without risk for those involved.

Phase VI: Transition of Former Socialist Economies to the Market System, 1990 to Date

The end of the Cold War resulted in some 30 former socialist countries [mostly in Eastern Europe and the former Soviet Union] applying for membership of the IMF and World Bank. The economies of these countries (and of other socialist countries that were already members) were in extremely bad shape due to years of gross inefficiency and it became apparent that a significant amount of outside assistance would be needed to alleviate the resulting appalling conditions of poverty for millions of people. Yet again the G7 industrial countries gave the IMF and World Bank, along with the newly created European Development Bank, key responsibility in responding to this need.

At the core of the IMF response was a new ***Systematic Transformation Facility*** tailor made to meet the special needs of these new members. In negotiating conditions for use of IMF [and Bank] resources, emphasis was placed not simply on the normal terms but on reducing regulation of the market, including introduction of free market pricing, privatization of the huge and highly inefficient state sector, and the establishment of a clear and open commercial law which could give confidence in enforcement of contracts. Such advice, which was a logical development of the earlier structural adjustment programs, was also given to member countries elsewhere in the world which for several decades had followed economic policies similar to those of the former Soviet bloc, in terms of state ownership of enterprizes, market regulation, price fixing and protectionism. This all represented a considerable breakthrough for the international organizations, because previously, especially during the Cold War, the period when many countries were still newly independent, such advice would have been seen as an affront to national sovereignty. Now concern for economic efficiency was the prime criteria for nearly all members.

Partly in response to past criticisms, the IMF would also encourage "safety net" policies to protect and provide for the unemployed and pensioners, groups that were likely to be particularly vulnerable during the period of transition. Both institutions also expressed concern about military expenditures when they seemed excessive in relation to basic social expenditures of economic importance such as education and health, as well as about environment matters. More broadly, there was an emphasis on "good governance", particularly with regard to corruption and human rights issues on the grounds that these are fundamental to the efficient running of an economy. Failure to meet these requirements by one country has, for the first time, led to suspension of a planned loan. However, it is evident that there has been some inconsistancy, on account of political pressure, in application of such principles especially in Russia where the rise of "mafia" style capitalism is a threat to the success of the whole transition to democracy and the market economy.

Three other developments in this period are worthy of note. First there was the continuing problem of indebted poor countries that had failed to recover from the crises of the 1970s and 1980s. One aspect of this problem was the difficult issue of debt of national governments to the IMF and the World Bank themselves. The IMF, in particular has taken a tough stand on the issue on the principle that rescheduling this type of debt would undermine the credibility of operations and it is simply unethical to routinely write off the contributions of all nations and peoples. After all, IMF loans had been given to assist the debtor, not to make a profit or gain other advantage. As a result, a third amendment to the Articles was approved in 1992 which imposed sanctions against borrowing members that failed to meet their repayment obligations to the IMF, including loss of voting rights and further access to IMF financial resources. Nevertheless, most recently the IMF, following the lead of the World Bank, has agreed to concessions to **Highly Indebted Poor Nations** (HIPCs), a very limited group, provided they carry out strong remedial actions to put their economies on a sound basis.

The second development of interest, has been the recognition of the vast increase in the international flow of private capital and the impact this can have on balance of payments and the functioning of the global economy. Such movements help to make for a more efficient global economy but can cause problems when they are restricted by government protectionist style regulation. Accordingly, consideration is being given to a fourth amendment of the Articles that would require members to liberalise their capital accounts as well as current accounts as in the original Articles.

The third important development in this period has been a greater degree of openness on the part of the IMF itself, for long following the traditional "confidential" culture of central banks and other financial institutions. The External Affairs Department has made increased effort to reach out to the media and interested non government organizations, mission chiefs were given more leeway to talk to the press, and the Managing Director, whose father was a journalist, spends a great deal of time explaining the IMF to the world and listening to the reaction. In 1997 a policy was approved to issue **Press Information Notices** (PINs) after consultation missions with a view to letting the general public know the IMF view of an economy of a member whilst still preserving the "integrity and confidentiality of the consultation process".

Postscript on the Collapse of the "Asian Tiger" Model, 1997

Since this presentation was made in 1994, the most important new IMF story has been its lead role in responding to the financial crisis in East Asia that came about in the second half of 1997. The countries involved had for some time had some of the fastest growing economies in the world. However, secretive and close ties, sometimes corrupt, between the government, the banking system and industry (so called "crony capitalism") led eventually to an unsupportable amount of bad debt because of non market tested investments and loans. The situation was aggravated by complex arrangements and practices, sometimes described as justified on grounds of tradition and culture, to keep out foreign competition. As a result of the crisis domestic and foreign investors alike, including most notably mutual funds and pension plans as well as commercial banks, withdrew large amounts of investments, and in consequence the value of currencies and of the stockmarket began a steep fall. This group of Asian countries, in effect represented a fourth major category of members turning to the IMF for financial assistance, the other three being: (i) the very poorest countries that often lacked the basic infrastructure to operate effectively in a global market economy (mostly in sub Sahel Africa), (ii) countries in debt because of unsustainable public deficits (mostly in Latin America), and (iii) nations in transition from centrally planned to market economies (mostly in Eastern Europe and the former Soviet Union).

The Asian countries involved are relatively wealthy but as a result of the crisis had need of large amounts of foreign currency to cover debt falling due and to restore investor confidence in the financial system. In response, over a six month period, the IMF organized some $118 billions of assistance for the 4 countries in immediate trouble (Phillipines, Thailand, Indonesia, and Korea), of which some $35 billion came from its own resources (including by far the largest loan in its history: $21 billion for Korea), and the rest came from other international banks and individual national governments[14]. The conditions being required by the IMF though similar to past remedies put special emphasis on the banking sector of the economy[15]. The borrowing countries were required to remove limits on interest rates, so as to re-attract investors and thereby steady the value of their currencies; to reduce public sector deficits, generally not a serious matter in these countries; to have much greater transparency and tighter control in the banking sector; and to allow the weakest banks and industrial corporations to go bankrupt and be open to sale to foreigners as well as nationals.

The IMF intervention, though welcomed by many has also attracted a considerable amount of criticism. Part of that is a continuation of the long running concerns of the left and religious constituencies, and part is a growing volume from the center and the right. Typical of the center argument is expression of concern that the IMF conditions unnecessarily deflate the economy and slows down production. Concern is also expressed about hasty action to close down ailing banks which it is said adds to the panic rather than the reverse. On the right there are nationalists and protectionists who object to "tax payer" money being used to "bail out" foreigners. Libertarians assert that Fund financial assistance involves "moral hazard" ie protects bankers etc from the consequencies of their own unwise actions and thereby encourages them to repeat their mistakes at the risk of the general public. They, therefore, argue for letting banks, industrial corporations and national governments go bankrupt to teach everyone a good lesson. In the US Congress, such arguments are being mooted as reason to reject the proposed 45 percent increase in quotas and the New Arrangement to Borrow (see footnote 8). Defenders of the IMF, including the ***Economist,*** concede the moral hazard argument, which is a long standing theoretical problem of central banks and insurance companies, but they point out (i) that creditors do, in fact, lose in such situations, (ii) that there is some risk that without corrective action by the IMF the financial crisis in these countries could spread around the world and cause a major economic dislocation, and finally (iii) that the tax payer far from losing may well gain in terms of repayment interest as in the Mexico rescue operation of 1995.

Overview: Past Achievements and Future Challenges

The IMF is an international public sector organization directed by representatives of the governments of 181 member nations, which between them contain most of the peoples of the world. As such, it functions in a manner very similar to any government department in a national democracy. It has a high quality professional management and staff as shown by the efficient and swift way it carries out its mission. It is not some "out of control" dictatorial bureaucracy. It is tightly controlled by national government representatives and it is sensitive over the long run to outside criticism, especially when it is soundly based.

Generally, it has been successful in carrying out its mission. Along with other international public sector economic agencies such as GATT/WTO and the World Bank, it has played a vital role in over fifty years not only in avoiding a repetition of the Great Depression (which was after all the main goal of the founders) but also in facilitating a nearly six fold increase in the real size of the world economy[16] from which most of the world's population has benefited. Acting as the engine for that growth has been international trade, which 50 years ago was less than 10 percent of the world economy and which today is more than 20 percent. With regard to the international monetary system, the IMF has acted effectively to restore confidence after three major critical occurrences: (i) the collapse of the par value system, (ii) the quadrupling of world oil prices, and (iii) the international debt crisis, as well as playing a leading role in the tast of helping the former socialist countries make the transition into the global market system. Slowly but surely it has moved the system in the direction of more openness and greater efficiency. Though it has been subject to much criticism over the years from both the left and the right, it has generally won the confidence of most governments as shown by the fact that it was entrusted with a central role in managing the Asian as well earlier crises mentioned above.

Nevertheless, it is clear that improvements will have to come if it is to successfully meet the challenges of the future and the needs of all the peoples of the world. So far, IMF interventions in balance of payments situations have generally lacked symmetry and have been more onerous to debtors and favorable to creditors, be they nations with favorable balances of payments or individual investors or banks. This is deplorable because of the moral hazard issue, the fact that it is evident that often the actions of the creditors are as much a cause of a crisis as the actions of the debtors, and worst of all, because the resulting burden is most heavy on those least able to bear it: the very poorest. Policies of the IMF and the World Bank seem to have been particularly unsuccessful in sub Sahel Africa, although most recently this may have been changing. It is true that since the end of the Cold War, the IMF, along with the World Bank, has paid much closer attention to poverty, human rights and environmental issues, but the concern still tends to be marginal rather than central and fundamental to efforts to achieve economic efficiency. Failure to improve on this aspect of its activities will in the long run undermine not only the IMF itself but international cooperation generally. The solution lies not with an expansion of the IMF so as to incorporte skills in new areas of competence, at the cost of internal efficiency, but rather to vastly improve cooperation with other bodies that do have such skills. Imaginative ideas, such as use of credit to finance equitable ownership of stock could be more thoroughly considered perhaps in cooperation with the World Bank, especially in connection with privatization programs.

More generally, the IMF should act less like a fireman putting out fires as they occur and more like a forward thinking organization that can warn and take defensive action against looming problems before they occur. The IMF must be given more independence to criticise members, even the most powerful (it gave glowing reports on the Asian countries only months before the 1997 crisis exploded into full view), and have the ability to impose sanctions on creditors acting against the general interest. At the same time the IMF itself should be subject to more detailed independent "evaluation" of its policies to see which are working and which are not. Most important, it should be planning for a more stable international monetary system free of the periodic crises of the last few decades, and the eventual evolution of the ultimate monetary tool of an efficient global economy: a single world currency—perhaps growing out of the SDR. In summary, the IMF should be moving forward to fulfill its potential to be a true world central bank acting to promote the well being of all humanity.

NOTES

1. In recent years the most systematic forecasts of the IMF have been the semi annual *World Economic Outlook*.
2. Initially, for instance, the USA had 30 percent of Quotas, but with increased membership and other adjustments the figure has fallen to about 18 percent (1997). Presently the G7 industrial countries have about 46 percent of the total. The Quotas of India and China are each between 2 and 3 percent.
3. In 1997 the membership was considering an increase of about 45 percent (approximately $90 billion)
4. The eight are (i) the five with the largest quotas (USA, Japan, Germany, France and the UK), and (ii) three others (China, Russia, and Saudi Arabia). Several others which dominate their constituencies also have in effect permanent representation eg. Canda Australia and India (the latter is grouped with Bangladesh, Bhutan and Sri Lanka).
5. Specific conditions for a loan are negotiated with the borrowing government which then incorporates them into a "Letter of Intent" for approval by the IMF.
6. In the last three decades, on average some 20-35 percent of the member countries make use of IMF resources each year.
7. By 1997, 140 members were in compliance with Article VIII,

including 63 that had made the transition since 1993.

8. The GAB has been renewed on several occasions. It in turn has been supplemented by other such arrangements as the direct resources of the IMF have failed to keep pace with possible needs: a special arrangement with Saudi Arabia in 1981 when it was flush with oil money, and a proposed New Agreement to Borrow (NAB) now (1997) being negotiated with 25 members.

9. The latter allows members to borrow to pay their contributions to the financing of international buffer stocks designed to stabilize commodity prices (rubber and tin)

10. In 1997 a proposal is being considered that would provide a new distribution of SDRs for the 40 members that have not had a distribution because they joined the IMF after the last distribution in 1981.

11. At this time a 12 point guideline for conditionality was adopted which put emphasis on encouraging members to undertake corrective measures at an early stage, and which while maintaining the principle of equal treatment for like situations, also allowed flexibility in the interest of an individual member's domestic objectives. Quantifiable targets were to be established with regard to key aggregate economic variables for domestic credit, public sector deficits, international reserves, external debt, exchange rates, and interest rates.

12. Named after two succesive Secretarys of the US Treasury.

13. It should be noted that the IMF, unlike the World Bank, is a true world institution, and on occasion has made conditional loans to industrial members e.g. the UK, France, Italy and even the USA itself.

14. Japan and China, the two largest economies in the region, have had similar internal deficiencies in their economies, but because they have favourable balances of external payments they have not needed to call on the IMF for assistance.

15. IMF records show that in the last two decades some two thirds of the membership have had troubles with their banking systems, including the USA with its savings and loan debacle.

16. *Vital Signs 1997: the environmental trends that are shaping our future,* World Watch Institute, Washington D.C., p.67.

CURING WORLD POVERTY

A review, printed in the March 1995 issue of "Finance and Development", a quarterly magazine of the International Monetary Fund and the World Bank, of the book "Curing World Poverty", edited by John Miller and published by the Social Justice Review and the Center for Economic and Social Justice, St Louis, Missouri, 1994.

This book contains 18 essays on various aspects of "binary" economics, a system developed by Louis Kelso (1913-1991) and his associates starting in the 1950s. Binary economics is a market based system that advocates, among other things, global free trade, a stable monetary system, a simplified and economically efficient tax system, elimination of monopolies, and a reduced state sector. What is distinctive about binary economics is its approach to the problems of poverty, unemployment, and extremes of wealth that the market system tends to produce, especially in the short and medium term.

At the core of binary economics is the idea that every person should have equal access to capital ownership, starting with employees as owners of shares in the corporations for which they work, and that purchases of these shares should be financed with credit. The recognition of credit as an essential "social good" that influences growth and future ownership patterns in a market economy is the key innovation of this model.

Employee profit-sharing and share-ownership schemes have been around since the early 19th

century and are generally intended to encourage a
spirit of partnership and hard work in the common
interest. The Kelso school goes further, and argues
that these schemes make the worker-owner less
dependent on wages and do away with the competition
between technology and labor.

Traditional employee stock-ownership schemes are
normally financed through either deductions from
wages or dilution of stock of existing shareholders,
making them less attractive to workers and
shareholders. The Kelso school believes that workers
should be allowed to purchase their shares on credit.
It argues that credit is as important a financial
invention as money itself, and that lack of access to
credit for purchase of productive assets causes the
poor to remain poor.

According to the standard Kelso model, a company
raises the capital it needs for modernization and
expansion by creating new shares for employees. The
shares are placed in a trust fund and paid for by a
loan, normally from a bank; the newly acquired assets
and profits from their use serve as collateral. As new
assets bought with the borrowed money become
productive, the debt is first paid off, and then fully
paid-up shares and supplemental dividend income
can be distributed to employees. During this period,
the employees not only make no down payment, but
are also protected from risk of default— which is
carried by the company, the bank, and the insurer.

Three other major benefits are claimed for the
credit-financed employee stock-ownership plan. First,
it gradually leads to greater equaliztion of wealth
without confiscation of the assets of present owners.
Second, it facilitates the transfer of the benefits of
technology to developing countries through
distribution of shares to local employees by
international corporations. Third, creation of wealth

or credit for the less wealthy stimulates demand for goods and services. Higher demand, coupled with increased capital formation and supply capacity, will create an expanding economy without inflation and will reduce pressure on government-redistribution programs.

Binary economics also provides for variations on the employee stock-ownership plan for different social circumstances— for example, a stock-ownership plan for consumers receiving continuing service from a corporation, a community investment corporation that develops and manages community property, and an individual stock ownership plan that supplements social security.

Because such systems are so obviously in the general interest, its supporters argue that the state should encourage them. First, the state should provide watertight laws to protect all parties. Second, it should provide last-resort insurance of credit. Third, the central bank should encourage expanded bank credit for financing capital growth linked to expanded ownership. Finally, the state should implement tax reforms that encourage broader ownership of private sector assets.

Curing World Poverty notes that employee stock-ownership plans are not merely theory. There are about 10,000 such plans in the United States alone, covering some 11 million workers. Several of the essays in this book analyze specific schemes in Egypt and Guatemala as well as in the United States.

With a large number of contributors, the book has a depth that might not have been achieved by a single author. Although it is not free of repetition and contains some gaps, it is stimulating. It describes a system that is simple and elegant (like all great ideas), that is based in market economics elevated by the injection of democratic and spiritual values, and that has appeal for the entire political spectrum. *Curing World Poverty* deserves to be taken seriously. It has a particular immediacy for those searching for a solid underpinning for economic reform in the former socialist countries.

MANAGING ECONOMIC INTERDEPENDENCE

**A Presentation at the Indian International Center,
New Delhi, India, 1995**

The subject I have been asked to address tonight is one which seems most timely for at least two reasons. First, as we all know, India in the last few years has taken steps to integrate its economy into the global economy in a way that represents a reversal of policy that had previously been followed since independence. Second as this is a key policy matter it seems appropriate to be talking about such developments in this distinguished center which focuses on major policy issues affecting the people of India.

Of course, I am somewhat hesitant as an outsider to come and give such a presentation, but I hope I can suggest some useful global perspectives for you that come from my experiences of some thirty years as both an international civil servant and a member of the Bahá'í Community which has as its priority the unity of humanity on the basis of peace and justice. The approach I propose in discussing this topic is to offer a few thoughts on the evolution of international trade, the benefits and costs of integrating into the world trade system for the less wealthy countries, and finally to offer some thoughts on what needs to be done to best take account of these factors.

The first point I should like to make about economic interdependence is that global integration, economic, social, and political is one of the most powerful trends of our time. Furthermore, the economy is undoubtedly a major driving engine of this process. There are at least two key factors bearing on this drive of the world economy. The first is science and technology. The second is economic efficiency.

Science and technology as a factor in integrating the global economy goes back several hundred years. Clearly a critical stage was the so called European "Age of Reconnaissance", the age of Vasco de Gama, Columbus and Magellan which resulted for the first time in the history of civilization, in societies in the continents of the Americas, Africa and Australasia being linked to those of the main landmass and population center of Euroasia. The process of strengthening those links accelerated greatly in the nineteenth century with the Industrial Revolution. That revolution, of course, brought vastly improved means of communication and transportation: the railway engine, the steamship, the refrigeration ship, the telegraph, the telephone, radio, cinema, the automobile and the aeroplane. It also brought a vast new productive capacity and a range of new goods for trading. Today we are experiencing a third period of acceleration towards global economic integration with the post industrial revolution with its television, satellites and computers.

Closely related to the evolution of science and technology has been the development of economic theory and practice. Until the European "Age of Reconnaissance", most cross border trade was basically expensive and risky, and therefore tended to be restricted to essential needs that could not be provided domestically, eg. for some states such goods as grains and timber, or high value to weight luxury items such as spices, silks, dyes, gems, etc. With the rise of the modern state in the seventeenth century a more conscious policy of "competitive advantage" began to emerge. This new policy of "mercantilism" promoted exports and discouraged imports. The prime purpose was to earn gold which the state would use to pay for a strong military force to be used both for expansion of territory and for domestic control/ suppression. It was a theory most suited to authoritarian imperialistic regimes and it assumed the Hobbesian philosophy of the jungle: for one state to gain, another must lose: the zero sum game.

That system was challenged by Adam Smith and other Western economists at the beginning of the nineteenth century. Their perspective was that the idea of specialization in what we do best, long acknowledged to be efficient at the individual level, also applied to the economy at the collective level. If nations freely traded with one another in the goods and services that they could produce most efficiently then all would benefit and the wealth of all humanity would increase. The main role of the state should be to ensure the free working of market forces, including competition as a spur to enterprise and innovation. It is no coincidence that this theory caught on at the time of the Industrial Revolution and vast improvements in communications and transportation, as well as the rise of democracy. The market philosophy is more in tune with the freedom and equality of opportunity of democracy than with the control of the authoritarian state. Clearly, too, the theory goes along with peace between nations and the rule of international law which are necessary preconditions if the system is to work most efficiently. It is no coincidence that the early free traders—the Manchester school in Great Britain, such as Cobden and Bright—were amongst the strongest early supporters of the popular peace movements of the nineteenth century.

The logic of free trade market theory soon became evident as the Industrial Revolution spread. In the mid nineteenth century Great Britain abandoned mercantilistic policies for free trade and was followed to a considerable extent by much of Western Europe. As a result international trade grew even faster than industrialization and, in effect, became the engine pulling along the world economy.

This process was temporarily halted and reversed in the first half of the twentieth century by the rise of nationalism, imperialism and militarism which resulted not only in two world wars but also in the Great Depression and a slow down in the growth of the world economy, with all that this implied for the struggle to eliminate poverty.

The lesson was understood. After the Second World War, the United States, now by far the most important national economy in the world, adopted the free trade principle [more or less], and the new international institutions of the United Nations included several with the mission of promoting the integration of the world economy. These included the General Agreement on Trade and Tarriffs (GATT) with the mission of negotiating reductions in physical barriers to trade such as tariffs and quotas; the International Monetary Fund (IMF) with the mandate to manage stable relationships between national currencies and to reduce such damaging practices as currency manipulation and barriers to free flow of capital; and the World Bank which was to facilitate the transfer of low cost capital and technology to the least wealthy countries so as to speed up their ability to take maximum advantage of an integrated global economy. A major recent advance for these institutions has been the replacement of GATT with a much stronger World Trade Organization which has increased powers of arbitration and enforcement.

As a result of techonological advances and free trade policies, international trade has expanded in real terms by about 12 times in the second half of the twentieth century, as compared with a six fold increase in the size of the global economy as a whole. In other words, as in the nineteenth century, it is international trade which is the prime locomotive pulling along the global economy. Those economies that have benefited least from this process tended to be those that chose to impose "protectionist" state management so as to insulate themselves to a large extent from the dynamism of the global system. By the eighties the cost of such policies had become so evident that change was almost inevitable, and during the last decade there has been a major change of direction in many of these countries, including not only the most the extremes practitioners of protectionist policies, the nations of the former Soviet bloc, but also many other countries which after independence from the old European empires had put so much emphasis on "economic self sufficiency"—of which India is a leading example.

This brings me to the second subject which I should like to briefly mention in this discussion of managing economic interdependency : namely the specific advantages and disadvantages of integration which are generally identified, especially as they pertain to less wealthy countries.

One theoretical advantage is that less wealthy countries usually have a competitive advantage from low wage costs which help to make their goods potentially cheaper than those of other countries. Opponents see this as exploitation of the poor, but it is argued by supporters that low wages are a lot better than been unemployed; furthermore as unemployment is reduced the opportunity arises for increasing wage levels as a matter of the normal working of the law of supply and demand. As capital and technology comes into the countries from abroad there is the additional benefit that such competition forces domestic producers to become more efficient. As wealth builds up the educated middle class expands and becomes confident enough to resist dictatorial government and to insist on freedom and democracy with regard to political and social issues as well as economic. As suggested earlier, such a constituency, in the long run, is likely to extend its demand for the rule of law domestically to the international stage as well.

The arguments against economic interdependence are well known. One is the possibility of reduced sovereignty and control over the national economy. An extreme example often quoted are the so called "banana republics" of Central America in the interwar period, tiny countries with undue dependency on one or two basic commodities which were virtually taken over by powerful foreign corporations. Closely related is the question of national security, particularly with regard to food or perhaps an arms industry. Critics point to the destruction of British agriculture in the late nineteenth century because under free trade policies it could not compete with the prices of agricultural imports from the Americas and Australasia. Another variation on this theme of loss of sovereignty is a perceived concern that opening up the economy poses a threat to the welfare state the cost of which adds to the operating expense of the economy which, in turn, might be a handicap in competing with less enlightened countries. Another argument is the risk of losing high wage jobs and the forcing down of wage levels. A more recent addition to the standard criticisms of free trade is that it undermines measures to protect the environment, as countries that do not observe basic environmental protection gain a competitive advantage and thereby put pressure on those that do to relax them.

What is striking about most of these arguments is that they are typically the concerns of wealthy countries when opening up their economies to competition from less wealthy countries. The first one, of course, is a "third world" concern but this pertains essentially to smaller countries and is hardly a risk for larger countries such as India. Furthermore, it has become evident that powerful as some of the arguments seem they lose their weight when the practical costs of protectionism in terms of stagnant economies are compared with the relative success of countries that follow free trade policies in achieving economic growth.

So what should a nation do to manage economic interdependence in its own best interest? Market economists, including those working at the Bretton Woods institutions, put emphasis on competitive efficiency and attraction of outside capital. A nation should make itself more efficient by giving high priority to literacy and primary education so that the general population has at least the minimum skills required of a modern economy. It should also invest in other infrastructure such as transportion, communications and "preventive" health care. Women should be given equal rights so that they have an opportunity to effectively contribute to the development of the economy. In the case of economies experiencing major readjustment, such as those of the former Soviet bloc, safety net social policies should be instigated, particularly with regard to pensions and unemployment benefits, so as to soften the impact of change. Job retraining may also be a necessary cost of adjustment. With regard to the goal of attracting capital for productive purposes, both domestic and overseas, there is advocacy of a clear and comprehensive code of commercial law, properly enforced without favoritism, strong action to ensure competition and to minimize monopoly, elimination of corruption and public sector deficits, efficient governments, low taxation which is broadly based, and a monetary policy that results in low inflation.

I would suggest that there are also other important policies to consider in addition to the standards just mentioned. First, there is a need to give strong encouragement to high levels of business ethics because this creates trust which attracts business and makes the economy more efficient. Second, there is a need to promote the idea of service, rather than the self destructive idea that service is somehow demeaning because it has been associated with the old "master servant relationship", an attitude that did so much to make socialist bureaucracy arrogant and inefficient. Third, I suggest, is a need to give strong support to the international institutions in their mission of ensuring a level playing field for all nations taking part in the global economy and in upholding the rule of international commercial law. Tempting though it may be sometimes, it is not in the long term interest of any nation, large or small, rich or poor, to indulge in unilateral action against another in defiance of due process and international law. In the international organizations such as the WTO, the IMF, the World Bank, the UNEP, all nations should work to strengthen objective arbitration, a single world currency, symmetry in responsibility and burden sharing between borrowers and lenders, and fair means to uphold protection of the environment. Beyond all this there, is a need, I would suggest, to think about the larger picture and the longer term. By this I mean those conditions of peace and the general rule of international law which ultimately are a necessary condition for the working of an interdependent global economy. This means amongst other factors the conversion of the United Nations from the present confederal model to a federal democratic structure which would have the necessary power and authority to maintain world peace. This would include, at a minimum, a world legislative assembly, democratically elected by all peoples of the world, which would have the moral authority to speak for all humankind; a strengthened World Court with compulsory powers of arbitration to give nations with grievances a real peaceful alternative to the use of force in trying to resolve those grievances; and a directly recruited world police force which would have the ability to act quickly and decisively against any aggressor group or nation.

Beyond these hard edged policy recommendations pertaining to the management of economic integration are the much more profound moral or spiritual questions, of which the most important is what is the purpose of life? If we get that wrong then no amount of concrete arrangements will guarantee a successful outcome. If we get that right and take it seriously then the right spirit behind concrete policies will eventually ensure their success. For a Bahá'í the spiritual perspective revolves around the idea of the brotherhood of man, and the twin purposes of life: for each to acquire the qualities of nobility, to grow towards God, and collectively to create an ever advancing civilization.

THE POLITICS OF PEACE

A JUST SYSTEM OF GOVERNMENT: THE THIRD DIMENSION TO WORLD PEACE

A presentation at a conference on the Bahá'í Faith and Marxism, Louhelen, Michigan, U.S.A., 1986

Introduction

The Bahá'í approach to government or collective action is a vast subject that cannot be adequately dealt with in a short paper. Accordingly, this brief presentation will be confined to a few highlights, which might be of special interest in the context of the general discussion this weekend.

There are at least three dimensions to the Bahá'í plan for the establishment of a permanent world peace based on justice, or in Bahá'í terminology, "The Most Great Peace." The first dimension is the creation of a new race of men: the adoption of the highest ethical standards by every man, woman and child on the planet. It is irrational to suppose that a just society can be achieved unless the people of that society are themselves just individuals.

A second dimension to the Bahá'í plan are broad policies to ensure that every person in the world has equal opportunity and encouragement to develop fully his or her physical, mental, and spiritual potential. One important aspect of this issue is the abolition of extremes of wealth and poverty within nations and between nations. Another is the elimination of racist and other prejudices that crush the human spirit.

A third dimension of the plan is a new system of government based on spiritual values and a world perspective. It must be clear by now to every thinking person that the present political system corrupts even the noblest of people and is not capable of dealing with the major issues that face humanity today. The most important characteristic of the present political scene is its division into some 170 sovereign states (the approximate number in 1986), the so-called Westphalian system[1]. Many of these states have authoritarian governments that exploit and oppress rather than serve their peoples. Even more appalling is the fact that the system is so out of step with the needs of the time that it risks the destruction of most, if not all, of mankind for causes, which, by comparison and in the perspective of history, can only be called frivolous. Establishment of a permanent peace based on justice is, in the Bahá'í view, only possible if we move to an entirely new system of government.

The Bahá'í Community has already established a new system of government to manage its own affairs. This system, known as the Bahá'í Administrative Order, is offered to mankind as an alternative model to conventional methods. Ultimately, it is envisaged that this model will evolve into a full-fledged system featuring a world legislature, a world executive backed by a world police force, and a world judiciary, with subsidiary branches at national and local levels in every part of the world. Meanwhile, Bahá'ís are acquiring, within their own communities, experience on how to work their radically different system of managing the collective affairs of society.

I propose to discuss the Bahá'í Administrative

Order in two parts: first by briefly recapitulating its main features, and second by suggesting some aspects that make it uniquely fitted for the needs of the day. There are three key elements in the Bahá'í approach to government: (i) a world structure; (ii) an electoral system, which puts emphasis on spiritual and collective qualities rather than on individual self-interest; and (iii) full, objective consultation as the basis for decision-making.

Three Principal Elements of the Bahá'í Administrative Order

Structure

The administrative structure has two parts: an elected wing responsible for running the affairs of the community, and an appointed wing responsible for monitoring the community's spiritual health. The elected wing is a three-tier structure with local spiritual assemblies to manage the affairs of local communities, national spiritual assemblies to coordinate the affairs of each cultural or national grouping of communities, and finally a Universal House of Justice to give guidance and direction to the whole world community. The other wing of the structure consists of Continental Boards of Counselors, appointed by the Universal House of Justice, which in turn appoint subsidiary bodies at regional and local levels. Members of these boards are carefully chosen for their spiritual qualities, abilities, and loyalty to the Faith. Their role is to observe and to advise the elected wing but not to intervene directly in community affairs.

Elections

The electoral system has both direct and indirect elements. The Local Spiritual Assembly is elected annually at a local convention by direct secret ballot

of all adult members of the community. The National
Spiritual Assembly is elected annually at a national
convention consisting of delegates elected on a
regional basis by the national community. The
Universal House of Justice is elected every five years
by an International Convention composed of the
members of all the national spiritual assemblies.
Each body has nine members, and to be valid, each
ballot cast must list nine names. All members of the
local, national, or world community, as the case may
be, who are in good standing, are eligible for
election, except for members of the boards of
counselors and their auxiliary boards, and in the
case of the Universal House of Justice, women[2]. All
qualified adults have a sacred duty to vote unless
there is a special circumstance, as happens, for
instance, when a move into a new community makes
it impossible to have an informed view. To preclude
divisiveness, nominations, forming of parties, and
campaigning are all strictly forbidden practices.

Consultation

At all levels of the Bahá'í administrative structure,
comprehensive consultation is practiced with a view
to increasing the probability of arriving at the best
decision. The first principle of Bahá'í consultation is
universal participation so as to benefit from the widest
range of experience and wisdom. It is the
responsibility of all members of the body involved, not
just the chairperson, to see that everyone present has
an equal opportunity to contribute. Everyone is
encouraged to speak frankly, though with calmness
and courtesy.

The second principle is detachment and
objectivity. The discussion should follow a logical
sequence: prayer to set the tone and perspective,
and then the normal steps of scientific enquiry:

determining the exact nature of the problem, ascertaining the relevant facts, agreeing on the spiritual or administrative principles involved, a full and frank discussion, the offering and voting on a resolution, and finally action to put the resolution into effect. All should feel that the ideas put forward belong to the community, and not to the person who first presented them; indeed, a participant may well speak against his original suggestion if he subsequently hears a superior suggestion.

The third principle is the need for unity in carrying out a decision. Decisions can be made by majority vote, but Bahá'ís are encouraged to strive for one approved unanimously. If a decision is by majority vote, a person in the minority should nevertheless wholeheartedly support the implementation of the decision and should not campaign to stop it, as this would only cause dissension and undermine the unity of the community, which is held to be far more essential than avoiding a possible short-term mistake. If proper consultation procedures have been followed, the chance that a mistake has been made should be low. In any case, such mistakes can always be reversed if further consultation is brought about as a result of proper appeal procedures, first through the body that made the decision and then, if that fails to bring satisfaction, through higher bodies.

Comparison with the Conventional Political System

Structure

I should now like to comment on each of the three main elements of the Bahá'í administrative order: the structure, the electoral system, and consultation, with stress on those aspects that seem particularly important in the context of the needs of the time. Perhaps the most important feature of the structure of the Administrative Order is that it is unified on a world scale. There is a single supreme world body, the Universal House of Justice, responsible for policy direction and coordination of the affairs of the whole community. This model structure contrasts sharply with that of the established political system, which is divided into some 170 independent nations that are often in conflict with one another.

A second important feature of the structure is that the short-term, day-to-day administration of the community is undertaken in the perspective of long-term principles and policies for the welfare of all mankind, which are laid down in the writings of the central figures of the Faith and which are the ultimate source of authority for all institutions of the Bahá'í Administrative Order. The long-term perspective is quite different from that which prevails in conventional politics, where to our immense cost nearly all concern is centered on short-term material gains for sectarian interests.

A third feature worthy of note is that, though the Administrative Order is unified at a world level, it is essentially a highly decentralized system with most of the day-to-day affairs of the community being handled at the local level where the decision makers are in constant communion with the other members of the community. Conversely, it is typical of the political system that the majority of important decisions are highly centralized at the national level, and there is little real contact with ordinary people.

A fourth feature is that the structure is simple and can therefore be put into practice in every type of society, from the most complex and sophisticated to those where the majority is illiterate-a fact already demonstrated in many places. There is a contrast here again between the successful experience of the Bahá'í community building up from the grass roots level, and for instance, the attempt in recent decades by Western democracies to impose from above their complex parliamentary systems on societies that have quite different traditions of govenment.

A final feature of the structure, which should be noted, is that the Continental Board of Counselors and their assistants, who form the second wing of the Administrative Order, keep a close watch on the spiritual well-being of all aspects of the community. This function is a vital protection for any society and illustrates the fact that the Bahá'í approach has realism as a well as idealism in that it recognizes that the highest standards will take time to achieve. In conventional politics such appointed guardians of the public good can degenerate into bullying commissars. This has not happened in the Bahá'í community because the counselors are chosen for their spiritual maturity as well as their other abilities, because their role is purely advisory, and because they are excluded from office in the elective wing of the order and thus have no self-interest to promote.

Elections

Perhaps the most important feature of the electoral system is that it does not permit the rise of individual leaders, who throughout history have caused great harm to society because of "hubris" and conflict between selfish individual interest and the welfare of society as a whole. Society has always been in great danger from kings, dictators, priests, and even powerful politicans in democracies. Some of the features of the Bahá'í Administrative Order that preclude the emergence of the individual leaders are (i) the ban on nominations and compaigning for elections; (ii) the indirect election for the two higher echelons of the administrative structure, which makes widespread publicity about individuals much less necessary than would be the case for direct elections[3]; (iii) the teaching that electors should vote for those who have spiritual qualities (such as humility and self-effacement) as well as administrative skills and a record of service; (iv) the fact that decisions taken by elected assemblies are confidential with regard to the voting of individual members; and finally (v) the fact that members of elected assemblies only have special status in the community when functioning as an assembly and not when speaking as individuals. Furthermore, it is noteworthy that the chairperson of a spiritual assembly is mainly a coordinator and does not use his or her position to gain more influence in a discussion than other members of an assembly. In the case of the Universal House of Justice, the chairman is changed frequently, and his name is not made known to the world at large, so as to avoid the possibility of anyone being construed as "president" of the Bahá'í world.

A second important aspect of the electoral system is that it encourages diversity of background in those who are elected to governing bodies. The requirement that each elector vote for nine names focuses attention on the individual elector's responsibility for the make up of the total assembly rather than on selecting a few individuals, and this focus is inevitably affected by the Bahá'í teachings on unity and diversity: the greater the diversity, the greater the richness of the community, just as a garden with a multitude of different flowers has greater beauty than one with flowers of just one type or color. A good example of such diversity was the 1985 National Spiritual Assembly of the United States which had, in terms of race, four blacks, two whites, one Asian, one Native American, and one Persian; and in tems of sex, four women and five men. They come from a diversity of regions and occupational backgound. This result, which is perhaps unique for an elected body in the United States, was achieved without any sort of quota system. The tendency to diversify is strengthened by the directive that in the event of a tied vote, "priority should unhesitatingly be accorded the party representing the minority"[4].

Finally, it might be observed that the voting system has the potential for eliminating that age-old problem of what is the correct balance between continuity and change in government, ie. how to adapt to changing conditions without turmoil and inefficiency of sudden breaks in continuity. Predemocratic systems always had the great risk of misrule when an individual or group held power for a long period of time and then of violent conflict when the ruler died or the regime became intolerable. Present-day democracies frequently do not achieve the right balance either and suffer when there are long periods of dominance by one political party, or when there is a complete change in government personnel following a major shift in power. Government by assembly, frequent elections, and the absence of subgroupings are all features of the Bahá'í Administrative Order, which tend to create situations in which continued membership of the governing body is balanced by new membership.

Consultation

The Bahá'í system of consultation has several features of immense importance for effective government. First, it encourages consideration, before a decision is made, of a wide range of options including those that are based on the experiences and view of those who in conventional society are rarely heard: the poor, minorities, women, the uneducated. Only too often, as many of us have witnessed personally, such breadth of discussion acts as a healthy corrective to the views of the forceful, the rich, and the educated who are sometimes too self-absorbed and not rooted in the hard realities of life. It is sometimes argued that government by a strong dictator is more efficient than democratic government. In the short run, it is true that one man may be able to decide on a course of action more quickly than a group, but in the longer run it is the depth of consultation on the Bahá'í model that is likely to lead to the most efficient results[5]. It might be noted in this context that an assembly of nine (which is the present Baha'i practice) is close to the optimal size for efficiency, because it is large enough to allow for a wide spectrum of opinion and small enough to allow all members to give their view in a relatively short period of time.

A second important feature of Bahá'í consultation is that it involves constant contact between the ruling bodies and the wider community, particularly at the local level where the community meets together on a regular basis at the Nineteen-Day Feast, at which time the assembly members hear the ideas and views of the other members of the community. The Feast is also a time when the assembly reports on its activities and plans, and thus in effect makes itself accountable on a regular basis.

Of course, a perfect working model cannot be created overnight, and Bahá'í administration is still only at the beginning of its evolution. It takes time for Bahá'ís to shed all of their "old world" habits and ways of thinking, and there is no doubt that there are many consultations that do not follow the ideal model. On the one hand, in cultures where ordinary people have been traditionally told what to do by others, it is not easy for them to change their ways and start taking responsibility, through the assembly, for their own community affairs. In addition, there are some countries where the membership of the National Spiritual Assembly does not change for years at a time except when there is death or emigration, and as result fresh ideas tend to wither in the face of exhaustion and lack of new experience. On the other hand, most of us who have been in the Bahá'í community even a few years, soon become aware from personal experience just how much quiet progress is being made and how the administrative system ultimately brings out the best in the individual and vice versa, in what might be called a progressive spiral. One of the most tangible signs of such progress has been the increasingly active role of women on local and national spiritual assemblies in countries where women have traditionally had a subservient role in public affairs—a development that has been reported to the United Nations in connection with the International Women's Decade.

Summary

To summarize, the Bahá'í Administrative Order has a series of features that would be essential in a government system charged with maintaining a lasting world peace. First, it focuses attention on the long-term spiritual and material interests of all peoples of the world (with particular attention to the interests of the weak and poor), rather than the short-term material interests of powerful sectarian groups, which is the normal goal of conventional politics.

Second, by putting authority in the hands of assemblies, democratically elected in accordance with spiritual principles, it removes the threat of individual leadership, which since the beginning of civilization has brought corruption and placement of individual interest before that of the community supposedly being served.

Third, principles of consultation and centralization ensure that the government is continually in dialogue with the whole community, and thus makes decisions on the basis of the widest range of experience and knowledge. Its whole character is one of organic unity with society and, indeed, with the pulse of creation. If the Hegelian model were to be applied to the situation, it might be argued that the thesis is the traditional autocratic form of government with legitimacy flowing from the ruler (God's anointed) down to those who are ruled; that the antithesis is democracy in which legitimacy flows upwards from the people to their rulers; and that the synthesis is the Bahá'í Administrative Order, in which there is a combination of both spiritual authority coming from God, through the teachings of his Manifestation, Bahá'u'lláh, to the Universal House of Justice; and a highly democratic process of collective responsibility and universal participation in election and consultation, which closely unites institutions with the community they serve.

NOTES

1. After the Treaty of Westphalia (1648), which is credited with formally recognizing that there is no superior authority to the territorial ruler (see for instance, Lynn H. Miller, *Global Order,* Westview Press, 1985).
2. 'Abdu'l-Bahá stated that the reason for this rule concerning the Universal House of Justice would become apparent in the future.
3. Put another way, rational election of the higher echelons would almost certainly not be possible if there were to be both direct suffrage and a ban on campaigning.
4. Shoghi Effendi, *The Advent of Divine Justice,* pp.29-30.

5. Thus, in an experiment carried out at Harvard University in the 1960s, it was observed that a group of non-Bahá'í students trained in the rudiments of Bahá'í consultation performed significantly better than other groups working on the same problem.

WAR AND PEACE: A PROPOSAL

**A presentation at the Annual Meeting of the
International Society of Political Psychology,
Washington D.C., 1990**

The proposal is that an international plan be drawn up to abolish war between nations. The goal would be to achieve this objective by the year 2000— a decade from now.

Such an agreed plan is needed to give a sense of purpose and direction to disarmament negotiations and related activities. Otherwise, as Henry Kissinger has pointed out, there is a risk that ad hoc and pragmatic initiatives in response to a rapidly changing situation will result in contradictions and dangerous road blocs. In addition, a publicly stated plan could make it easier for the general public to hold their governments accountable. Individuals and governments alike have plans for most activities. This practice should be extended to the most pressing issue on the public agenda: the need to abolish war.

Until recently talk of abolishing war seemed utopian and unreal (except perhaps for a short period at the end of World War I). Three events have modified that perception:

(a) The apparent end to the Cold War and associated radical changes in Europe and in various regional conflicts.

(b) A more realistic public awareness of the consequences of war, especially when there is use of weapons of mass destruction.

(c) A growing awareness that a deteriorating environment has become a major threat to our well being and that amelioration will require an unprecedented degree of international cooperation. This puts quarrels between nations into a different perspective.

Since 1945 there has always been the risk that weapons of mass destruction would be used as a result of miscalculation, accident, etc. It may seem that the risk has been reduced as a result of lower tensions between the superpowers. Against this has to be weighed the proliferation of such weapons and the means of their delivery, usually into regions where there are intense grievances and perhaps low appreciation of the consequences involved in their use. In addition, the unstable situation in the Soviet Union could easily lead to new dangers. In short, there is a real risk that we are in a window of opportunity which may close down if we do not make use of it in good time. Choice of the year 2000 is, of course, arbitrary but has the advantage of focusing public attention whilst giving ample time (a decade) to complete the process.

Such a plan has to win widespread public support so as to build up impetus for implementation and, therefore, interest in its maintenance. The plan should be broadly based so as not be blown away by rapidly changing ideas and circumstances. It should take advantage of the fact that the sovereign state is not the only political level to inspire popular loyalty: there are also strong loyalties at local and regional levels, and it is probable that in the coming decade more and more people will have a strong sense of being world citizens. All this would suggest that the plan should be based on moral principle. Past experience shows that real-politik obsession with immediate material self-interest tends to be unstable (because of changing power relationships) and induces cynicism (ie. lack of public support). A policy based on the general long term interest of all humanity will make it difficult for a rogue government to win the support of its own citizens and accordingly make for constraint.

It should also be transparent and easily understood by government and public alike. This means strong logic and consistency and a minimum of opportunity for lawyers to twist complex terms to selfish advantage. It also means, as President Wilson rightly insisted, that there be no secret covenants.

The plan must be global in its perspectives. A plan confined to the superpowers and their allies would be hampered because they would always have to consider the need for defense against third parties. Furthermore, regional conflicts in the rest of the world have the potential not only for immense local destruction but for dragging down with them the rest of the world.

Realistic in recognizing the fears and concerns of all nations, a peace plan must give a sense of security which is, at a minimum, marginally better than present arrangements. It has to be recognized that some nations still see force as a useful option in remedying deep felt grievances. There has to be a peaoeful alternative which is perceived to be workable and just.

The plan should not be free floating but rather provide a link between the present situation and desired goals.

Bearing in mind these desirable underlying characteristics it is suggested that the Peace Plan be built on two main pillars: one being a comprehensive and logical program of disarmament and confidence building and the other being the development of minimum basic procedures for peaceful resolution of disputes between nations.

The basic suggestion is that all offensive weapons of all nations be abolished without exception, and that all nations be permitted whatever defensive weapons they feel necessary.

Over the last few decades, weapons have become increasingly more important than personnel (hence the decline of mass conscript armies): furthermore advancing technology has led to increased specialization so that weapons can be classified quite easily as primarily offensive or defensive. Of course, almost all types of weapons can be used offensively but some are clearly more efficient for that purpose than others, and if they are abolished confidence in attack would be drastically reduced. These considerations have come into increasing focus in the last year (1990) in the security negotiations taking place in Europe (e.g. the significance of the Soviet decision to withdraw riverbridging equipment from forward areas). Military experts in the past have argued that the offense is the best means of defense but it is offensive weapons which cause fear and tension on the other side.

It is necessary that the ban apply to all conventional offensive weapons, not just weapons of mass destruction, not least because one key argument justifying nuclear weapons is that they are an affordable counter to, say, a mass tank army.

Whatever may be the reason in the interim, it is clear that there cannot be exceptions which allow a few powers to retain even a few nuclear weapons as an ultimate insurance. The rest of the world will not willingly acknowledge such privileges as has been demonstrated in the widespread resistance to the nuclear non-proliferation treaty.

The first line of security should be a comprehensive verfication system. Methods now

available can give assurance that verification systems
will be sufficiently effective to prevent the secret
manufacture, maintenance and deployment of a large
number of offensive weapons. Verification can be
strengthened by a system clearly based on moral
principle because that would increase the possibility
that citizens will blow the whistle on their own
government if they should try to cheat.

Retention of as many defensive weapons as desired
offers a second line of defense against cheating by
rogue governments, and, no doubt, will be necessary
to induce governments to give up all their offensive
weapons. This approach has the additional advantage
that as time passes and governments begin to feel
secure, there would be a natural, rather than
imposed, pressure to reduce such defensive forces in
the name of economy and more important priorities.

The third line of security might be to introduce
neutral forces between nations which are hostile to
one another. These could be provided by other nations
acceptable to both sides. Such a system can
complicate and slow down aggressive action. Recent
suggestions for multi-national forces to be stationed
in each country in Europe may make such a device
unnecessary on that continent, but it could be
beneficial if applied, for instance, between Israel and
her neighbors, between India and Pakistan, between
the two Koreas, etc.

There are a wide range of possibilities to achieve
peaceful resolution of conflicts but it would seem that
they should include, systematic development of
centers for study and management already existing
in universities and elsewhere, as well as formal
undertakings by nations to make use of such services
when in dispute with other nations: agreement by all
nations that any dispute not settled through peaceful
conflict management be submitted to the World Court

for arbitration. The World Court has a record of acknowledged fairness and objectivity and any perceived surrender of national sovereignty involved in agreeing to abide by its decisions would seem to be a small price to pay for permanent abolition of war. It is of particular importance that (i) an example be set by the major nations including the USA which supposedly stands for the rule of law and which has played a major role in the establishment of the World Court; (ii) there be a meaningful system of sanctions against government which try to wage war or refuse to accept the rulings of the World Court. Ultimately this may entail (a) military force and the need for a prior committed international police force (e.g. in case of invasion and occupation); (b) restructuring of the UN so as to establish an organ which has a true global perspective and which is able to make swift decisions in times of emergency with the support of the majority (some suggestions on this point are given in the book **Achieving Peace by the Year 2000**); and (c) a revival and strengthening of the Briand-Kellog pact outlawing war so as to give a watertight legal as well as moral base to the whole peace system proposed.

Humanity now has an unprecedented opportunity to abolish war between nations, one of the great scourges of civilization, just as in the 19th century it abolished slavery, that other great scourge which for so long had seemed to be an inevitable aspect of the human condition. What is needed is a collective act of will to make abolition of war the highest priority. Let's be clear: priority for peace means that when necessary other interests, no matter how important they may seem, will be put aside so as to achieve the common goal. Once threats of war between nations have been finally removed then humanity can concentrate on the other great issues of the time-the environment, poverty, etc.-with a view to ultimately establishing a true spiritual peace based on justice.

THE ELEMENTS OF WORLD GOVERNMENT

A presentation at the Earth is But One Country, a Conference on a New World Order, the Environment, and Development, Dublin, Ireland, 1992

Basic Assumptions

Community and Government

My first assumption is that government in principle is about the community acting together in cooperation to solve community problems that cannot be solved at the individual level eg. enforcement of law and order. Logically this applies at the world as well as at the national and local levels. In other words the government is not "them" but "us". I feel it is necessary to say this up front because we live in a time of extreme hostility to government. Of course, there always has been a significant part of the world population that has traditionally seen "government" as the enemy — and with good reason. Most people until recently have lived under authoritarian regimes which have been oppressive and arbitrary. In consequence defeating the will of government has been a way of life: corruption, evasion of taxes, throwing trash on to the street, running red lights—often by people who otherwise are honorable in their relationships with family and friends, and who take their shoes off when entering a home. In short, oppressive government is not conducive to a community spirit.

What is different today is that hostility to government has become rampant in democracy as well. It has been provoked by heavy handed, insensitive, inefficient big government. But instead of a rational response of looking for reform, we have a large part of the political spectrum demonising all public servants and arguing as if there is barely a need for government at all. The assumption seems to be that individuals can pursue their own needs without conflict with one another, and that the bigger issues can best be handled by "efficient" private organizations with a little help from voluntary charity organizations (I am a strong believer in the role of voluntary oganizations, but history has shown that this scenario is simply not real). This perspective has provoked extremist, so called private "militias who preach armed resistance to government regulation (but not to government benefits when they are the beneficiaries) and in some cases terrorist attacks on government personnel. World government is seen as the ultimate evil—a view encouraged by some Christian Fundamentalists who see it as a sign of the Anti-Christ. This is a serious matter because the worst excesses are in the United States, which being the only superpower, is clearly a lead player on the international stage.

Democracy

My second assumption is that any world government will have to be democratic. There are two basic reasons for making this assumption. First, replacement of traditional authoritarian forms of government is a key aspect of modern society. The wealth and education brought by the Industrial Revolution has meant that more and more people demand freedom and control over community affairs—

they simply will not put up with dictatorship anymore. This is humanity growing from childhood (when we were told what to do) to adulthood when we are in charge of our own affairs. Two hundred years ago the number of states that could be labeled "democratic" or "constitutional" was no more than a handful. Today, the majority of nations, containing the majority of humanity, are democratic. The mighty empires of the nineteenth century that tried to resist this tide of history have been swept into oblivion. The second reason for this assumption is that the very idea of a world dictatorship is so frightening that it is inconceivable that existing governments and the peoples of the world would accept such an outcome, especially as now the majority of peoples live under democratic regimes. Opponents of world government who try to frighten ordinary people with such a scenario are simply setting up a straw man.

Federal Democracy

My third assumption is that a democratic world government would have a federal structure. Consider the main alternatives: confederation or a unitary state. A confederation is a structure where there is very little central power and there is effectively veto power by the component states that make up the confederacy. This is in essence the system that we have had since the League of Nations was created in 1918. Clearly this has been a major advance over what went before, but it did not prevent the Second World War, nor the regional conflicts of the Cold War. Furthermore, it clearly is not adequate to meet the challenges we face today, as has been demonstrated repeatedly in the weak, divided responses to wars in Eastern Europe, the Former Soviet Union, and Africa, as well as to the immense issues of poverty and the environment.

The classic example of the democratic unitary state have been the French republics since the 1789 Revolution. The advantage of this model where the people vest all real power in the central government is that it would be able to enforce equality of treatment between all regions of the world. The problem is that such a system becomes remote from the people and thereby authoritarian and ham handed, even in democracy and even at the national level, let alone at the world level. Furthermore, such a model would be very much against the spirit of the time, with its emphasis on devolution to the local community level and on national self determination.

It seems reasonable to conclude, therefore, that the best model is the one in between confederation and union. ie. a federation in which there is a division of function and authority between various levels of government: world, national and local. In short, following the example of the newly independent states of North America in the 1780's, the present world government structure should be moved forward from confederation to federation. Clearly, we Bahá'ís are at one with our friends, the World Federalists, on this issue, and as a result many of us are members, of their association including myself.

In making these assumptions, we have to be very conscious of the basic flaws of democracy so as to be on our guard. One a is tendency for dictatorship of the majority, at the expense of minorities, as pointed out in the 1830's by Alexandre de Tocqueville when he visited the United States. Another is a tendency to parochialism and division as a consequence of the drive by both the executive and the legislator to seek reelection by ingratiating themselves with their constituencies. This rapidly becomes what the Americans call "pork barrel" politics. Edmund Burke gave warning of the dangers of this tendency some

200 hundred years ago. For the same reason, perspectives also tend to be short sighted—long term plans do not yield the "goodies" a politician needs for the next election in 2, 4, 5 or 6, years time, as the case may be.

Details

Having spelt out some very basic assumptions about world government, I should now like to pose some questions that will help fill in some of the more important detail. In doing so let me just highlight two aspects of the world government which make it unique, ie. what makes it different from all other forms of government. The first is that there is only one world government, as compared with about 190 national governments and literally thousands of local governments. This means that we have to get the answers to our questions right otherwise we are likely to have major trouble. The second aspect is that world government would be concerned for the well-being of all humanity (including future generations), rather than particular constituencies as is the case with national and local government.

The first and most obvious question concerning a federal structure is how best to optimize distribution of authority and power. This question has at least three dimensions: distribution by level of government (world, national, local etc); distribution by function (legislative, executive, judicial, etc); and distribution between the public sector and the private/voluntary sector—the latter being the key issue in recent years, as already observed.

Levels of Government and Subsidiarity

With regard to distribution by level, there seem to be certain functions that would of necessity go to the world level simply because that would be the only one with the necessary "reach". The most obvious such political function is the maintenance of international law and order and the peace. This would mean it would have to have a strong independent police force and a world court with complusory powers of arbitration.

The key economic function at the world level would be to manage the global economy, as a matter of efficiency and fairness. This would involve at a minimum, supervision of an international commercial code and establishment of a single world currency and system of weights and measures—all extensions of functions already assigned to the World Trade Organization and the International Monetary Fund. It would also involve a key role in management of the transition from the partial global economy which we have today, to one which is fully integrated, so as to ensure fairness in distribution of the cost of transition. This is necessary because if left to national governments there will be overwhelming pressure to slow down the process at great cost to the common good. It will also involve a major role in reducing extremes of wealth and poverty within and, particularly, between nations—a necessity for the establishment of a lasting peace. This implies such matters as making sure that the mineral resources of the world (humanity's inheritance) are used for the general good, and openness in transfer of resources and technology. Thirdly it would involve a major role in protection of the natural environment, especially with regard to such global concerns as the warming of the planet, protection of the ozone layer and management of the international commons, such as the oceans.

The world level of government would also have to have some major social functions, including upholding of universal standards of human rights (presumably based on the Universal Declaration of 1948), and in choosing an auxiliary world language, an important means for nourishing the idea that we are all "world citizens" as well as members of a particular national culture.

The role of the national level in a world federation is likely to be reduced as compared with that of national sovereign states belonging to a confederation, as is the case today, because one of its main basic functions, providing security against external threat, would have been largely transferred to the world level. This would allow the national level to be more relaxed about its authority and make it easier to be flexible in responding to the needs of minorities. An example of such a situation is the easing with regard to the two parts of Ireland that is now possible with membership of the European Community. In other words, a world federal government will make easier national self determination for minorities, and opens up possibilities of innovative models to meet different circumstances. For instance, it would be possible for a minority group, not concentrated in one geographic location, as is often the case, to be allowed to manage its own internal affairs, including social services. The new situation would also facilitate the process of pushing responsibility down to the local level— "subsidiarity"—whenever justified by the function. This is desirable as a way of making "government" more "human" and encouraging participation by ordinary citizens, as with the models of the Swiss canton, the town hall meeting in New England, and tribal government among many indigenous peoples.

The Branches of Government

Now for a few words about the various branches of government in a federal world system. With regard to the *legislative* branch, an obvious issue is should it be unicameral or bicameral. A unicameral model would presumably be less costly and more speedy in decision making, and therefore it is one traditionally favored by those who wish to make radical reforms in society. The bicameral model has the advantage that it usually ensures more reflection on proposed legislation to correct oversights that arise from undue haste, and typically has made for a better balance between the popular general will and local culture, for instance, by having the lower house representation allocated on the basis of population and the upper house allocated on set numbers for each component state in the federation, regardless of relative size of population, as in the United States. Certainly this seems like an appropriate model for a world government.

With regard to the ***excecutive*** branch, a basic question is should this be elected directly by the population (as in the US model) or indirectly by the legislature (as in the Westminster and other European models)? A second question is what sort of person do we wish to have as head of the Executive: an influential politician who might take initiatives and in effect be the world leader, or simply a bureaucrat who carries out the instructions of the legislature. President Wilson was inclined to the former and even toyed with the idea of putting himself forward for such a position. The idea was still born because member nations were reluctant to take the risk of too strong a leadership, and the alternative bureaucratic model has been the general experience of both the League and the United Nations, although Dag Hammerskold (Secretary General, 1953 to 1962) was led by circumstances of the time to take an unusually strong leadership role. A third alternative would be to have a collective presidency. At the national level such a model has not been very successful in the Soviet

Union and Yugoslavia, but on the otherhand there is the relative success of the Swiss experience.

Turning to the third branch of government, the **judiciary**, it is clear that under any reformed system of international institutions, this branch would have to have authority to pass judgment on the actions of the other two branches to see if they are in accordance with the "constitution". By contrast with the present World Court, it would have to have compulsory powers of arbitration of disputes between nations. Another important consideration would be how best to incorporate into the global judicial system the lessons that have been learnt over the last 40-50 years with regard to conflict resolution, which gives first priority to understanding and accommodating underlying emotional issues such as security fears and the need for genuine mutual respect, before addressing specific, material, issues. There would also be a need to consider an ombudsman function to mediate disputes between individuals and the bureaucracy of government.

In addition to the three traditional branches of government, there would be a need to address two other vital aspects of government. One is the place of the **central bank** charged with managing the world currency. Today at the national level there is a trend towards giving the central bank independence from the rest of the government, so that it can focus on minimizing inflation and protecting the value of the currency without political interference. This is clearly a desirable goal but the solution may be slightly undemocratic, though parallels might be drawn with the independence of the judiciary branch. The question is how far this issue needs to be taken at the world level—a question which is now (1992) preoccupying the European Community? Another function often referred to as an unofficial branch of

government is the **news media,** because it plays such
a vital role in providing information on public affairs
which is needed for the proper functioning of
democracy. What guarantees are necessary to
safeguard the independence and objectivity of the
news media? Probably of all techniques tried so far,
encouragement of diversity of ownership and
viewpoint are perhaps the most important.

Public, Private and Voluntary Sectors

A third dimension to the question of distribution
of functions and authority in a federal system is that
basic criterion: the division between the public and
private sectors. Until recently there was a tendency
to give the state an increasingly large influence in
society—in terms of the economy, managing up to 50
or 60 percent, sometimes as much as 70 percent, even
in democratic societies, let alone in Communist
countries where the figure typically has been in excess
of 90 percent. This was seen as necessary to achieve
economic justice, or at least that aspect of it that is
to do with equality. In recent years, as already noted,
there has been a strong reaction against such a role
for the public sector because it was perceived to be
an inefficient manager of the economy. It provided
little incentive to work hard or take initiative or
innovate, because of heavy taxation of the individual
and guarantees of employment in the public sector
regardless of performance. From a Bahá'í perspective,
with its emphasis on service to others as the highest
form of service, there was a deplorable tendency for
egalitarian socialists to despise service as a reminder
of the old master servant relationship, and the result
all too often was the arrogance and sloppiness of
public servants in dealing with the general public, rich
and poor alike. Some would also argue that central
control of the economy by the state whilst feasible

when economies were relatively small and simple, as in the early days of the Industrial Revolution, is becoming increasingly difficult as economies have become more complex and sophisticated, and is becoming a barrier in itself to economic development and the creation of wealth for the benefit of all.

We are still in the midst of the struggle to reduce the role of the state in the economy, and it may be a few years before the dust settles and we are able to take a cool long objective look at the optimum balance over the long run. One role that almost certainly will have to be continued and strengthened by the state will be supervision of monopoly type situations to prevent uneconomic exploitation of society as a whole. Another might be to ensure that long term protection of the environment is built into the pricing system and general functioning of the economy. There may have to be a broader mandate embracing the establishment of socially desirable goals over the long term including the achievement of a reasonable balance between freedom in the market place and the need not to allow differences in wealth to become so extreme as to weaken the fabric of society. One device for such a goal is counter cyclical fiscal policies which to a degree are already built into the functioning of the welfare state e.g. the rise in unemployment expenditures during a recession. What all this means in terms of an eventual balance between the state and the private sector is hard to estimate, but it may well mean that the state will come to represent say a quarter or one third of the economy instead of the typical half to two thirds of the mid twentieth century.

Spiritual Issues
So far the discussion has been about the formal surface structure of a future world government: the trunk and branches of the tree so to speak. But no

matter how perfect such a structure is, the key issue ultimately is the spirit with which it is managed: the spiritual sustenance that come through the roots. So often a fine political structure is corrupted because the people who operate it lack moral principle. Thus the ideals of an egalitarian and just society which inspired the Communist Revolution and the creation of the Soviet Union were destroyed from within by apparatiks, following the cynical philosophy that the end justifies the means. This brings us to the role of religion, which historically has always been a major factor in the ethical sustenance of society, not only because of the teachings of religion but because of its unparalleled ability to reach into the very hearts of people over an extended period of time. Looking at religion objectively, and without the undoubted prejudice of much of the educated elite of our society, so influenced by the conflict of science and religion in modern times, there are at least three contributions that religion can make which are of central importance to the effective functioning of a federal world government.

The first is that religion has a vision, the absence of which is one of the main deficiencies of democracy. The Holy Books of religion speak of a time when swords shall be beaten into ploughshares, a new Jerusalem—a time of peace and justice. This gives hope and therefore motivation to strive for a better world. A most obvious area where this longer perspective is immediately relevant is the environment.

The second contribution of religion is the basic concept of the brotherhood of man, the human family, the children of God, which is at the heart of the teachings of all the great religions, though often, of course, this has become obscured by the clutter of practices added by man. This concept is of immense significance. When we have such an idea we cannot casually dismiss from our thoughts the poverty of others who live on the other side of the planet and are of a different race, or culture or nation. They are our brothers and sisters and we have no choice but to give them every assistance.

This brings me to the third contribution of religion that is a nourishment of a world community and a sense of purpose. Religion teaches that the purpose of life is not simply to survive and consume things: the more we consume the happier we are is a materialistic philosophy. The religious view is that our purpose is to grow towards God, to acquire spiritual qualities, to become noble beings, to develop ourselves to our full capacity. This is most explicit in the Bahá'í Faith, the latest of the world religions, where it is further refined to include a collective dimension of creating an ever advancing civilization. With such purposes we have a powerful spiritual and intellectual tool for overcoming all the material barriers to world unity and peace.

There are two subsidiary aspects of the spiritual nourishment of the tree of world unity that should also be mentioned. The first is the family. It may seem odd to mention the family when discussing world government, but experience shows that it is the basic buidling block of society: two or more living together in mutual cooperation, indeed as one flesh, and in support of the resulting children—the weak and helpless. It is in the family, when it is functioning properly, that a child grows up to have a loving attitude towards others. When the family structure is absent, as is increasingly the case in Western society, children all too often lack this positive experience, and as a result slide into indifference to the welfare of others, and this in turn can lead to careless brutality. In Washington DC, where I live, kids kill and expect to be killed, with neither remorse nor hope, living as if characters on TV. But to restore the family, it has to be recognized that the old authoritarian model has failed, and we have to build a new model based on the equality of the sexes and a balance between the best of male and female characteristics.

This leads to the second subsidiary spiritual issue and that is the role of women in contributing to a peaceful society and the establishment of a democratic federal world government. This is not just a matter of equality ie. women as half the world population should have equal input and benefit from government, important as that is as a matter of elementary justice. Equally important is the special contribution that women can make on the basis of their experience, both as individuals and from the collective historical experience e.g. the feminine tendency to be constructive, nourishing, mutually supportive, maternal and loving—qualities that are sometimes given lower priority in the traditional male perspective. That this is not just sentimentality is born out by numerous opinion polls over the years, in the United States and elsewhere, which show such perspective affecting such specific issues as welfare, arms control, the environment and the United Nations.

What Now?

These are, of course, very general comments and there is the question, yes but what specific actions do we need to take now. Let me make a couple of suggestions.

The first is to give strong support to reform and strengthening of the United Nations so as to make it more effective. Some of the most obvious needs are (i) to reform the Security Council so that it is more representative of the peoples and nations of the world as it is today, not as it was 50 years ago at the end of the Second World War, and (ii) to purge the bureaucracy of waste and corruption so that once again it has the trust and respect of national governments. Other urgently required reforms, as previously observed, would be the strengthening of the World Court and remodeling of peace keeping forces. Just as important, we have to start a public dialogue about how to move from a world confederation to a world federation. The conventional and boring, myopic views that so dominate public discussion today must be challenged, and a full account given of the consequences of such views over the long period for all humanity.

The second suggestion is to find already working models of global communities and institutions. This is where, I suggest, the Bahá'í world community has something of real values to offer. For many years the community has had an administrative and political structure which is in effect a world federal democratic system that is strongly nourished by religious or spiritual values as discussed earlier. One particularly valuable feature of the system is the process of public discussion: **consultation,** which I suggest, is a significant advance over the democratic process of debate. Though debate is more open and healthy than the old system of the general population simply taking orders from some authoritarian institution, it does tend to create division, to divide participants into winners and losers, and to encourage biased rhetoric rather than objective analysis. The Bahá'í process of consultation is very different. It is consciously aimed at arriving at the truth through (i) open and frank discussion but within the framework of maintaining unity of spirit; (ii) universal participation, including even the most humble; and (iii) spiritual detachment from the ego. Experience over seventy years in the Bahá'í community shows that ordinary people can gradually learn this method of discussion and the results are remarkable. The model offered by the Bahá'í community has the added advantage that Bahá'ís are not a threat or rivals to anyone; it's objective is to reach out and cooperate with all who have the common interest at heart.

The Role of Ireland

I should like to end with a few words about Ireland and its possible role in helping humanity move towards the rule of law at the global level. It is, of course, obvious that the United States has to be a lead player in the process because of its power and influence and because of its past magnificent contributions, and indeed this is confirmed in the Bahá'í Writings. But it is also clear that each nation has something special to contribute to the process as well, on the basis of its own individual culture and experience. A world federation will be voluntary and not imposed from outside, so these contributions will have to be listened to, as will be especially true if there is particular respect for a country because of its "track record". Such respect is already accorded to Ireland in international circles, as I have seen from working in an internaional institution for 30 years, along with other countries that spiritually punch "above their weight" (if I may be allowed to borrow from Mrs Thatcher!): Canada, the Scandinavian countries, the Netherlands, Costa Rica, Sri Lanka, and so on. This respect for Ireland undoubtedly is connected with such factors as its spiritual leadership of Western Europe during the "Dark Ages", as well as with its struggle for independence, an experience which it has in common with many of the nations of the "Third World". The recent visit of your President to Somalia is an example of this mutual empathy and this nation's concern for the general well being of humanity. Ireland has a lot to offer and we must make sure that this is not overlooked.

Conclusion

The purpose of this presentation has been not so much to entertain but to prompt questions of the conventional and meditation on the logical next step in the process of strengthening the rule of law and the achievement of a just society. This conference should not end with words, but lead to each one of us leaving this place determined to take action to advance the cause of a world democratic federal commonwealth.

THE ENVIRONMENT AND THE INTERNATIONAL AGENCIES

**A presentation at the Association for Bahá'í Studies-
Japan Conference, Tokyo, June 12, 1994**

Widespread concern about the need to protect our natural environment is a comparatively recent phenomenon. It is true that man has caused damage to the environment, often serious, for thousands of years, at least since the coming of agriculture and permanent settlements: deforestations, soil erosion, soil salination, etc, and this has been given as one of the major factors accounting for the fall of great civilizations in Mesopotamia, the Indus Valley, and Central America[1]. Generally, however, the process was slow and incremental, stretching out over several centuries before becoming a catastrophe, and no single generation would be especially conscious of what was happening until the very end. Even when damage was comparatively rapid, as in the case of overfishing or hunting of animals to extinction for fur or oil, there always was another region to turn to, even if it presented more difficulty.

All this began to change with the coming of the Scientific and Industrial Revolution in Europe, especially after it acquired real momentum in the nineteenth and twentieth centuries. This revolution brought unprecedented power in terms of productivity and communications; it made possible, for the first time in history, the abolition of poverty,[2] and it has brought together the various continents and regions, previously barely in contact with each other, into what is rapidly becoming a global society. The impact on the natural environment has been and continues to be immense. Industry itself brought pollution, including new toxic wastes, of land, water, and air; business based agriculture often resulted in pollution and erosion of the land and the destruction of traditional diverse cultures, especially when following in the wake of colonialism; whilst fishig and hunting to extinction became more systematic and global. This process was aggravated by the dominance of a "new" consumer philosophy which encourages demand for material goods far in excess of basic needs, and by an unprecedented growth in population size arising from a fall in death rates of rich and poor alike because of improved methods of health care, but with little reduction in birth rates, at least among the poor.

As the destructive effects of the Industrial Revolution became increasingly apparent, societies took a growing number of counter measures. These were either at the local community level or at the national level, eg. measures in the USA and the UK in the late nineteenth and early twentieth centuries to establish national parks and to manage forests. Only slowly would it be recognized that the damage being done was so widespread that its effects crossed frontiers and affected peoples perhaps thousands of miles away, and that therefore there would be a need to take corrective measures through international cooperation.

One critical side effect of the Industrial Revolution was the development of increasingly powerful machines of war, a process that eventually led to weapons of mass destruction, including the nuclear bomb, which threatened the very existence of civilization, perhaps all life on the planet. It was to be the resulting concern about the need to reduce the risk of war between nations, with important indirect implications with regard to the safeguarding of the environment, which was to lead to the first efforts at systematic international cooperation. This process began at the end of the revolutionary wars in Europe, 1792-1815, with the Congress System, an arrangement for periodic consultation between the Great Powers of Europe (other nations were brought in later) when there were major issues of concern. A second stage was the creation, at the Hague Conference in 1899, of a permanent international institution for voluntary arbitration of disputes between nations. A third was the establishment of the League of Nations, after the First World War, which had as its core the concept of collective security. A fourth was the replacement of the League, after the Second World War, with a more global and otherwise strengthened United Nations.

An aspect of this movement towards collective security and peace keeping international organizations was the quest to reduce national armaments. Of vital significance for the environment were steps taken with regard to weapons of mass destruction: conventions concerning biological and chemical weapons, and above all, agreements on limiting testing, non-proliferation (managed by the International Atomic Energy Agency), and reduction in numbers of nuclear weapons.

Though the international "peace-keeping" organizations represent a major step forward in the history of civilization, wars still happen, and it is clear that much more needs to be done. There is, for instance, a need to convert the present weak confederation of national sovereign states into a federation of the peoples of the world, to make arbitration by the World Court compulsory, to make much greater use of real conflict resolution techniques, to create a directly recruited and finanaced peace making force, and to have a more equitable and systematic approach to national disarmament[3].

A very important improvement associated with the United Nations as compared with the League, was a more direct attempt to tackle the causes of war, an attempt coordinated through a new high level Economic and Social Council (ECOSOC), with the assistance of associated agencies and offices. A basic element in this approach was to stimulate the growth of the world economy, and thereby raise average standards of living, by systematically removing state imposed barriers to trade. The two lead institutions were (i) the General Agreement on Trade and Tariffs (GATT), now (1994) being converted into a stronger World Trade Organization (WTO), which has been responsible for reducing "physical" barriers to international trade eg. tariffs, quotas, etc., and (ii) the International Monetary Fund, which is responsible for managing a stable relationship between currencies, so as to reduce the Financial risk and cost of international transactions, as well as to give financial and technical assistance to countries with balance of payments difficulties.

Though there have been deep disappointments, both institutions have been comparatively successful, as is reflected in the fact that international trade has consistently grown faster than domestic trade since they were created some fifty years ago. Environmentalists have, however, expressed concerns about both organiztions. With regard to GATT, it is argued that the recently concluded "Uruguary Round" will make more difficult the enforcement of environment protection in connection with imports, e.g. US concern about importation of tuna harvested in conditions which kill dolphins that swim with them.

It remains to be seen if provisions of the new WTO for arbitration of such disputes will meet this concern adequately. With regard to the IMF, it is vehemently argued that its conditions for giving temporary balance of payments financial assistance can be detrimental to the environment, especially when they involve large cuts in public expenditures. The IMF counter argues that its emphasis on market efficiency, on balance, is favorable to the environment because it forces a nation to put a true value on its natural assets, and conserve them accordingly. Some are sceptical of such a response, especially bearing in mind that most market prices do not reflect depreciation of natural assets and pollution costs, and in any case there is always a need for case by case review with regard to public expenditures. It is somewhat encouraging that more recently the IMF (and the World Bank) has shown greater willingness to advise in favor of enviromental protection and social safety net expenditures and against military expenditures in certain circumstances.

The UN concern to address the economic causes of conflict extend beyond encouragement of free international trade, to include active programs to transfer financial and technical assistance to countries in need, with a view to eventually eliminating poverty. Such programs involve a series of international agencies including the Food and Agricultural Organization (FAO), the World Health Organization (WHO), the UN Development Program (UNDP), and international and regional development banks, led by the World Bank. Undoubtedly these programs have had some major successes[4]. From the environmental perspective, a key consideration is that when average per capita income in a country reaches a given threshold (about US$1,500), experience suggests that it will pay much more attention to environmental questions and the protection of its natural capital assets. Nevertheless, the World Bank and the other development banks continue to be severely criticized by environmentalists, e.g. most recently by the Environment Defense Fund[5], for many of their policies and projects. Though much of the criticism may be justified, it is to the credit of the Bank that it does seem to listen to it critics, and in recent years has strengthened its Environmental Department and has increased the number of its loans directed at environmental protection, e.g. in FY1993, such loans were increased by 67% to 8.4% of the total.

The UN's advance, as compared with the League, in addressing the basic causes of international conflict had a second pillar, human rights: the Universal Declaration of Human Rights and associated conventions, supported by various executive agencies such as the UN Human Rights Commission, the UN Education, Science and Cultural Organization (UNESCO), the UN International Children's Fund (UNICEF), the International Labor Organization (ILO), the UN High Commission for Refugees, etc. Proposals made in 1919 by Japan that the League Covenant should incorporate a statement on human rights had been vetoed by the Western powers, fearful that this might undermine their colonial empires. However, the Holocaust of European Jewry and the other terrible evils of the fascist dictators in the Second World War, made human rights a fundamental requirement in 1945 for the new United Nations.

There are at least three major reasons why the human rights question is important for protection of the environment. First, it has enhanced the status of women world wide. Women, with their strong universal tradition of protecting children as the highest priority, and of working together in a peaceful and constructive way to make the best use of land and other resources, are quick to understand the wisdom of protecting their natural environment. Investment in the education of girls at primary, secondary and tertiary levels has a steadily increasing impact on the number of children they are likely to have, and it is recognized now to be the most effective way to reduce the growth in population. Second, human rights consciousness is leading gradually to an improved position for indigenous peoples (e.g. the holding of the first UN conference on indigenous peoples in Vienna in 1993). Such peoples, hunter-gatherers, and agriculturists alike, have cultures which are far more in harmony with nature than the massive and insensitive systems of the modern consumer society. Humanity needs the wisdom and diversity of such cultures to make the best use of the resources available, perhaps even to survive. It may be that this is an important aspect of the Bahá'í teaching that the American Indian "will become so enlightened that the whole earth will be illumined"[6]. Third, at the heart of the human rights concept is the idea of democracy and an open society, and experience suggests that in the long run this is a much better protection for the environment than authoritarian government. It is surely not by chance that some of the worst damage to the environment in modern times occurred inside the secretive communist empire.

So far the discussion has been about the international organizations and an indirect connection with the environmental question, ie. where the environmental concern was not primary, although, as noted, the environmental impact could often be significant. It was not until the 1970s that the environment became a major item on the international agenda in its own right, although there had been occasional earlier activity, e.g. the establishment of the International Whaling Commission in 1946-an institution bedeviled to this day by the old problem of lack of a sense of responsibility for the commons especially on the part of competing users whose short term interest blinds them to their more important long term interest. The new international agenda had its roots in the growing understanding of the complexity and global significance of environmental degradation which came to public notice with publication of such books as ***The Silent Spring*** by Rachel Carson, ***Small is Beautiful*** by E.F. Schumacher, and ***The Limits to Growth*** by Dennis Meadows and the Club of Rome.

The first UN "Conference on the Human Environment" took place in Stockholm in 1972[7]. As a result of that conference an "UN Environmental Program" office was established in Nairobi (1974) to monitor the global environment. In addition, it prompted, over time, most national governments to nominate one ministry or department to be responsible for overall public policy on the environment. The same year the first conference on global population was held in Bucharest a second was held in Mexico in 1984, and a third is scheduled for Cairo this autumn (1994). This critical issue for the environment has involved a great deal of controversy, partly because of adamant opposition to artificial contraception and abortion by powerful religious institutions eg. the Catholic Church and Islám—a position strengthened by crude methods in India and China—and partly because of a suspicion among some Third World leaders that the issue was a devious device of the former colonial powers to maintain ascendancy (after all, population size has always been one key indicator of national power). Another important international debate taking place at this time with profound implications for the environment was in connection with the long running preparation of a new Law at Sea which covers such issues as dumping waste at sea and ocean mining as well as fishing rights.

Commitment of the international community to the environmental agenda moved into a second phase in 1983 when the UN General Assembly authorized the appointment of a World Commission on the Environment and Development with Gro Brundtland (later first woman prime minister of Norway) as chairperson. In its 1987 report, called *Our Common Future,* the Commission recommended the goal of sustainable development, which was defined as a policy to "meet the needs of the present without compromising the ability of future generations to meet their own needs". An important aspect of the report was encouragement of environmental and economic viewpoints to converge, a necessary change from a long and destructive practice of separation and near hostility. At last, serious discussions were beginning on such key matters as including natural assets in national accounts, and how best to adapt the market so that it would serve to protect the environment rather than damage it.

There were two tangible consequences arising from the report. First, it was agreed to establish a new Global Environmental Facility, a joint arrangement between UNEP, UNDP, and the World Bank, to finance global environmental projects. The second was a 1990 decision of the General Assembly to hold a World Summit to discuss implementation of the Commission's recommendations. A sense of urgency was added for the latter as new information began to emerge about damage to the ozone layer and the apparent warming of the planet as a result of human activity.

By now, the momentum of concern about global environmental problems was gathering force, and a wide range of special issues were being addressed

even as plans were being laid for the comprehensive
summit. Such activity included:

1. A "Protocol on Substances that Deplete the Ozone
   Layer" agreed in Montreal in 1987, which was
   subsequently strengthened by an agreement in
   London in 1990;
2. "The Basle Convention on Control of Transfrontier
   Movement of Hazardous Waste" (many experts
   now see waste as a greater environmental
   problem than consumption of non-renewable
   resources);
3. An "International Tropical Timber Agreement" (it
   is calculated that the world has lost more than
   50% of its tropical forest since 1950: a disaster
   of many dimensions, not least of which is the loss
   of biological diversity involved because of its high
   concentration in tropical forests);
4. Establishment of a "World Commission on Global
   Governance", consisting of a group of highly
   distinguished world leaders with Ingvar Carlsson,
   prime minister of Sweden as chairman, which
   was mandated to report on how best to improve
   international institutions especially with regard
   to safeguarding the global environment.

The UN Conference on Environment and
Development, or Earth Summit, held in Rio in 1992
was attended by representatives from 175 nations,
including 105 heads of state. All told, when
participants in the parallel Global Forum for Non-
Government Organizations (NGOs) are added, the total
number in attendance was about 30,000, making it
by far the most representative world conference in
history. The Conference resulted in six broad
agreements:

1. A Declaration of 27 principles defining rights and
   responsibilities of nations as they pursue human
   development and well-being;

2. a statement of principles on forestry management (there was failure to agree on a convention);
3. a convention on climate change (agreement to limit greenhouse gases to 1990 levels by the end of the century[8].);
4. a convention on bio-diversity (originally opposed by the USA because of disagreements about rights and benefits to be derived from exploitation of bio diverse assets in Third World countries);
5. a start on negotiation of a convention on combating desertification (progress has been slow because original assumptions that the focus would be on Africa is now being questioned by nations from other continents);
6. Agenda 21, a 40-chapter blue print on how to make development socially, economically and environmentally sustainable (though very comprehensive, the plan has been criticized for being weak on such controversial matters as population, energy consumption, patterns of production and consumption, etc).

To carry forward the achievements of Rio, a series of new international institutional arrangements were made. First, a new "Commission on Sustainable Development" was established, with representation from 53 nations, which has as its main function the monitoring of progress in implementation of Agenda 21, locally, nationally, and at the world level. It reports directly to ECOSOC. Second, the Commission is to be given technical advice by a "High Level Advisory Board" of experts. Third, the Commission is also to be given secretarial help by a new "Department of Policy Coordination and Sustainable Development" (about 100 staff) which has been added to the UN Secretariat. It is estimated that full implementation of Agenda 21 would cost about $625 billion per annum, of which some 80 percent would come from domestic resources, and about 20 percent ($125 billion) from international transfers of aid. The latter figure, which is more than twice the present level of official international assistance, would require rich countries to give about 1% of their GNP, an aid target agreed in principle, though never achieved, in the halycon days of the sixties.

Agenda 21 depends for success not only on action by all levels of government, local, city, provincial, national and international, but also on initiatives by private citizens and business. In their own activities there is a need for citizens and businesses to implement new strategies to protect the environment, over and beyond the traditional role of prodding government organizations into taking action. An important example is being given at the international level by Global Forum, a private sector organization based in Costa Rica which is headed by Maurice Strong, the main organizer of the Earth Summit. Other examples of initiatives by private sector international organizations are: the International Chamber of Commerce, which has already adopted a "Business Charter for Sustainable Development" and the Business Council for Sustainable Development which has recently published "Changing Course", a global business perspective on development and the environment.

In making this brief review of the international organizations and the environment, there is no doubt a sense of achievement, especially with regard to the flurry of activity in the last five years or so. Clearly concern about protecting the environment is now very much on the public agenda, and in principle at least, there is a global unity that was clearly lacking twenty, may be ten years ago. Yet major differences still exist as shown in the compromises and failures at Rio, and it is apparent that what has been achieved so far is very superficial when compared with the great dangers that threaten, which are likely to intensify in the coming decades rather than moderate. So what should be done to get more into line with the need?

One obvious concern is the weakness of the international organizations, hence the numerous studies of the UN in the last few decades, including the present one being prepared by the World Commission on Global Governance. With regard to activity directly aimed at protecting the environment, a minimum need, as suggested by Hilary French of the World Watch Institute, is for a central UN Environmental Agency, with the coordinating, legislative, executive, and general status of an IMF or WTO[9]. But daily experience, most notably in the area of peace making, shows that the problem is much broader and the present weak confederation model for the UN, with its numerous free floating agencies, is, in toto, increasingly inadequate for the global challenges of our time. The real question then is how to persuade the peoples of the world that a democratic world federation is an absolute necessity and would be conducive to the well being of all.

A second major concern is how to persuade the wealthier countries that giving serious assistance (trade outlets, technical assistance, investment and concessionary finance, etc) to the least well off countries, so as to help them abolish extremes of poverty and strengthen environmental protection of global significance, is in their own best interest, and should rank as one of their highest priorities, along with military security and public safety.

On the other hand, it would be significantly easier to persuade nations to take these steps, which can involve some sacrifice, if (i) the UN were to undertake a major effort to cut unnecessary and low priority expenditures, and (ii) Third World countries were to make good governance one of their own top priorities, and otherwise demonstrate that assistance given from outside will be used effectively for the intended purpose.

These desirable outcomes, however, depend to a large extent on changing the general mindset and vision of modern society. First, there is a need for everyone to see themselves as world citizens, with all the responsibilities that implies, as well as members of a local culture. Second, there is a need to have a holistic view of life on earth, with recognition of the spiritual as well as the material dimension, a way of bringing together knowledge in specialized fields, so that there is mutual support and cross fertilization rather than proceeding at cross purposes. Third, there is a need to re-examine the assumptions of the consumer society, and to see that harmony with nature must imply confining our material demands essentially to basic needs of food, clothing, shelter, and health care, and that surplus wealth is most satisfactorily spent on education, the arts and sciences, and on service of those least well off and of nature itself. This leads back to the fundamental question: what is the purpose of life? All the great world religions, including most specifically the Bahá'í Faith, which claims to give teachings for this age, identify the purpose of life to be: to grow towards God, to become noble beings, and to create an ever advancing civilization. When this vision becomes the common experience, the role of the global organizations in protecting the environment will be truly fulfilled.

NOTES

1. *A Green History of the World,* by Clive Ponting, Penguin, 1993.

2. For instance, the World Bank states that the number of people living in absolute poverty (about I billion) could be halved in twenty years (*Washington Post,* November 30, 1993).

3. For instance, with regard to nuclear non-proliferation, it seems unreasonable to allow China to have such weapons, but not India, her cross Himalayan rival. And if an adjustment for India, then what about Pakistan? And if Pakistan, what about Irán? And so on.

4. Some achievements in "developing" countries as a whole over the last 25 years have been: (i) a reduction in infant mortality from 120 per thousand to 60 per thousand, and increased life expectancy of 12 years; (ii) a doubling of food production and an increase in average nutritional intake per person of 20 percent; (iii) a doubling of secondary school enrollments (a triplinng for girls), and a substantial rise in literacy; (iv) clean water made available to 1 billion who previously lacked it; (v) a doubling of average incomes; and (vi) a dramatic trend towards democratic forms of government (*Earth Times,* May 14, 1994).

5. *Mortgaging the Earth: The World Bank, Environmental Impoverishment and the Crisis of Development,* by Bruce Rich, 1994.

6. Shoghi Effendi: *Advent of Divine Justice,* page 46.

7. The Scandinavian countries have played a distinguished leadership role in environmental matters for several decades, both domestically and internationally.

8. This has been replaced by a less ambitious agreement reached at the Kyoto Conference in December, 1997.

9. *Uniting the Peoples and Nations,* compiled by Barbara Walker, World Federalists Association, 1993.

WORKING TO ESTABLISH A PERMANENT PEACE

A presentation at Addis Ababa Univesity, Ethiopia, 1995

I appreciate very much being invited to address you today on the subject of peace. This is a subject which is very close to my heart because of personal experience, as I am sure it is for all of you. In my case, I was a child living during the Second World War, and I remember very much the terrible disasters of that time and the almost universal feeling after it was all over of "never again". I am also a Bahá'í, perhaps partly on account of that experience, because the highest priority of the Bahá'í Teachings is the establishment of the "Most Great Peace", based on justice "the most beloved thing in my sight". The attraction of the Bahá'í Faith was not just the nobility of this aspiration but its very practical approach to the achievement of such a peace.

It is also rewarding for me to be speaking on such matters at a university because students, being young and trained to be objective, and having inquiring minds are perhaps more open to discussion of new and radical ideas than is normal in the population at large. University students, because of their privilege of learning are likely to be the leaders and thinkers of tomorrow. It is a particular honor to speak at this university, because as the potential future leaders of this country, you may very well have a very special impact on the wider world community. Ethiopia is a leading nation of Africa with a long and distinguished history which commands outside respect, not least because of the way you have recently brought to a peaceful conclusion the horrendous turmoil of the last two decades.

Of course, in this period of national reconstruction, it is natural that much of your attention will inevitably by focused on domestic issues, and this is only right and praiseworthy. However, I would like to suggest that it is very important not to forget that events in the outside world could have a major impact, for good or bad, on the domestic scene. Accordingly it would be prudent to pay attention and to become actively involved in them. This is particularly of concern because the world remains a very dangerous place despite the end of the Cold War. There are still fierce regional conflicts, some not too far from here. Furthermore, there is potential for new and even more dangerous conflicts to arise in the coming years as a result of nationalistic and religious passions, or major clashes of material interest over economic development and the environment, or simply a struggle for political dominance. The situation is all the more dangerous because of the continuing availability of weapons of mas destruction, nuclear, chemical, and biological, which almost certainly in the coming decades are going to become cheaper, more portable and generally more available unless there is concerted action to prevent such a development.

And that brings me to the other side of the present situation, namely that the end of the Cold War presents an extraordinary opportunity, perhaps the first real one, globally since the 1920s, to establish an improved and more effective international system to reduce the risk of war and strengthen the rule of law. To coin the fashionable term it is a "window of opportunity" which if not used, may well be closed again as circumstances change.

In discussing the challenge of establishing a permanent peace, I should like to address three broad aspects. First the past, where we have come from, what progress has been made and lessons learnt so as to help decide what needs to be done next. Second, and this follows logically from the first, the future and a sense of vision, of what can and should be, so that we have a clear sense of direction and we do not get diverted down useless cul de sacs. And then in the context of these two themes some practical suggestions on what needs to be done now to take advantage of the "window of opportunity" to establish a solid base for a permanent peace.

Looking to humanity's past experience, I think it is reasonable to see the conscious struggle to establish world peace as beginning in Europe after the French Revolutionary wars of the late eighteenth and early nineteenth centuries. It is true that the need for some international structure to reduce the risk of war between sovereign states had been discussed spasmodically in Western Europe among leading thinkers since the end of the great religious wars of the 16th and 17th centuries as a replacement for the spiritual authority of the pope which was no longer universally acknowledged, but such ideas had not been translated into action prior to 1815. From that point on the history of the "peace process can be divided into four broad periods: (1) 1815-1918, from the end of the Napoleonic Wars to the end of the First World War; (2) 1918-1945, from the end of the First World War to the end of the Second World War; (3) 1945-1989, from the end of the Second World War to the end of the Cold War; and (4) the post Cold War period.

The first of these periods may be generally

associated with the European Congress System. In broad terms there were four significant innovations during this period. First, the Congress System established the practice of governments meeting to discuss international disputes and other issues before they had escalated into violence and war. Hitherto large international conferences had almost invariably been called only to establish the terms of peace AFTER a major conflict. Second, during this period the first permanent international institutions were established to coordinate technical aspects of economic and social interaction between states which were becoming increasingly important with evolution of industry and international commerce e.g. the International Telegraph Union (1865) and the Universal Postal Union (1874). Such institutions employed the first international civil servants, people who in quite a formal sense were the first world citizens. Third, there were the first of a growing number of international conventions establishing agreed rules on the conduct of war with a view to reducing excessive violence and cruelty, practices that were perceived to serve little military purpose and were morally repugnant. The roots of such ideas were in the values of chivalry promoted by Christian churches in the Middle Ages. The first conventions dealt with the treatment of civilians and the wounded on the battlefield and were the result of a campaign by the Swiss based Red Cross, whose founder, Henri Dunant, had witnessed the horrors of the battles of Solferino and Magenta in Northern Italy in the late 1850s. The fourth development was associated with the Hague Conferences at the end of the century which resulted in Conventions that established f acilities for international arbitration and international commissions of inquiry, a development of ad hoc arrangements that had periodically occurred in the nineteenth century, e.g. in connection with British arms sales to the South during the American Civil War.

It is evident that these innovations as a whole contributed to a reduction in the incidence of war during this period as compared with the experience during previous centuries. Nevertheless, much of the system was based on voluntary compliance and was otherwise weakly structured. As a result it was ultimately overwhelmed by powerful forces of violence that spread in the latter part of the period: nationalism, imperialism, and militarism, and as a consequence humanity had the experience of the First World War, which with its 20 million dead and untold destruction was one of the worst incidents of violence in the history of humanity.

In response to that horror, governments of the world, pushed forward by voluntary organizations and popular pressure, established the League of Nations, the key institution of the second of the broad periods of struggle to establish world peace. The League incorporated two important innovations to strengthen peaceful relations between nations. The first was to replace the ad hoc and only occasional international congresses with a permanent international assembly for consultation on international issues. The second was agreement to the principle of collective security, involving international economic and, in extremis, military sanctions against any state that attacked another. These characteristics in effect meant that the League was a world confederation, and as such represented a major advance in the history of humanity.

It is well known that the League ultimately failed to live up to the early high hopes that were placed on it, but it should be noted that in its first decade it had quite a successful record in resolving several potentially dangerous international disputes e.g., between Germany and Poland over Silesia and between Greece and Italy, and it did encourage for the first time the emergence of a constituency of ordinary citizens of many countries who saw themselves as world citizens as well as subjects of their own individual countries.

But like the Congress System it did have major weaknesses. It relied unduly on the voluntary compliance of members and its membership was far from universal; indeed for much of its life only a minority of the critically important Great Powers were members, with the absence of the United States being the most serious deficiency. As a result it was not able to withstand the stress of the Great Depression and the associated rise of a new wave of militarism. A major failure was its response to the invasion of Ethiopia by fascist Italy, when after initially showing signs of resistance, the League, led by France and Great Britain, faltered and gave way to short term nationalistic considerations. The ultimate price of this failure was the most terrible self inflicted wound on humanity in the history of civilization: the Second World War which resulted in some 60 million deaths.

To avoid repetition of such a disaster, the victorious Allies agreed to establish a new United Nations which was structured to avoid some of the more obvious weaknesses of the League of Nations which it replaced.

First there was a conscious effort to make membership more universal. This time all the most powerful nations have been members (with short periods of absence on the part of China and Indonesia), and today virtually every sovereign state is a member.

Second, there was a major effort to address two of the main causes of war: abuse of human rights and poverty. Horrified by the Nazi Holocaust of the Jews, the nations of the world unanimously approved a Universal Declaration of Human Rights, to spell out clearly what standards are expected of governments and other power centers in dealing·with their peoples. The approach to the problem of reducing poverty had two broad elements. One was to avoid the deadly competitive nationalist policies of the 1930s which enormously damaged the well being of practitioners as well as those targeted, and instead to move towards a global economy with all the efficiency and broadened economic opportunity for all nations that would be entailed.

To that end, two new subsidiary institutions were to be established: an International Trade Organization (ITO) to coordinate reductions in physical barriers to trade, such as tariffs and quotas, and an International Monetary Fund (IMF) to manage smooth and non disruptive relationships between currencies. After further consideration, governments initially backed away from the ITO concept and settled for a much weaker General Agreement on Trade and Tariffs (GATT), but in the last few years the original concept has been in essence revived with the establishment of a new World Trade Organization (WTO).

The second element in the strategy of reducing global poverty was the creation of the World Bank, later supported by similar organizations at the regional level, such as the African Development Bank, to help transfer technology and top up the supply of capital from the private sector with public multilateral funds for economic and social development and reconstruction after the War. Voluntary transfers of resources prior to this time had almost always been in connection with military alliances and other immediate self interest motivations and, very occasionally, in connection with humanitarian concerns at times of major natural disasters. These approaches to poverty were themselves a major step forward in the process of global solidarity and responsibility.

The United Nations has clearly had some significant successes during its first 45 years. In terms of human rights, a major success was the speedy dismantling of the great European overseas empires and the emergence of a multitude of newly independent nations, all with far less violence than might initially have been expected on the basis of prior experience. With regard to poverty, there have significant rises in the level of life expectancy in most countries, elimination or reduction in the incidence of disease, improved nutrition and a significant rise in the level of real incomes in many parts of the world, partly as a result of international aid through the World Bank and specialized agencies such as the World Health Organization, UNICEF etc, and partly on account of the vast growth in internatinal trade which acted like a locomotive to speed up the development of the world economy as a whole, all under the protective guardianship of GATT and the IMF.

Yet like the League, the UN was not able to live up to initial hopes with regard to its prime mission of maintaining peace and during this period there were some 150 significant armed conflicts around the world which cost the lives of some 15 million people. In addition poverty remained a major problem in several regions of the world, a problem compounded by large increases in the size of population especially in poorer countries, ironically as a consequence of impoved medical and sanitation facilities. This all resulted in large measure from the near paralysis of the organization induced by (i) the Cold War with the First World (the western industrial nations) in head on confrontation with the Second World (the

communist countries), which had its main
manifestation in the Security Council; and (ii) the
related North South Conflict which pitted the First
World against the Third World (the developing
nations), which was most clearly manifested at the UN
in the General Assembly.

With the end of the Cold War, there was an initial
renewal of confidence in the UN, a hope that at long
last it would be able to function as originally intended.
Indeed there were considerable successes. The UN
contributed to the reestablishment of peace in Central
America, Southern Africa and Cambodia and the
establishment of an international war crimes court in
connection with events in Yugoslavia and Rwanda is
of considerable significance. It played useful role in
advancement of the process of banning the
manufacture, storage and use of chemical and
biological weapons and in the renewal of the nuclear
test ban treaty. The UN Conference at Rio on the
environment represented a major step forward in
raising general consciousness of the issue and
securing some broad agreements from governments
on what is needed to be done.

Nevertheless, there have been some profound
disappointments. The UN's peacekeeping operations
in Yugoslavia, Somalia and Rwanda were deeply
flawed. The international arms trade continues to be
a threat. The practical follow up to the Rio Conference
has been minimal. There has been little if any advance
in response to demands that the Security Council be
made more representative of the peoples and nations
of the world. Many member states, led by the United
States, have fallen into arrears with their annual
membership dues which are clearly not regarded as
very important. It is obvious that governments have
little vision of what will be required of the UN in
coming decades in response to rapidly changing

situations, and that they are preoccupied with narrow and purely pragmatic concerns. The result is, as always, too little too late. Overarching the situation is the obvious fact that the confederation model, introduced 75 years ago, is reaching the limits of its capacity in relation to need, as happened also with the American confederation in the 1780's.

I should now like to say a few words about the second point of this presentation, and that is what vision do we have of the future? Clearly there are many ideas on various aspects of the question of how to establish a permanent peace. However, my impression is that the most comprehensive and realistic over the long run is the vision provided by the Bahá'í Faith. Accordingly I should like to briefly discuss this vision with you.

It seems to me there are at least three aspects of the Baha'i vision that are important in this context:

- a sense of the meaning of history;
- a vision for the future that connects with that historical view point and sees that vision being achieved on a step by step basis;
- a practical goal for the coming years.

The Bahá'í picture of history is essentially to see the evolution of civilization as following a life cycle similar to that of individual human beings: infancy, childhood, adolescence and maturity. May be these four stages can be identified with (i) the hunting and fishing era before agriculture, (ii) the agricultural revolution, (iii) the industrial age, and (iv) the future post industrial age. We are today in the period of adolescence when we have the great physical strength of industry but lack the wisdom and skill to manage that strength without hurting ourselves. The time has now come when we have to move on to maturity, acquiring the spiritual qualities that are necessary to survive and progress: how to avoid wars now that

weapons of mass destruction are available;
cooperating to manage the abolition of poverty whilst
living in harmony with nature; acquiring a sense of
internal peace which makes sense of the meaning of
life.

The vision is of an ultimate peace based on justice,
"The Most Great Peace" when all will be united by an
acceptance of the twofold purpose of life:

- for each and everyone to achieve our full potential
  in life: physical, intellectual and above all,
  spiritually growing towards God, becoming noble
  beings;
- collectively to build an ever advancing civilization
  to which each one of us contributes, no matter
  how humble we may think we are.

The first steps towards such a permanent peace
are related to the abolition of war. A major phase was
the creation of the League, a world confederation. As
in the American experience that now needs to evolve
into a more effective federation. The Baha'i picture of
that Federation includes such features as:

- a world parliament elected directly by the peoples
  of the world, with the represenatives being then
  confirmed in office by the national govenments;
- a supreme tribunal whose members are selected
  by the national assemblies of the world, and
  whose decisions would be binding and
  compulsory;
- a world executive appointed to carry out the
  decisions of the world parliament and world
  court, with the backing of an international police
  force;
- education of all peoples to be true world citizens
  free of prejudice, appreciative of cultural diversity
  and united by communication through an
  auxiliary world language to be chosen by the
  world parliament;

● a world economic system which benefits all, in which, in particular, arrangement are made so that the worlds natural resources are used for the benefit of all and not just for groups sitting in the right place at the right time, and where arrangements are made to prevent extremes of wealth and poverty.

Finally, let me make some suggestions on priorities in the immediate future:

(i) The holding of a mighty convocation to consult on what needs to be done in the post Cold War age. Such a conference might be compared with those held at the end of the earlier great conflicts of this century: in 1918 and 1945, and with the global conference on the environment at Rio. Such a conference has been recommended, for instance, by the Carlsson Commission on International Institutions. Its mandate should be to convert the UN into a world federation.

(ii) Agreement to make decisions of the World Court compulsory. This is necessary so that nations with grievances may feel there is a realistic peaceful alternative to war in obtaining justice. This is a critical element in the establishment of the rule of law in international relations. It is practical because the World Court has already established a reputation in its judgements for fairness and objectivity. It should also be strengthened by converting the present ad hoc criminal court into a permanent court. Such improvements are clearly in the interest of all nations.

(iii) The establishment of a directly recruited and effective international police force which would be financed out of some independent income source so that it would not be weakened by the arbitrary action of individual govenments. Such a force is necessary because experience has shown how totally inadequate are present arrangements, whereby the UN creates temporary peacekeeping forces by asking members to

contribute units from their national militry forces.
Such forces can take time to assemble and may well
arrive too late; they tend to be overly cautious because
national politicians continually interfere, fearing that
"our boys" will be killed in other peoples quarrels; they
are inefficient because they often have different
equipment and procedures, they have little experience
of joint action and they are reluctant to accept an
effective joint command; they are also unaccountable
as the UN is fearful to be critical in case the national
unit is withdrawn in retaliation—and so on.
Establishment of such a directly recruited standing
force would strengthen the credibility of the UN in the
eyes of potential aggressors and would pay for itself
by making it possible for national govenments to
reduce their defense expenditures.

I hope Ethiopia will use the high moral prestige it
has won as a result of recent events and join other
progressive and enlightened nations in persuading the
world community to take these actions. Thank you.

DEMOCRACY AND THE RULE OF LAW

A presentation at the Police Headquarters, Bangalore, India, 1995

The subject that I have been asked to address tonight at this venue seems most appropriate for several reasons. First, the Indian police profession has the responsibility of maintaining the law in the context of democracy. Second, as a Bahá'í I regard obedience to the law of the land as a basic spiritual principle because it is essential for social unity. Thus when the Islamic Republic of Irán ordered the Iranian Bahá'í community to dissolve its institutions, it was obeyed immediately. The only order from the state which we as Bahá'ís cannot obey is to deny our Faith. Third, making democracy and the rule of law work is a necessity for ultimate survival and the advancement of civilization.

The law is one of several concepts designed to regulate public affairs in the interest of order and peace. Other concepts include custom, ethics and values (both of which have their roots in religion) and the idea of justice itself. The idea of justice has many dimensions, including "just deserts", or reward for behavior which is conducive to the well-being of society, and withholding of reward when conduct is socially prejudicial. Another idea of justice has been for each one to choose a craft or profession to which he or she is best suited: the origin of the caste system;

an idea of Plato; and the theme of society in Medieval Europe. A third concept is economic justice: the need to reduce extremes of wealth and poverty. Perhaps the best way to bring together all ideas on justice into a single theme is to say it is that condition when all humans are encouraged and supported in the quest to fulfill their full potential: physical, intellectual, and above all, spiritual, ie the process of becoming noble beings.

Clearly the rule of law has long preceded democracy. But without democracy it is inevitably incomplete. Under authoritarian regimes there is almost certainly an attitude on the part of rulers that the state and privileged groups are above the law. Any challenge to that privilege will result in disproportionate and arbitrary punishment. Such injustice provoked the great revolutions in England, America and France at the beginning of modern times and the rise of democracy.

The rule of law is a key characteristic of democracy because it is about equality and the absence of privilege. It is intimately linked for its effectiveness with other characteristics of democracy e.g. all the people taking part in the management of their community affairs, usually indirectly through election of representatives to a legislative assembly or parliament; accountability of government to the people especially with regard to taxation, military service, general laws and human rights; transparency of government including freedom of speech and information; and, not least, the establishment of universal literacy so that all citizens can be fully aware of the issues when making decisions about their representatives and other matters.

It is only in modern times that democracy has become the prevailing philosophy and practice of government, so that the complete rule of law could become a practical goal. The modern movement began with those revolutions in England, North America and France, already mentioned. In the nineteenth century it spread to other parts of Europe, America and Australasia. After the Second War it spread further to the defeated Axis powers: Germany, Italy and Japan, and to some of the newly independent nations in Africa and Asia, including most notably, India, the most populous democracy in the world. Most recently it has embraced Latin America, South and Eastern Europe, much of the former Soviet Union, and parts of East Asia and Africa. As a result, today the majority of sovereign nations, which include the majority of the world's population are either democratic or are truly aspiring to be democratic.

At the same time, the quality of democracy has improved. The suffrage has expanded to be universal, including women; voting is now largely secret so as to reduce the risk of intimidation; the press is freer to shine the light of truth on the activities of government; and an educated population is progressively demanding higher and higher accountability from government, and so on.

And yet it is clear that much more has to be done. My view is that major improvements need to be made on two "fronts" if we are to have an effective free society and the rule of law.

The first is a need for a further significant advance in the quality of democracy. Democracy itself tends to be short sighted (the focus is usually on the next election), parochial (most legislators are primarily concerned with the well being of their own constituency because it elects them), and too concerned for the majority interest at the expense of the minority (especially when the minority are a different religion or culture). The rule of law is often weak because of slowness in adapting from the practices and custom of an agricultural society to those needed in an industrial society (especially when industrialization has been fast), and because of a decline in moral values associated with consumer materialism. The result has been corruption, a rise in general crime and in particular violence and use of drugs.

To deal with this problem we need to give top priority to the moral as well scientific and techonological education of all our children in all nations of the world. This is a proposal that has been made by the Bahá'í Community in connection with the 50th Anniversary of the United Nations. This means first emphasis on the traditional moral values: honesty, truthfulness, hard work, reliability, compassion, etc, without which no society can function properly. It also means conscious abolition of prejudice, equality for men and women, appreciation that we all are enriched by cultural diversity, responsibility for community affairs, a sense of being world citizens, the idea that we should all serve the interests of humanity and not be exploitive and abusive, and finally have a deep love of justice. One result that would come from such an education in world citizenship would be protection of the indep·ndence of the judiciary, a police force viewed as a friend and protector of the people and not as an oppressor, and a prison system which protects society and encourages criminals to reform rather than one that makes criminals worse.

The second major improvement that Bahá'ís believe is necessary if we are to have true democracy and the rule of law is to extend the concept from the national level to the global level. We need to strengthen the United Nations so that it is more democratic, and thereby uphold the rule of international law for the benefit of all peoples. We need to move forward from the confederate model, introduced in 1918 with the League of Nations, to a model of a world federal democracy, built on the pillars of national democracies. First, need a world parliament elected directly by the peoples of the world with the approval of national governments. Second, need to enhance the effectiveness of the World Court by making its decisions binding, not voluntary, as is generally the case today, so that nations which have grievances will feel that they can get objective justice peacefully and therefore do not need to try and obtain their goals through military force and war. Third, we need to give the executive a world police force so that it can enforce the will of the world parliament and the World Court. Clearly, present ad hoc arrangements whereby the Secretary General has to beg member governments to provide national military units for peacekeeping operations is totally inadequate as has been shown in Yugoslavia, Somalia and Rwanda. We need a strong, directly recruited, military force under the control of the world parliament which can, if necessary, stop aggression by an individual nation and give reality to the concept of collective security.

These then are some of the Bahá'í ideas on making a free society and the rule of law a greater reality. I hope you find these ideas useful and worthy of consideration by you in both your individual capacities as world citizens and your collective role as maintainers of the rule of law in a free society which encourages all humanity to achieve its full potential. The police force plays a vital role in helping civilization to advance. I know from my friends who are policemen around the world and from my own limited experience in the military that it is very easy for a policeman to have a sceptical, perhaps cynical, view of life, because so often he is dealing with criminals and the baser side of human nature. But it is very important for the well-being of society that policemen have a balanced assessment of human nature and recognize that human beings, when encouraged and supported, especially by true religion and a sound moral education for children, have a spiritual side which has no limit in what it can do to create nobility and a civilization of light.

WORLD CITIZENSHIP AND SUSTAINABLE DEVELOPMENT

A presentation at the Conference on Sustainable Development in the Twenty First Century, Rekyjavik, Iceland, 1996

World citizenship is more than a dry legal term; it is also an expression of the oneness of the human family and comes from the heart as well as the head. Accordingly, in talking about this subject, it seems inadequate to formally address you as "ladies and gentlemen"; it seems more fitting to simply say "Dear Friends". I am encouraged to do so by my sense of unity and warmth of feeling in this room, not something, if I may say so, that is normally experienced at an academic or professionally oriented conference!

The sense of unity and commitment that emanates from our gathering this afternoon reminds me that effective communication is best achieved if both parties to a dialogue, listeners as well as speaker, know something of the other before the presentation begins. I have had opportunity to learn something about others taking part in this conference in the last two days. Now it is time for me to tell you something about myself which is relevant to the subject at hand.

To be direct, my whole life experience has made world citizenship a subject which is very close to my heart. As a child, I experienced the Second World War and was one of that post war generation which had a mind set of "never again". That way of thinking prompted me to choose a career as an international civil servant, which, over thirty years, has strongly reinforced my inclination to a global perspective. I found as I traveled around the world in connection with that job that I would begin to identify with each country that I visited: that I would think of it as my country in the same way as I felt about the land where I was born, England. Years after being in a country I closely follow the news from there and am concerned about its well-being. For instance, I last visited Iceland some twenty years ago but still feel very much that I am an Icelander. This global perspective has been further reinforced by my family experience: I am English, my wife is Persian, and my children are American citizens because they were born in the United States. Finally, of course, there is the commitment to world citizenship that comes from being a Bahá'í. The Bahá'í Faith, which is the most recent of the world's great religions, gives the highest priority to working for the unity of humankind and the establishment of world peace based on justice. Bahá'u'lláh, its Founder Prophet said more than one hundred years ago.

"The Earth is But One Country and Mankind Its Citizens"

As time is limited and we are near the end of the day, I will focus my presentation on the issue of citizenship and limit comment on the other aspect of my title: "sustainable development", which has already received extensive treatment from other speakers. Suffice to say that I interpret the phrase to refer to the total evolution of civilization and not just to the economy in relation to the natural environment. There are three broad points that I should like to touch on:

- the concept of citizenship;

- the vital relationship between citizenship and sustainable development;
- some practical aspects of world citizenship.

The Concept of Citizenship

The concept of citizenship has two broad characteristics. The first is a sense of social solidarity, a sense of being part of a larger group than the immediate family, and a concern for the general well-being of that larger group. This idea was originally associated with the cities of Ancient Greece, Athens in particular, but in modern times, certainly since the eighteenth century republican revolutions in North America and France, it is very much associated with the nation, a people who perceive themselves to have a common culture.

The second general characteristic of citizenship, is that it involves active participation in community affairs—enfranchisement—and in this sense it is different from the idea of being a "subject". In short citizenship is associated not only with the nation but with democracy.

Such active involvement brings certain rights and benefits. The most fundamental right is to participate in community decision making i.e. through "town hall meetings", referendums or, more typically, in voting for representatives who in turn make such decisions on behalf of all citizens in an elected legislative assembly or parliament. The idea is clearly enunciated in the famous demand of the American Revolution. "No taxation without representation". Closely linked to enfranchisement are "civil rights", as laid out in the Universal Declaration of Human Rights, such as equality before the law, without distinction of any kind, and freedom of thought, expression and peaceful assembly, and so on. Other benefits include most importantly collective protection against physical violence, both external and internal. In modern times this concept of protection has been significantly extended to include protection against extreme poverty.

Citizenship also involves certain duties, obligations, and sacrifice which have symmetrical relationships to rights and benefits. There is an obligation to obey the law and to pay taxes as approved by the community. When necessary there is an obligation to defend the nation against external attack, to the point where even life may have to be sacrificed for the common good. This obligation was clearly expressed during the French Revolution when it was in extremis, with the stirring and unforgettable appeal: "aux armes citoyens". In modern times the idea of sacrifice has been broadened to include restraint in our demands on the natural environment for the common good of ourselves and of future generations.

In the last two hundred years the concept of citizenship has spread rapidly and today is accepted almost universally. Empires have been replaced by the Nation State in most parts of the world, although the final stages of this advancement are still in bloody process. Simultaneously, authoritarian forms of government have been replaced by democracy. We have experienced a major surge forward in this process in the last twenty years or so. Thus the Interparliamentary Union has recently reported that 179 out of 192 sovereign states now have popularly elected legislative assemblies, one of the key indicators of democracy[1]. Another Assessment provided is the 1995 edition of the Penguin **State of the World Atlas,** using a somewhat more rigorous standard, concludes that of 189 sovereign states, 129 practice multi-party democracy i.e. some 68 percent of all nations, which between them contain some 60 percent of the world's population[2].

Citizenship and Its Relationship to Sustainable Development

I should now like to move on to my second topic: the vital relationship between citizenship and achievement of sustainable development. There are at least six interlinked aspects of the condition of the world today, which it seems to me, have important bearing on this proposition.

The first is that humanity is rapidly acquiring the character of one people, one culture, one nation, as a result of its experience and converging bases of well-being. On the economic plane, jobs, goods and services, environment and health, and indeed, overall living standads are all matters which are deeply affected by the global market. Similarly on the social plane, values and culture freely cross national frontiers e.g. attitudes towards family, equality of the sexes, religious tolerance, race, drugs, crime and even such matters as food, music and movies. On the political plane, local and regional conflicts are increasingly taking on a global dimension as protagonists play the terrorist card and strike anywhere in the world where they think they can most effectively draw attention to their grievances. Even the most powerful nations and the most passionate defenders of the past are unable to long resist these economic, social and political trends towards the merging of humanity into one people.

The second point is that these are not temporary trends that could come to a stop or even go into reverse. On the contrary they are but the most recent manifestations of a great tide of history moving towards globalisation which began at least four hundred years ago with the "Age of Reconnaissance" and the linking together for the first time of the five continents and their peoples. What is evident about this mighty tide of modern times is that it shows no sign of slowing down; on the contrary it appears to be accelerating.

Thirdly, there is the question of what adjustments should be made to the sytem of international institutions that we now have, to respond to the changes that have taken place since they were established and to the changes that are likely to occur in the coming decades. Many useful suggestions have been made in connection with the recent celebration of the 50th anniversary of the founding of the United Nations, including, most notably, the report of the Commission on Global Governance, which was co-chaired by Mr. Ramphal and former Prime Minister Carlsson of Sweden. Despite some protestations to the contrary, many ideas aimed at strengthening the United Nations and its' agencies are ultimately pointing in the direction of a democratic federal world commonwealth. This is clearly logical because without such an advance the international system, at a minimum, lacks an ability to coordinate the various specialized agencies so as to avoid contradictions and duplication. Far more important, it cannot systematically enforce international law and establish a permanent peace based on justice. Ultimately this is a question of survival and it is ignored at our peril. Faced with a similar challenge in the seventeen eighties, the newly independent states of North America quickly recognized the ineffectiveness of the confederation model and they had the courage and vision to replace it with a federal system. Today, humanity is faced with the same challenge of moving forward from the confederation model which we have had since 1918.

This brings me to the fourth point which concerns timing. With the end of the Cold War, the third great global conflict of this century, we have a "window of opportunity" to make international cooperation more effective in the interest of all humanity, just as we did in 1918 and 1945. If we do not take such an opportunity now, there is a real risk that the moment will be lost. It is not difficult to imagine scenarios in the coming years in which major confrontations between nations would make strengthening of international cooperation impossible, as during the Cold War, and so put all humanity at risk.

The fifth point is that the political system is clearly failing to respond to the challenge as can be seen not only with regard to the issue of reform of the institutions of the United Nations but also in the ineffective handling of such critical matters as regional peace keeping operations, abolition of extreme poverty, and protection of the natural environment. To some extent this is because democracy, now the prevalent political system, tends to encourage a parochial and short term outlook. But there are other important factors at play also. One is a general ignorance on the part of many of the world's peoples of the vital necessity for global cooperation, a result, partly, of a failure of the education system and, partly, of manipulation of public discourse by a media and political establishment which feels more comfortable with past ways of doing things than with facing the challenges of the future. In the constant battle for office it is all too tempting to promote xenophobic attitudes at the expense of the United Nations and foreigners who do not have the vote. A second, and perhaps more fundamental, factor is the decline of religion and associated spiritual values so that material greed, ambition and cynicism have gotten out of hand and are tearing apart the very fabric of civil society.

The sixth point is that this situation, alarming as it is, does offer opportunity for change, if there is a clear vision and sufficient commitment to achieve that vision. Whatever its faults, democracy does allow free discussion of ideas and will eventually respond to popular concerns, as we have seen with regard to human rights issues and local environment matters, despite initial opposition on the part of political forces that take pride in being "realistic" and in practicing "real politik". The key issue here is that ordinary citizens have to expand their concept of themselves so that they are indeed world citizens. If we want our leaders to seriously consult on the issue of global planning for the future they have to be persuaded by pressure coming from the grass roots of society: the ordinary citizen.

Practical Aspects of World Citizenship

The question is how do we bring this about? This is the third issue that I should like to briefly discuss in this presentation: practical aspects of world citizenship. Many are coming to the view that the most effective way to promote widespread consciousness of world citizenship is to incorporate the concept into the curriculum of all education systems, world wide. The logic is clear: education has always been associated with democracy because it is recognized as being essential for the exercise of citizenship, hence the close correlation between universal suffrage and the introduction of universal compulsory elementary education in nineteenth century Western democracies.

A good example of such advocacy is a statement called ***World Citizenship: A Global Ethic for Sustainable Development*** which was submitted to the Commission on Sustainable Development by the Bahá'í Community. The statement urges concerted action to build "world citizenship" concepts into all education systems, formal, informal and non formal. It proposes national commissions to implement the process with coordination by a UN Commission. Such commissions would initiate pre-and in-service training for teachers, prepare necessary materials, and facilitate involvement of interested NGOs. Such activity should be supplemented with guidelines for the media in prompting the concept and by a much bolder effort on the part of the UN to explain to the public its role and identity.

The purpose of such broadening of education systems would be to strengthen the two key aspects of citizenship discussed earlier. First, the sense of social solidarity would be expanded to the global level by universal teaching of: (i) the history of all humanity and the evolution of civilization; (ii) the conscious abolition of prejudice on account of race, nation, class, sex and religion, and (iii) an auxiliary world language. The latter is of great importance, not simply because it would improve communication between all peoples, but because, as we have learnt at the national level, it is a key factor in social bonding and the creation of a sense of common culture.

The second aspect to citizenship previously discussed, enfranchisement and active participation in community affairs, would be enhanced by the teaching of two themes. The first is that a peaceful society will only last if based on justice, and that a just society requires citizens who are just at the personal level: a just society imposed from above will never work as the Communist experience has shown. This means emphasis on such moral qualities as trustworthiness, compassion, service to others, and a much greater willingness to make sacrifice for the common good e.g. with regard to helping the poor and protecting the natural environment. The second is to improve our way of communication and discussion of public issues, so that the right decisions can be made whilst maintaining unity. This means advancing from "debate", the system of discourse in democracy with all its divisiveness and loaded rhetoric, to a new system of consultation, which puts emphasis on (i) universal participation, (ii) detachment and a willingness to review proposals on their merit rather than on the basis of who made the proposal, and (iii) a systematic approach to the order of discussion, starting, for instance, with the facts and principles that should apply, and ending with agreed action and post action review.

Roles of Iceland and of Religion

I would like to end my remarks on the practical aspects of world citizenship with two supplementary comments.

The first, which is prompted by the location of this conference, is the role of the people of Iceland in this process. In the struggle to achieve a peaceful and just world civilization, there is clearly a role for every nation, each unique on account of its circumstance and historical experience. I would like to suggest that Iceland's particular contribution is molded by it's established reputation for enlightenment with regard to both management of domestic issues and its role on the international stage. Such reputation means that in general other nations are more likely to listen to its viewpoint than if this was not the case. Secondly, and reinforcing the first point, Iceland is, in effect, a bridge between the Old World and the New World, both geographically (as we all know, the two continental plates actually meet here in Iceland) and historically (Icelanders were the first Europeans known to have reached the Americas). In short, Iceland potentially has the ability, despite its relatively small size, to exercise significant influence in international affairs if it chooses: "to punch above its weight" to borrow that useful, if combative, phrase of Prime Minister Margaret Thatcher.

This all suggests that Iceland can play a most useful role in promoting the idea of world citizenship not only in educating its own succeeding generations but also in influencing other nations, and most particularly, its neighbor to the west, the United States, the most powerful nation in the world. The people of the United States need to be reminded of their historical experience and spiritual inheritance which has uniquely prepared them for the task of leading humanity to freedom, peace and unity. To this end, Iceland can take the initiative in focusing on the enlightened side of the American role in global affairs: its leadership in bringing about the Hague Conventions, the League of Nations, the United Nations, and the Universal Declaration of Human Rights, to name just the most obvious, rather than joining in the destructive and useless clamor about America's dark side. Like individuals, all nations have a dark side as well as an enlightened one. Any psychologist will acknowledge, however, that to encourage good behavior it is best to talk mostly about strengths rather than weaknesses; this surely is true of nations as well as individuals. Americans today are being prompted to look inward and to have an almost hostile attitude towards the rest of humanity. This is contrary to the American spirit and Americans need to be encouraged to be true to themselves for the sake of all humanity.

My final remarks concern the vital role of religion in creating a sense of world citizenship. This is so important that I make no apology for perhaps repeating some of the thoughts expressed by Daniel Gomez-Ibanez and Jim Kenney in their presentations. Religions with their particular perspective, which at heart is common to them all, have the potential to counter the obvious weaknesses of democracy with regard to short range focus and parochialism. In the last few years it has become noticeable, that religion has been a major voice in expression of global concern to promote peace, literacy and education, abolition of poverty, and protection of the environment[3]. This needs to be greatly encouraged.

The Bahá'í Community has a special, additional, contribution, in that it offers itself as a working model of a global community and world citizenship, and so demonstrates that such ideas are not just pipe dreams but can and are reality. This is a community totally dedicated to the unity of humanity and having as its explicit purpose the task (i) at the individual level to achieve nobility, and (ii) at the collective level to create an ever advancing civilization. It is drawn from every conceivable background in just about every country in the world[4] and practices everyday the art of consultation at both the family and community level. It is a community where there is indeed a real sense of world family and world citizenship.

NOTES

1. *Washington Post,* August 18, 1996
2. *State of the World Atlas,* 5th edition, by Michael Kidron and Ronald Seagal, Penguin Books, 1995.
3. For example articles on *Interfaith Environmentalism,* Washington Post, April 23, 1994, and *Resurrecting Peace: Religion's Service to the Political World,* Washington Post, April, 16, 1995.
4. According to the *1992 Encyclopaedia Book of the Year,* the Bahá'í Faith is established in 205 sovereign countries and dependent territories, a figure for religions which is exceeded only by that for Christianity.

CONSULTATION: THE BAHÁ'Í PERSPECTIVE ON RESOLVING CONFLICTS

A presentation at the 20th Annual Conference of the Association of Bahá'í Studies, Alberta, Canada, 1996

Introduction

The term "consultation" is now in common usage. Generally, it is understood to mean: informing, advising, or seeking an opinion. Each of these practices is clearly helpful in reducing the risk of conflict as becomes evident when they are absent, e.g. diplomatic clashes that occur when the United States fails to "consult" with it's allies before it takes some unilateral action which affects their interests as well as it's own.

A review of the Bahá'í Writings shows that the Bahá'í concept of "consultation" is much broader and deeper than implied by the common understanding of the term and is thereby a potentially more effective instrument for reducing conflict and facilitating unity. In fact its potential is so great that it seems reasonable to argue that it represents a new stage in the evolution of humanity's practice of discussion of common affairs and collective decision making.

To use the analogy of 'Abdu'l-Bahá, during the period of humanity's childhood, the normal form of public and private dialogue was for decisions to be made by some superior authority, a king or the patriarch of the family, and for everyone to obey the decision without question. This is the model which is applied almost universally to small children on the basis that they are not mature enough to take part in the decision making process.

A more advanced stage of discussion and decision making is that developed with the coming of democracy—essentially in the last two hundred years—as humanity has grown into adolescence and has acquired great physical power as a result of advances in science and technology. This stage of discussion is called "debate", a term which covers not only political discussion, but also the adversary practice of Anglo Saxon law and negotiation between opposing parties, e.g. trade unions and employers. "Debate", in principle, is more just and conducive to identification of the truth than the authoritarian model because it generally allows greater numbers of individuals to participate in decision making, as well as much freer discussion of ideas and identification of the facts. But it is also often characterized by the turbulence associated with adolescence. The discussion is usually heavily weighted in favor of powerful special interests, e.g. economic, class, regional, and military, which leads to such unhelpful practices as intimidation, corruption, bias, oversimplification, exclusion of inconvenient facts, exaggeration, straightforward lies, and ad hominem diversions. In short debate often deteriorates into demagoguery:

"In the parliamentary meeting mentioned, altercation and useless quibbling were frequent; the result mostly confusion and turmoil; even in one instance a physical encounter took place between two members. It was not consultation but comedy".

'Abdu'l-Bahá[1]

Public perception that this is the case is no doubt one of the reasons for the present widespread disillusionment with the democratic process. The Bahá'í model of consultation overcomes these deficiencies and responds to the need of society to become united on a global level in order to meet the challenge of our time and to advance towards the true civilization which humanity has the potential to achieve. In short, Bahá'í consultation is a model for discussion and decision making as humanity comes to maturity.

This model has so much potential for eliminating conflict and achieving unity, both key goals of the Bahá'í Faith, that it is seen as an essential part of the every day life of the Bahá'í Community:

"In all things it is necessary to consult...inasmuch as it is and will always be a cause of awareness and a source of good and well-being..." Bahá'u'lláh[2]

Thus Bahá'í consultation is flexible and simple and can be used in a wide range of situations, for instance, by a married couple, by an individual or group in relation to an institution, or by an institution itself. Most aspects of Bahá'í consultation apply in all situations where there is a call for discussion and collective decision making. However, in some situations there may be special circumstances, e.g. decision making for a couple requires consensus whilst when larger numbers of people are involved majority decision making is a practicality. As time is limited this afternoon, this presentation will focus on those characteristics that are required when consultation is at the community level, especially as it applies to the work of elected institutions.

There is one more general point that should be made before reviewing the main elements of Bahá'í consultation and that is to note that it is only one dimension, albeit an important one, in the vision given to us by Bahá'u'lláh, of a future civilization, the coming of the "Most Great Peace", a time when society

will be based on justice:
"The most beloved thing in my sight is justice."

Bahá'u'lláh[3]

Justice, of course, is the basis for elimination of conflict. Being just is to be noble, the purpose of life at the individual level:

"...the purpose of life is to prepare the soul for the next"

The Universal House of Justice[4]

The experience of this century alone has surely taught us that a "just" society cannot be created without people who themselves are just as individuals. A second part of the vision is a new way of managing our collective affairs, which includes in addition to consultation such features as a new world federal administrative structure, a new system of elections designed to bring forth ethical as well as managerial qualities, and a political, social and economic plan which will promote the physical, intellectual and spiritual well being of all humankind.

For the purposes of this short presentation it is proposed to group the main characteristics of Bahá'í consultation around three themes: purpose; preconditions, and general guidelines with regard to practice. The focus will be on four purposes, two preconditions and nine guidelines for the practice of consultation.

Purposes

Four purposes of Bahá'í consultation are clearly identifiable. They are closely inter linked and mutually dependent. The first is to find the TRUTH:

"consultation must have for its object the investigation of truth"

'Abdu'l-Bahá[5]

Establishment of the true facts and principles that apply in a particular situation are key aspects of establishing JUSTICE which is a second main objective of Bahá'í consultation:

"consultation is the operating expression of justice in human affairs."

Prosperity of Humankind[6]

Justice in turn is a prerequisite for UNITY which is a third purpose of consultation, and indeed, as already noted, the key theme of the teachings of the Faith as a whole:

"If they agree upon a subject, even though it be wrong, it is better than to disagree and be in the right, for this difference will produce the demolition of the Divine foundation...it is in unity the truth will be revealed and the wrong made right"

'Abdu'l-Bahá[7]

Finally, it is to be noted that Bahá'í consultation has as its purpose some CONCLUSION AND DECISION; it is not simply discussion for its own sake—gossip or confession, for instance:

"...all consultation is aimed at arriving at a solution to the problem"

Universal House of Justice[8]

Preconditions

Let us now turn to two clear preconditions for Bahá'í consultation. 'Abdu'l-Bahá was quite explicit about this question: the first is harmony and the second is prayer, and obviously there is a close link between the two.

"The first condition is absolute love and harmony amongst members of the assembly. They must be wholly free from estrangement. . .Should harmony of thought and absolute unity be non existent, that gathering shall be dispersed and that assembly brought to naught".[9]

"The second condition: They must when coming together turn their faces to the Kingdom on High and ask aid from the Realm of Glory".[10]

The first of these conditions is now generally acknowledged to be necessary in standard conflict resolution practice outside the Bahá'í Community; the significance of the second in establishing the right frame of mind for consultation still seems to be underestimated presumably because of widespread scepticism about religion especially in Western intellectual circles.

Guidelines for Practicing Consultation

As suggested earlier, it is possible to identify at least nine practical characteristics of Bahá'í consultation beyond purposes and preconditions. Three of these can be seen as contributing to clear and open discussion; another three are about attitudes on the part of participants which are conducive to smooth and efficient consultation; two are to do with democratic and orderly procedures; and the last is about the necessity for unity in decision making.

The first three are (i) frank and open discussion including most importantly encouragement of questions (a quality of God); (ii) being straightforward and avoidance of old style lobbying; and (iii) taking care to listen carefully to what others are saying as well as being as clear as possible in making one's own contribution to the discussion:

"The shining spark of truth cometh forth only after the clash of differing opinions"

'Abdu'l-Bahá[1]

"To give up asking other members to voice your opinion"

Shoghi Effendi[12]

"You have. . .to be a sensitive receiving instrument that will pick up the seekers correct wavelength".

Ruhhiyih Khanum[13]

I should like to add some comment on the "listening" question [point iii], because it is not usually given special emphasis in Bahá'í references to consultation, although it is mentioned elsewhere in Bahá'í literature and clearly it is an important aspect of communication, as anyone knows who, for instance, has been interviewed by the media without benefit of a supporting audio recording. If I could make a personal comment, I remember my mother-in-law saying, presumably because she had sympathy with me on account of my beautiful wife's tendency to have a great deal to say for herself, that we should always remember that God gave us all one mouth and two ears. This meant that we should spend more time listening than talking! A second point is what we should be listening for. Dwight Allen has pointed out that, contrary to the way we are trained today in a cynical society, we should focus on what is actually said rather than why it is said, what is the hidden agenda. Having said that I should add that, nevertheless, we should be alert to the feelings behind peoples' words, especially when they come from a different culture where there are different assumptions and different ways of expressing thoughts. It is particularly important that we not miss any expressions of pain or hurt.

The second group of characteristics, which might be called those to do with making the process more smooth and efficient, are: (iv) detachment; (v) patience, humility and refraining from feeling hurt by others, and (vi) courtesy, respect and trust. 'Abdu'l-Bahá gave the following advise on these aspects of consultation: "The prime requisites for them that take counsel together are purity of motive, radiance of spirit, DETACHMENT from all else save God...he must on NO ACCOUNT FEEL HURT."[14]
"...HUMILITY...PATIENCE and long suffering in

difficulties and servitude to His exalted Threshold".[15]
"They must then proceed with the utmost devotion,
COURTESY, care and moderation to express the
views...and it is in no wise permissible to belittle the
thought of another..."[16]

Some of these qualities of consultation can present
particular difficulty. For instance, being humble and
curbing the ego, is not always easy, in this age of
meritocracy, for members of the academic world. After
all, a person with a doctorate is an expert in his/her
field and feels therefore he/she knows best—perhaps
forgetting the numerous occasions when the experts
have proved to be totally wrong in their assessment
of situations eg the complete failure of political experts
to foresee the imminent fall of the Soviet Empire. This
is hardly surprising considering the spiritual
wasteland that academia has generally become along
with much of the political and business worlds. In
short, those working in academia have to be especially
on guard against their own egoist tendencies in
consultation as in every activity. The problem is
compounded by the culture of the consumer society
which increasingly rewards "stars" at the expense of
others; excessive praise for stars puts such persons
at abnormal spiritual risk.

The other requirement mentioned above that is
particularly difficult is "not being hurt by others". I
remember when I first became a Bahá'í, being warned
by that wonderful lady, Sarah Pereira, who served for
many years on the United States National Spiritual
Assembly and then as a member of the Continental
Board of Counselors, that it is relatively easy to learn
not to hurt others but it is much more difficult not to
be hurt by others. With her experiences as a black
woman living in the United States in the mid twentieth
century, she knew what she was talking about.

The next group of practical points on the conduct

of consultation are (vii) universal participation and (viii) an orderly and scientific procedure. On universal participation, the Guardian wrote:

"...the most lowly untutored and inexperienced among the friends will by the sheer inspiring force of selfless and ardent devotion, contribute a distinct and memorable share to a highly involved discussion..."[17] Though the number of persons who take part in democratic debate is normally greater that had been involved in old style authoritarian decision making, it is still true that the majority are usually excluded. Thus most public debates are dominated by rich educated white males, whilst women, the poor, minorities, and the uneducated tend to have a small or non existent role. This is not only unjust and thereby likely to cause unrest on the part of those excluded, but in addition, it increases the chance that the truth is not properly identified because it does not give opportunity to hear the experience and views of those who are often much closer to the reality of life than those who live in comparative comfort.

With regard to the requirement for orderly discussion the Australian National Spiritual Assembly has identified[18] such key steps as:

   i. Define the matter to be decided;
   ii. Ascertain all the facts of the matter and agree on them;
  iii. Identify the spiritual and administrative principles that relate to the issue;
   iv. Consult together;
    v. Make a clear statement of the provisional conclusion;
   vi. Make a decision by consensus or majority vote;
  vii. Record the decision in the minutes;
 viii. Decide how the decision will be carried out.

There is clearly a sharp contrast between the orderly process of Bahá'í consultation and the chaos of normal democratic debate. This is a characteristic that has important implications with regard to arriving at the true facts of a situation and a logical and just decision.

The ninth practical aspect of Bahá'í consultation is the emphasis on unity when a decision is to be made, after the procedures outlined above have been followed. Three key aspects of unity in decision making are:

(i) Dissenting positions : votes are not recorded:

"There are no dissenting votes in the Cause". Shoghi Effendi[19]

"The whole question of abstaining does not arise in Bahá'í voting".

Universal House of Justice[20]

(ii) There should be no public criticism of an elected assembly outside of the assembly or properly constituted convention:

"They must not go around undermining the Aseembly by saying they disagreed with the majority. In other words they must put the Cause first and not their own opinion."

Shoghi Effendi[21]

(iii) Instead, those who are dissatisfied with a decision should follow an orderly appeal process:

"The friends should take up the matter (appeals against decisions) with the assembly concerned...This is both their privilege and their duty".

Shoghi Effendi[22]

"An individual who is unhappy with a decision of the local assembly should first appeal to that assembly for reconsideration. If he or she is still not happy with the decision of the assembly an appeal may be made to the National Spiritual Assembly. Should the NSA's decision not be satisfactory, as a final recourse, appeal can be made to the Universal House of Justice.. In all instances the appeal must be channeled through the local assembly which is duty bound to pass it on."

Australian National Spiritual Assembly[23]

Conclusions

Of course, when non Bahá'ís first hear of the Bahá'í consultation process there is a tendency for them to say that this is all very nice but it will never work in the real world. There is ample experience now in the Bahá'í world community over some seven decades or more that this is not true. Certainly it has been my observation that very ordinary people, on becoming Bahá'ís, gradually learn the process through constant practice in their communities. It is remarkable how well a community or assembly can function, if there is unity, after just a year or two of experience. Furthermore, the simplicity and the spiritual basis of the system make it workable in a wide range of conditions, from, say, a village in Africa to a university campus in New England. Experiments have shown that even a non-Bahá'í group can more effectively consult together when following Bahá'í guidelines for consultation instead of conventional methods of discussion and decision making.[24]

This short review has only touched the surface of the Bahá'í system of consultation. Much more depth can be found by referring to:

Consultation: A Compilation, Research Department of the Universal House of Justice;

Consultation by John Kolstoe.

In addition there are valuable insights in such sources as:

The Prosperity of Humankind, (Section 3), the Bahá'í International Community.

A letter on the Covenant, dated July 2, 1996 from the Universal House of Justice.[25]

The Australian NSA *Handbook for Local Spiritual Assemblies.*

NOTES

1. *Consultation: a Compilation,* no.22.
2. ibid, no.5
3. *Hidden Words* (Arabic), no. 2.
4. *Bahá'í Marriage and Family Life,* p.25.
5. *Consultation: A Compilation,* no.22
6. *Prosperity of Humankind,* section 3.
7. *Consultation: A Compilation,* no.13
8. ibid, no.47.
9. ibid, no.10.
10. ibid, no.10.
11. ibid, no.10.
12. ibid, no.33.
13. *Success in Teaching,* pp.11-13.
14. *Consultation: A Compilation,* no.9
15. ibid, no.9.
16. ibid, no.10,
17. ibid, no.26.
18. *Local Spiritual Assembly Handbook* (Australia), 3rd edition, p.52.
19. *Consultation: A Compilation,* no.43.
20. ibid, no.46.
21. *Bahá'í News,* December, 1947, p.3.
22. *Guidelines for Local Spiritual Assemblies* (USA), 4.9.
23. *Local Spiritual Assembly Handbook* (Australia), pp.60-61.
24. *The Earth is But One Country,* Third Indian Abridged Edition, 1996, p.106.
25. *American Bahá'í,* volume 27, no.7, September 8, 1996.

RELIGION AND THE SPIRITUAL DIMENSION

THE CHALLENGE OF THE BAHÁ'Í FAITH AND YOUR RESPONSE

Article Published in Herald of the South Australia, January and April, 1986

Introduction

We live in an age of crises: the threat of physical obliteration in a nuclear war, the destruction of our environment by pollution, the breakdown of the economic system, and the collapse of social and ethical values. Such matters are hard to bear over a period of time and there is a natural tendency to push them to the backs of our minds. This tendency is reinforced by the deluge of information which falls on us each day in the form of news, commentary, propaganda and commercials. This is all far too much to absorb and therefore forces us to filter out and sometimes shut out a great deal of what is going on around us.

This glazed-eye lifestyle applies particularly to the claims to have the answer to our problems made by politicians, religious sects, scientists and others. It is perhaps not surprising, therefore, that most of mankind, though it may have heard something of the Bahá'í Faith, does not comprehend how great is its claim and how immensely important it is for all of us if its claim is valid. There are at least three aspects of the Bahá'í claim which are extraordinary by any standards.

The first is the position claimed by Bahá'u'lláh. There are many in the last century or so who have claimed to speak in the name of God, but none have put forward the claim of Bahá'u'lláh to be the Manifestation of God for this age and to be the fulfillment of the prophecies of all the great religions of the world:

"To Israel, He was neither more or less than the incarnation of the "Everlasting Father", the "Lord of Hosts"come down "with ten thousands of saints"; to Christendom, Christ returned "in the glory of the Father"; to Shiah Islám, the return of the Imám Husayn; to Sunni Islám, the descent of the "Spirit of God" (Jesus Christ); to the Zoroastrians, the promised Shah-Bahram; to the Hindus, the reincarnation of Krishna; to the Buddhists, the fifth Buddha"

Shoghi Effendi[1]

For a Christian, for example, if Bahá'u'lláh's claim is true, then His coming must be by far the most important event in history, the event for which all Christianity has been waiting for nearly 2,000 years. The significance of the claim is equally great for the adherents of the other great religions.

The second extraordinary aspect of the Bahá'í claim is that the teachings of Bahá'u'lláh offer a comprehensive solution to all the major problems that face mankind today. The Bahá'í theme is that mankind has been through childhood and has now reached the state of maturity when there must be unity on a world scale in order to solve the problems of the day and advance civilization. The Bahá'í Faith claims that it alone offers the means to achieving that unity:

'Let there be no mistake. The principle of the oneness of mankind - the pivot round which all the teachings of Bahá'u'lláh revolve - is no mere outburst of ignorant emotionalism or an expression of a vague and pious hope . . .It does not constitute merely the enunciation of an ideal, but stands inseparably associated with an institution adequate to embody its truth, demonstrate its validity, and perpetuate its influence.

'It implies an organic change in the structure of present day society, a change such as the world has not yet experienced. It constitutes a challenge, at once bold and universal, to outworn shibboleths of national creeds - creeds that have had their day and which must, in the ordinary course of events as shared and controlled by providence, give way to a new gospel, fundamentally different in form, and infinitely superior to, what the world has already conceived.

'It calls for no less than the reconstruction and demilitarization of the whole civilized world— a world organically unified in all the essentials aspects of its life, its political machinery, its spiritual aspiration, its trade and finance, its script and language, and yet infinite in the diversity of the national characteristics of its federated units.

Shoghi Effendi[2].

The third extraordinary aspect of the Faith is the promise of a spiritual life after the physical death. This has been a central theme of all the other great religions and it is still a belief of large numbers of people. Nevertheless, in the West and other parts of the world affected by Western rational thought, belief in the afterlife, along with other religious beliefs, has declined rapidly as part of the reaction— especially among educated peoples— against superstition associated with the established churches. Now a new religion has come stating that religious teachings which are contrary to true science must be wrong. At the same time it affirms the continued existence of the soul after physical death:

'Know thou of a truth that the soul, after separation from the body, will continue to progress until it attaineth the presence of God, in a state and condition which neither the revolution of ages and centuries, nor the changes and chances of this world can alter. It will endure as long as the Kingdom of God, His sovereignty, His dominion and power will endure. It will manifest the signs of God and His attributes, and will reveal His loving kindness and bounty...

'If any man be told that which hath been ordained for such a soul in the worlds of God, the Lord of the throne on high and of earth below, his whole being will instantly blaze out in great longing to attain that most exalted, that sanctified and resplendent station.'

Bahá'u'lláh[3]

These claims are of such fundamental importance to all mankind that no man or woman with intellectual and spiritual honesty can remain neutral or indifferent. There are essentially only three responses to this challenge.

The first is to agree that the claim of Bahá'u'lláh is true. In that case there is an overwhelming obligation to oneself, to one's children and indeed to the whole of humanity to become a Bahá'í and to do all in one's power to help build up a new world society.

The second possible response is to deny Bahá'u'lláh's claim and the truth of His teachings. However, the claims are of too great a significance for an off hand denial. There is a deep moral obligation to put aside prejudices and fear of what is new and to look at the claim with a detached and deeply penetrating eye and to see if the reasons for denial have validity.

The third response is to admit to being unsure as to whether or not the claim is true. This position brings little satisfaction when the issues are so great and there is, therefore, again a moral imperative to investigate thoroughly the issues so as to be able to come to a conclusion one way or the other.

When the challenge is seen in this light, it becomes apparent that the conventional response to the Bahá'í Faith is back to front. The usual question is, 'Why should I become a Bahá'í?' It really should be,'What reason do I have for not being a Bahá'í and helping build a just world society?' which puts the spotlight on the individual concerned and makes him look at his reasons and motives in the face of this great challenge.

The more frequent reservations that are expressed about the Faith fall into three broad groups:

- Those that are theological or cosmic in scope;
- Those that are social and political;
- Those that are of a personal nature.

Cosmic Reservations

The most fundamental of the 'cosmic' reservations is a doubt about the existence of God. Three important aspects of the issue should be mentioned. First, it is vital for a person considering this subject to try to free himself from the prejudices of the culture of which we are all part. It is useful in this context to recall how intellectual fashions change and things which were certain yesterday are ridiculed today (for instance, concepts about the relationship of the earth to the rest of universe; the nature of evolution; and what is the best balance between liberty and social constraint). Today 'Western' society, in particular, is heavily conditioned to view the universe from a materialistic perspective, largely as a reaction against traditional religion which appeared to be contrary to science and rational thought. This reaction has included disbelief in the anthropomorphic God described in the popular presentation of the churches. 'Abdu'l-Bahá (eldest son of Bahá'u'lláh and his appointed successor as leader of the Bahá'í community) is reported to have said to an agnostic that 'the God you do not believe in, I do not believe in either.' A second aspect of the issue is meditation on the complexity and order of the universe, ranging form the galaxies to the molecule to the human brain. Mathematically, the odds are extremely high against such order coming about by accident. This suggests some guiding force for order, and it would seem unreasonable to assume that force is any less subtle, complex and aware than the human brain it has created.

"Every created thing in the whole universe is but a door leading into his Knowledge, a sign of His sovereignty, a revelation of His name, a symbol of His majesty, a token of His power, a means of admittance into His straight Path". Bahá'u'lláh[4]

The third aspect to consider is the argument in the Bahá'í writings that God is on a quite different plane of existence from ourselves and it is, therefore, unreasonable to expect we can know of His Essence through the normal processes of human knowledge, such as the use of the senses and reason - just as an animal which is on a lower plane than man cannot comprehend the thought process of the latter.

"So perfect and comprehensive is His creation that no mind nor heart, however keen or pure, can ever grasp the nature of the most insignificant of His creatures, much less fathom the mystery of Him Who is the Day Star of Truth, Who is the invisible and unknowable Essence."

Bahá'u'lláh[5].

A second fundamental religious belief which has suffered under the assault of materialism is the spiritual life after the physical death. Clearly this belief is closely linked to the idea of God and if belief in God returns, then there is an enhanced probability that belief in an after life will also come back.

The Bahá'í approach to this issue has attraction for the rational person because its starting point can be observed by all to be anchored in historical experience. That starting point is the view that the nature of man has two sides, a spiritual and an animal or material, and that man is free to develop in either direction. This is different from traditional Christian views and the prevailing materialistic schools. The former sees man as innately sinful and only able to reach salvation through belief in the sacrifice of Jesus. This view causes offense to thinking people because it is so obviously unjust to the newly-born child and to others who have never had the opportunity to hear of Jesus. Furthermore, it fails to explain why there have been so many people in history of non-Christian background who have had the greatest virtues. Likewise, there is little satisfaction in the pessimistic, materialistic philosophy that man is essentially only a very intelligent animal or in the more optimistic view that he is a noble savage, only corrupted by institutions, who will become God-like when those institutions are changed— a view which has been completely undermined by the events of the 20th century.

The rational person will also be attracted by the logic of the next step in the Bahá'í philosophy of the soul. This is that the purpose of the physical life is for man to develop his spiritual qualities so that after the physical death he will be able to move towards God - just as an embryo in the womb develops the physical attributes needed after birth. It also explains that the idea of hell is a spiritual state of knowing one has not made proper use of life and failed to achieve one's full spiritual potential.

A rational person will not find it difficult either to
accept the Bahá'í teaching that man's spiritual side
is developed under the guidance of the founders of
the world's great religions. An objective assessment
shows that these have indeed been the source, directly
or indirectly, of nearly all the great ethical systems of
history. Many who have formerly condemned religion,
because of the terrible things that have been
committed in its name when it has been corrupted,
are now coming around to the view that it does, in
fact, have a vital role to play in giving a sense of
belonging, a purpose to life, and social cohesiveness,
and that without it society eventually falls apart.

This leads on to the third major cosmic or religious
issue that can cause reservations about the Bahá'í
Faith, and that is Bahá'u'lláh's claim to be the
Manifestation of God for this age. For many, the main
barrier to acceptance of the Faith is the religion which
they already have, which in most cases claims
superiority over all other religions and indeed often
condemns them as being false. Christians, for
instance, have at least two special features of their
own religion which make it difficult for them to see
other religions in an equal light: a belief that Jesus
was God incarnate and in addition, a special feeling
about the human Jesus as a model of all that is
compassionate, loving and just. A Bahá'í response is
that Christians have also an expectation of a Second
Coming which is fulfilled by Bahá'u'lláh and therefore,
there is no inherent conflict between Christianity and
the Bahá'í Faith - the latter is not a replacement but
a development of the former.

When a Christian becomes a Bahá'í, he does not
give up Jesus but continues to revere Him no less
profoundly, and perhaps more so, than when he was
a Christian. Furthermore, the theological issue of
whether or not Jesus was God incarnate is not as real

as it may seem at first sight, for although Bahá'í teachings do not accept the idea of the division of God or His limitation to the human form, they do accept that Jesus was a perfect mirror of God, that God did indeed speak through Him, and that one of His special titles was the Son of God. Jesus did not claim to be God and on several occasions made clear the distinction. The theory that Jesus was God developed only after the crucifixion and under the influence of Greek ideas of the time. The virgin birth and resurrection are both essentially side issues which, even if true, would not prove Jesus was God, as pointed out recently by the Bishop of Durham.

Two other religious questions which are closely related are:'Why is there a need for a new religion when there are so many in existence already?' and 'What is so new and special about the Bahá'í Faith which makes it different, for instance, from Christianity?"

These type of questions clearly lead into the theme of "progressive revelation". A new revelation is necessary today to restore spiritual inspiration which has largely died out in existing religion and to unite all religions to respond to the problems of today. All religions go through a spiritual cycle like the seasons of the year. When a messenger of God appears, He inspires such a spiritual wakening in His followers that it is like a springtime. This, in turn, leads to a summertime when that spiritual impetus leads to the flowering of a great civilization. Over time, however, men begin to elaborate on the original teachings of their Faith and obscure them with ritual and superstition. The original spiritual inspiration begins to fade. This is the autumn, which is inevitably followed by a cold spiritual winter when the institutions of the religion become but hollow shells and men feel lost and without direction. It is time for a new messenger of God to bring about a new spiritual springtime.

It is not difficult to see how this theme has worked itself out in the great religions of today, each of which has had its time of inspiration and glory, and each of which is now divided, clouded with corruptions of the original teachings and generally a force for reaction rather than for the development of humanity.

The theme of progressive revelation is more than a story of religious cycles; it is also a story of evolution. Each religion, in addition to renewing the great universal themes about man's relationship with God, his fellow human beings and the universe, also adapts these themes to the needs and capacities of the peoples of the time, and as civilization has advanced, so have the teachings of each succeeding religion. Contrary to the general perception, each new religion does not deny past religions, but rather builds on them, just as in school each teacher builds on what has been taught in the earlier classes. Twentieth century society is very different from that at the time of Muḥammad, Jesus or Moses, and there is a need for specific guidance with regard to the new conditions.

While the Baháʾí Faith reiterates, for instance, the universal themes of compassion and love taught by Jesus, it also brings into sharp focus specific areas of life where such themes need to be applied today (for instance, to remove all forms of prejudice against others, to establish the equality of men and women, to eliminate extremes of wealth and poverty). Above all, it stresses the need for mankind to achieve unity in order to survive and continue the advance of civilization. The Baháʾí Faith is, therefore, distinctive from all other religions because in addition to spiritual and ethical teachings for the individual it also has guidelines on collective action so as to achieve world justice and peace. It is also distinctive in that it recognizes the equal station of all founders of the great religions of the world and, therefore, has the potential to unite all religions into one - perhaps, the single most powerful principle for achieving world unity and peace.

This leads on to another common 'religious' question - why is there a need for religion to be organized and have a formal structure? This is a natural question for those disillusioned with corrupt and self-serving religious institutions, and is particularly common in the United States where many, whose forebears fled authoritarian regimes in Europe, have a sceptical view of any institution which appears to be interfering with their personal freedom. It is argued that the individual can seek God by himself through prayer and meditation without the intervention of a third party such as a priest.

Bahá'ís can agree with this view up to a point. After all, their Faith has no clergy and every individual is encouraged to investigate the truth independently. But here, as elsewhere, the golden rule of moderation applies. History shows that when men rely solely on their own intuition to find God, they often go badly astray and they need the guidance of a Jesus, a Moses or a Buddha. The prayers of a manifestation of God, for instance, are of a much greater order of spirituality than those composed by ordinary individuals. There is also another dimension to this issue: the problems which face mankind today (nuclear war, pollution of the environment, economic dislocation, the breakdown of law and order) are issues that can only be handled by men working together. It is totally unrealistic, not to say selfish, to imagine an individual can retire to his room and pray to God, and ignore the rest of the world. One of the attractions of the Bahá'í Faith is it shows that everyone, no matter how humble in the eyes of the world, has a vital part to play in working with his fellow humans to solve these problems.

Having accepted all of these arguments, a non-Bahá'í still might hesitate to embrace the Faith because of doubts about whether or not Bahá'u'lláh was a true prophet. For many used to the distance in time that separates us from Jesus, Moses and Muhammad, it is emotionally hard to accept the idea of a prophet in our time. Many are also very conscious of the large number of sects which have emerged in recent years and which have almost instantaneously attracted thousands of followers, despite some dubious teachings and practices, and they ask in what way does Bahá'u'lláh differ from the founders of these sects.

The short answer is the guidance given by Jesus when He said:

"Even so, every good tree bringeth forth good fruit; but a corrupt tree bringeth forth evil fruit...Wherefore by their fruits ye shall know them". (Matthew 7:17-20).

This test should be applied to the claimant, to the quality of His teachings, and to the effect there is on His followers. A review of the history of the Bahá'í Faith shows that Bahá'u'lláh had a great innate knowledge, a great sense of justice and vision, the utmost love and compassion for humanity, and that He never wavered on His claim or principles no matter how great the threats against him. His teachings are unrivaled in their comprehensiveness, particularly with regard to the establishment of a new worldwide civilization based on peace, justice, and spiritual development.

Many who were once spiritually lost have, on becoming followers of His, changed to a life of the highest moral principles. People coming from backgrounds with the deepest prejudices, racial, religious, national and cultural, have come to love, appreciate, and work in amity with those whom they once despised or feared. Bahá'í communities have distinguished themselves in backward countries by raising the standard of education and the place of women to levels far above the average. A worldwide network of communities has been established where adherents of the Faith practice a new system of administration based on the spiritual principles of consultation and universal participation and of electioneering for office. In Iran, thousands have accepted persecution including loss of jobs and property, denial of education and other facilities, imprisonment, torture, and execution rather than deny their Faith. Such strength is all the more remarkable in a materialistic age when the prevailing values encourage compromise of principle in order to keep life and liberty.

Viewed as a whole, the Bahá'í Faith is indeed surely something extraordinary, the like of which has not been seen since the time of Muhammad or Jesus, and perhaps not even then. In the face of such evidence how can there be doubt about the veracity of Bahá'u'lláh's claim?

Social and Political Reservations

The second broad group of reservations about the Bahá'í Faith are those which might be classified as social or political.

It is not infrequent, for instance, to hear someone of right-wing persuasion express the fear that the Faith is vaguely communistic because of its advocacy of a world government and of fair distribution of the world's resources (such people often accuse the United Nations of being a communist front organization). There are echoes here of the accusations made against the early Bahá'í by the Shi'ah mullas. To such people, it can be pointed out that the Faith puts great emphasis on personal responsibility, on work as the highest form of worship, on prohibition of begging, on the role of the entrepreneur, world free trade and a single world currency, and on a democratic and highly decentralized form of government. These are hardly the features of a communistic dictatorship.

On the other hand, radical reformers are sometimes critical of the Faith because it does not share their conviction that direct action is necessary in order to achieve a just society. An answer to this criticism is that the Bahá'ís have by far the most radical agenda of all (one going to the root of the matter), nothing less than the achievement of universal peace based on justice. As a hard-headed practical matter it is clear such a goal cannot be achieved by force applied from above (there are enough examples of revolutions which have failed to achieve lesser ends by force). What is needed is long-term commitment to the building of a new order from the grass roots upwards by winning the enthusiastic support of all peoples of the world, support which can only come from a spiritual reawakening inspired by a new revelation from God.

Others who are not at the extremes of the political spectrum and who perhaps recognize the validity of the Faith's long-term goals, nevertheless often ask why Bahá'ís do not enter into the political fray to help deal with immediate problems. A related question is:"Just what are the Bahá'í doing except talk?" If Bahá'ís became involved in politics, they would inevitably lose their unity which is one of their greatest assets for achieving their goals. How long would it be before there were serious differences between a Bahá'í Communist in Russia and a Bahá'í Republican in the USA? Furthermore, politics would divert the relatively small Bahá'í community from its main task and might even cause some to get involved in policies which would be contrary to Bahá'í teachings.

This is not to say that Bahá'ís are indifferent to what is going on today. There are many other ways in which Bahá'ís individually and collectively work to ameliorate the ills of society. Thus in answer to the question, 'What are Bahá'ís doing?', it can be said that they are encouraged as individuals to take up careers in such fields as education, medicine, agriculture, environmental sciences, etc, which are of direct service to humanity. They are also encouraged to give support to the United Nations and organizations for human rights, equality of men and women, etc, which are law-abiding and not tied to political parties. In addition, the community itself is now making a small but valuable and rapidly growing contribution to the worldwide process of economic and social development.

Even when these arguments are accepted there still is often a lingering doubt as to whether the Bahá'í Faith is too idealistic and not sufficiently down to earth. The Bahá'í philosophy of human nature is certainly not starry-eyed, and it is recognized that there is always the risk of individuals following the animal or material side of their nature: hence the provision in the Bahá'í world order for a world police force and other devices for the protection of society. It can be pointed out that though many of the Bahá'í teachings when first promulgated in the 19th century - such as progressive taxation, universal compulsory education, the equality of men and women, the conscious abolition of prejudice and the establishment of world institutions - seemed unreal and utopian at the time, they have now been accepted as practical goals and some have been implemented to a greater or lesser degree. It can also be argued that the reason why society and present-day institutions are so

obviously not functioning properly is that old style
'practical' politics of conflict is not a suitable device
for dealing with the massive world problems which
mankind faces today. By contrast, the low-key Bahá'í
approach of building up from the grassroots a new
worldwide community according to a detailed plan
does seem to be providing an alternative approach
that is working.

Reservations of a Personal Nature
    The third group of reservations about the Faith are
those of a personal nature. Many such reservations
concern particular laws of the Faith such as the one
forbidding use of alcohol except for medicinal
purposes. For vast numbers of the world's population,
alcohol has become a means for escape from the
strains of everyday life. Many argue that a little alcohol
does no harm especially when it is a 'social lubricant'
and ask why the Bahá'ís are 'fanatical' on this issue
when they follow the golden rule of moderation on
other matters. The answer is that the laws of the Faith
are to protect man, not to oppress him. Alcohol, like
other so-called pleasure drugs, not only does physical
damage to the individual but also affects his mind and
spirit and causes suffering and pain for the immediate
family and for those who come in contact with him.
There can be no compromise about giving
respectability and a huge market for a product which
ruins the lives of millions from all backgrounds
around the world. As for the desire to blur reality, this
is something that no longer has meaning when people
are kind and straight with one another (how many
non-Bahá'ís have expressed surprise at how much
they have enjoyed themselves at Bahá'í functions even
though there was no alcohol?) No more does it make
sense when considered in relation to the perspective
and purpose given by the Bahá'í faith. On the

contrary, there is a felt need to sharpen all one's faculties so that one can be as effective as possible in the struggle to remove the causes of pain in the world and to build a new society.

There are also some who have reservations about Bahá'í teachings concerning the family and marriage. Some want the freedom to have sexual relations with whomever they please. Others feel that it is unreasonable to require the consent of parents when Bahá'ís marry. Some feel that the man should be master of the house and do not like the teachings on equality of men and women. Yet others believe their children should be set free to find their own way in life without having Bahá'í teachings imposed on them when they are young. Nevertheless, personal lifetime experience and history itself confirm the wisdom of the Bahá'í teachings on the family. Most religions and philosophies since Confucius have seen the family as the setting where the child learns to have a loving and trusting relationship with others, which he will later take into his adult life when relating to the rest of humanity.

Promiscuous sexual relationships create comparisons and eventually end with the devaluation of feelings, boredom and degradation. Confined to the marital relationship, they create mutual trust and appreciation and thereby strengthen the bonds of love in the family as a whole. The law requiring the prior consent of parents for marriage gives the parents, who care but who are detached from the immediate emotions of the two most concerned, an opportunity to fulfill their responsibilities and to offer their judgment on the basis of experience, as to whether or not the proposed relationship is likely to flourish. Above all, this law cements the bonds of love in the extended family.

Men need not fear the concept of the equality of

the sexes in the Bahá'í marriage because the Bahá'í view differs from that of the women's movement in that it puts equal emphasis on duties as well as rights of both the parents and the children. In this way, the harshness often associated with a male-dominated family can be tempered with love and diversity without the father feeling that his position has been usurped.

The raising of children is a field where there is a need for moderation. The extreme liberal view that children should not have any values imposed on them is typically a reaction against narrow values which were beaten into earlier generations. Experience shows, however, that children want guidance and do not like to be left to themselves. For a Bahá'í, it would be a dereliction of responsibility to deny his child a Bahá'í education because this provides both the highest ethical standards and the sense of tolerance which the child will need if he is to be able then to make sound independent judgments when he grows up.

The Bahá'í case with regard to its teachings on marriage and the family is much strengthened when the non-Bahá'í can see for himself its success in the Bahá'í community with whom he is in touch. It does not help to see communities with badly brought up children and with more broken marriages than successful ones.

Though these are probably the most frequent reservations on the personal level, there are many others that occasionally come up - fear of having to mix with people of a different racial or cultural background, intimidation by the writings of Bahá'u'lláh or Shoghi Effendi, and inability to pray after a lifetime of unfamiliarity with such spiritual practices. What these often come down to is a feeling of personal inadequacy, a sense of not being able to live up to the Bahá'í teachings. In response it has been pointed out that Bahá'ís are ordinary people too. The difference is that they have been so inspired by the Faith and supported by their communities that they have been able to extend their reach far beyond what was previously possible. This is a continuing process because, with time, understanding increases and, with it, the ability to respond. Those who fear that they are inadequate should be helped by being shown that the important factor in the Bahá'í Faith is the effort to move forward from where one stands and not an expectation that everyone can have the same standard of qualities all at once. This is because each of us starts from a different base and has widely varying difficulties to overcome. Entering the Faith is like entering a life-long university - the challenge to improve continues to the very end.

Conclusion

This is by no means a complete list of reservations that are expressed about the faith nor of the responses which might be given, and readers may wish to develop the idea for their own use. That brings me to the main purpose of this exercise which is to focus attention on the need in presenting the Faith, to listen as well as to talk. Formal presentations are, of course, essential for dissemination of information and such presentations often attract those who are able to identify in them the answers to their own hopes and aspirations. Those who do not respond should be listened to so that the focus of attention can be narrowed and deepened to their particular concerns with a view to eventually helping them to answer their own questions. Sometimes when the focus is so sharpened, the person concerned may recognize that, in relation to the total picture, his concern is relatively minor. He may recognize that to hold up commitment to the faith on account of it would be a stunting

process and it would be better to make a commitment
with the expectation that growth and experience in the
Bahá'í Faith will gradually realize the answer that is
needed. This indeed was my own experience.

In such circumstances it is worth remembering
that all that is required on becoming a Bahá'í is
acknowledgment of the station of the central figures
of the Faith and an undertaking to follow the laws and
obey the elected institutions.

NOTES

1. God Passes By , Wilmette: Bahá'í Publishing Trust, 1944,
   p. 94.
2. World Order of Bahá'u'lláh, Wilmette: Bahá'í Publishing
   Trust, rev. ed 1955, pp.42-43.
3. Gleanings, London: UK Bahá'í Publishing Trust, 1949,
   p.155.
4. ibid, p. 160.
5. ibid, p. 62.

THE PHOENIX AND THE ASHES

A review, printed in Dialogue Magasine, Volume ii, no 2/3, 1988, U.S.A., of the book *The Phoenix and the Ashes: The Bahá'í Faith and the Modern Apocalypse,* by Geoffrey Nash, published by George Ronald, Oxford, 1984

During the last decade there have been growing signs that the Bahá'í community is coming of age. First, it has achieved worldwide recognition as a result of the incredible bravery of the Iranian Bahá'ís who have refused to recant their Faith in the face of brutal persecution. Second, there has emerged a strengthened Bahá'í program to promote the economic and social development of humankind, both through a long-term strategy and through numerous short-term, concrete projects. Third, there is a growing volume of literature addressing the complex relationship of the Bahá'í community to society - books designed to broaden the appreciation of Bahá'ís and to attract the interest of those, especially the educated, outside the Bahá'í community.

One of the distinguished books of this class is **The Phoenix and the Ashes** by Geoffrey Nash. This well-written book, which consists of five essays and a postscript, covers four basic themes: the optimism that permeated Western society in the first half of the nineteenth century; the sense of hopelessness that replaced that optimism in the second half of the nineteenth century and early twentieth century; the

immediate prospects for the world; and the promise
that the spiritual needs of all mankind will be
eventually fulfilled.

Geoffrey Nash examines these themes in the light
of history, literature, and politics. The essay format
creates some repetition but also provides an unusual
depth that comes from the multiplicity of approaches.
The author's low-key tone is likely to attract open-
minded non-Bahá'ís. The book also has the high
production standards we have come to expect from
its publisher: a thought provoking cover; good, clear
print; strong binding; and a reasonable price. The only
shortcoming is the absence of an index or detailed
table of contents.

The book's first essay, "The Lost Hope of the
Nineteenth Century," begins with a review of early
nineteenth-century romanticism, showing how its
essential optimism and spirituality were based on a
continuation of tolerance, a love of freedom, and a
respect for the individual themes adapted from the
Enlightenment movement of the eighteenth century.
The essay then describes the more pessimistic view
of life that developed among intellectuals, such as
Henrik Ibsen, in the latter half of the nineteenth
century as religious conviction faltered in the face of
a materialistic philosophy and scientific advances.
There were attempts to revitalize religion but most of
those efforts were backward looking and, therefore,
doomed to fail.

The one exception was the Bahá'í Faith, whose
remarkably advanced teachings looked to the future.
Unfortunately, though some educated Westerners
knew about the new Faith, they mistakenly assessed
it as little more than a rather dramatic reform
movement within Islám. As a result religion continued
to decline, and society lost its sense of purpose and
cohesion.

The main subject matter of the second essay, "From Vision to Nightmare," is disillusionment with present-day society as described by five leading writers of our time. This essay is perhaps the most original and stimulating of the five. Three of the writers - George Orwell, Arthur Koestler, and Alexander Solzhenitsyn - discuss the flaws in communism that they found through personal experience.

In ***Animal Farm*** and other works, George Orwell satirizes the shallowness of modern society, the gullibility of the vast majority, and the terrible hypocrisy of the communist movement as epitomized in the mock slogan, "All animals are equal but some are more equal than others." In ***Darkness at Noon***, Arthur Koestler criticizes the revolutionary and seductive principle that the end justifies the means and concludes: "And perhaps reason alone was a defective compass, which led one on such a winding, twisted course that the goal finally disappeared in the mist." Disillusionment with Communism becomes virtually complete in the detailed description by Alexander Solzhenitsyn of the Russian gulag, the ultimate nightmare of a dream gone wrong.

The final two writers whose works are analyzed in "From Vision to Nightmare" - Henry Miller and Aldous Huxley - are equally critical of Western capitalist society. Though remembered mostly for the strong language in his "Tropic" novels, Miller's primary message was indignation at the misery inflicted on the poor by unbridled capitalism and by insensitivity to the cultures of black peoples and the American Indians. He spoke harshly of American society as being like Moloch, devouring humanity in pursuit of all that is useless. He recognized how different were the teachings of the Bahá'í Faith and wrote: "It is for this reason that the Bahá'í movement is destined to outlast all the other religious organizations on this continent." In **Brave New World**, Aldous Huxley shows that, if society concentrates only on material desires and achieves its goal, our culture will lack depth and ultimately will fail because it does not meet the deep spiritual needs we all have.

Nash concludes that all five writers recognize, explicitly or implicitly, that man descends into savagery when civilization has no moral core. As Henry Miller puts it, "We are kept alive by men of faith, men of vision. they are like vital germs in the endless process of becoming. Make room, then, for the life-giving ones."

The third essay of the book, "The Bahá'í Faith and Philosophy of History," compares the Bahá'í view of history with that of other religions and humanism. Some religions such as Hinduism and Buddhism have little concern with history. Judaism, Christianity, and Islám, however, do have a historical dimension. Each sees the intervention of God in man's affairs but concludes that such interventions have been essentially completed until the Day of Judgment; as a result all three religions tend to look backward rather than forward. This has contributed to their failure to capture the minds and hearts of the many who have turned instead to a humanist faith in science that it is believed, will ultimately lead to a better society. The Bahá'í view of history is similar to that of Judaism, Christianity, and Islám in that it recognizes God's intervention in man's affairs through His Messengers, and sees a preordained pattern to evolution. But the Bahá'í view differs because it sees God's interventions as continuing indefinitely into the future and because it recognizes that, within the overall preordained pattern, the details of history are determined by human beings, who do have a choice as to how they will follow the guidance that has been given to them.

The Bahá'í Faith, Geoffrey Nash argues, does not pass responsibility to God for the way we run society. Man is at the apex of the animal kingdom and at the beginning of the spiritual kingdom. It is his responsibility to grow into the latter and the time is now. As Teilhard de Chardin recognized, it is not unrealistic to expect that humankind will grow spiritually: "It is finally the Utopians, not the 'realists', who make scientific sense. They at least, though their flights of fancy may cause us to smile, have a feeling for the true dimensions of the phenomenon of Man."

The book's fourth essay, "The Bahá'í Faith and Political Theory," reviews the main political movements of the day. The principle features of democratic capitalism are freedom of speech, of press, of association, and of religion - and equality before the law. The device of universal suffrage has made possible reform and change without revolutionary violence. Democracy is essentially a secular philosophy because established religions tended to be associated with old regimes and privileges, at least in the nineteenth century. As a result, the main deficiency of democratic capitalism is that it is largely devoid of spiritual values. Similarly, the revolutionary Left has a materialist philosophy, although it does have overtones of religious messianism. Like the Bahá'í Faith, the revolutionary Left places great importance on historical evolution and recognizes that the present day is the time for universal change. But the revolutionary Left differs radically from the Bahá'í Faith in its godlessness, cultivation of antagonisms between men, and willingness to use violence. Right-wing nationalism is another false political god of our times, and in its extreme form it is the direct opposite of what the Bahá'í Faith represents.

The conventional political perception today (1988)

is that the world is divided into two distinct systems: democratic capitalism and communism. But, Geoffrey Nash argues, this cannot be a permanent arrangement for a number of reasons, not least of which is the lack of agreement as to where the dividing line should be. The Bahá'í Movement, which is outside partisan politics, is a radical alternative to the established political system. It offers a new form of government and a spiritual approach to economic issues, though Geoffrey Nash observes that the latter are not very specific. This may be so if the comparison is with a program of a political party campaigning in an election, but it should be added: (i) that Bahá'í economics has many features, several of which are listed by Geoffrey Nash, which are certainly more specific than, say, those proposed by Karl Marx; and (ii) that anything more detailed cannot be expected of a system which has to be flexible enough to provide guidance for a variety of circumstances over at least one thousand years. The Bahá'í program, which is both idealistic and practical, will involve major changes in social and cultural attitudes. For these reasons its implementation will no doubt be painful and will likely not be achieved overnight.

For those who fear that the Bahá'í Faith will end in tyranny, as have other movements, Geoffrey Nash argues that it is protected by such basic principles as the individual conscience and the individuals right to investigate reality, the rights of minorities, and the theme of spiritual evolution.

The fifth essay, "The Modern Apocalypse," reviews the writing of Shoghi Effendi on the fate of humanity, and his interpretation of history, particularly in the **The Promised Day is Come**. Geoffrey Nash outlines Shoghi Effendi's explanation that the failure of the rulers and religious leaders to follow the exhortations of Bahá'u'lláh has resulted in their loss of power and an accompanying series of catastrophes for humankind. In the Bahá'í view, the immediate future is bleak, but humanity's long-term future promises to be glorious. This theme is as important in giving cohesion and a sense of purpose to the Bahá'í community as is the theory of class struggle for Marxists.

In a postscript, Geoffrey Nash expresses the belief that the world is heading toward a major catastrophe because the process of decline is too deeply ingrained to be diverted by remedial measures. Ultimately, however, the pain will make people see that a rebirth of spiritual values, as promulgated by the Bahá'í Faith, is the answer. Then there will be witnessed a spiritual civilization, "the new phoenix emerging from the ashes of man's inchoate historical past."

PERSPECTIVES, PURPOSES AND BROTHERHOOD: A SPIRITUAL FRAMEWORK FOR A GLOBAL SOCIETY

A presentation at the First International Dialogue on Transition to a Global Society, Landegg, Switzerland, 1990

Why We Need a Vision

In discussing a new vision and new values for an emerging world order, we might define vision as a spiritual insight of who we are, why we are, and where we are going. Values might be similarly defined as standards of spiritual worth by which we try to live in accordance with our vision. A society needs vision because it is a powerful motivator for forward movement; conversely in the absence of vision a society can slip backwards towards disintegration.

"Where there no vision, the people perish."[1]

A variation on this theme is the perception that a vision, like a strategic plan, helps a society to be more efficient and effective, because it provides a sense of direction, and thereby reduces the risk of inconsistencies and error. A good example of a need for such a vision or plan today is, as Henry Kissinger has pointed out, with regard to the whole process of disarmament: we need to know where are trying to go. Clearly such needs are of particular significance in times of rapid and radical change.

Religion and Vision

For most of history since the beginning of civilization and for the vast majority of humanity, vision and values have been intimately associated with the religious experience. Religion has presented a vision of a time when righteousness shall prevail (the coming of the New Jerusalem) and when there will be universal peace:

"They shall beat their swords into ploughshares, and their spears into pruning hooks. Nation shall not lift up sword against nation, neither shall they learn war any more."[2]

Such a time is usually connected in the human mind with the coming or return of a Manifestation or Messenger of God: The Second Coming of Christ, the Messiah, the Fifth Buddha, Shah Bahram, the Q'áim, the Mihdi, and so on. The deep values promulgated by the great religions have over and over again helped to propel civilization forward, ranging from ancient times when biblical prophets held up an independent system of morality against which to measure the activities of the state, to modern times when religious inspiration largely caused the abolition of slavery and gave great strength to the movement for human rights. However, it is undoubtedly true that in modern times, and especially in the west, established religion has lost much of its attraction. As is true of all living things, religions have a life cycle and with age they become corrupted with superstition, fanaticism, hypocrisy, division and oppression. Disillusioned, humanity has searched for inspiration in alternative secular philosophies.

The Democratic Capitalism Model

One of the great forces of modern times that has captured the imagination of millions is democratic capitalism. In reaction to the suffocating effects of mercantilism and absolute monarchy, legitimized as the viceroyalty of God, democratic capitalism has held up a vision of maximum freedom for all: political, economic and social. The goal has been to maximize human happiness. As Bentham put it:

"The greatest happiness of the greatest number is the foundation of morals and legislation."[3]

As each person is the best judge of what makes him or her happy, clearly the optimum social system is one that, within the bounds of maintaining basic law and order, maximizes individual freedom. Unfortunately all men and women are not born equal and maximum freedom tends to make differences more extreme and, in particular, to cause, on the one hand, many to be deprived of the basic economic necessities, and on the other hand, a few to have excess of power and influence.

And so we have, in reaction to the gross and obvious inequalities of early democratic capitalism, the emergence of a new socialist 'vision': an egalitarian society where there would be no poverty and no dominating rich. There were, of course, many variations on the socialist theme: co-operatives, trade unionism, anarchism, syndicalism and so on, but the one that became predominant was characterized by the highly centralized control of a bureaucratic state, with the Stalinist model being the most extreme example. This vision has failed, as we have all recently witnessed[4]. Beyond a certain point central control did not lead to economies of scale but rather to rigidities and reduced initiative and incentive. In extreme cases the system became highly inefficient and failed to create the additional wealth needed to raise everyone form poverty. Furthermore, those in control for too long apparently thought that they alone were exempt from Lord Acton's dictum:

"Power tends to corrupt, and absolute power

corrupts absolutely."[5]

Talk about a new Soviet Man first became a bad joke and then simply stopped. No wonder Vaclav Havel has felt compelled to say: 'Let us teach both ourselves and others that politics...can be the art of the impossible, that it is the art of making both ourselves and the world better.'

And so it seems that democratic capitalism is triumphant. After successes in Latin America, East Asia, and Southern Europe over the past decade or so, we have just witnessed amazing advances in Eastern Europe and the countries of the former Soviet Union. For the first time in history, democracies, in the loosest sense, may be a majority of the world's nations. As a jewel in the crown, we have a strengthened European Community and the promise of further European integration. The question now is: does democratic capitalism provide, after all, the vision and values needed for a new world order? Clearly there are positive things that can be said. For instance, it is argued from experience that democracies rarely instigate a war, and certainly their record in this respect is better that of authoritarian regimes. Second, it is fair to assume that evolution of international co-operation towards a federal world government is much more likely to happen if the majority of the member nations of such an organization are democratic, follow the rule of law in domestic affairs, and are accountable to their citizens.

However, I would suggest that democratic capitalism is essentially hollow at the center in the same way as socialism, and accordingly, its vision and system of values is inadequate for our time. The system lacks a soul. It rests on the assumption that man differs from animals only because of his superior intelligence. Bentham's 'happiness' fundamentally means material enjoyment and consumption. Indeed, we are proud of the fact that ours is a consumer society. But there is growing fear that the earth will not be able to sustain a world society where five billion persons would consume material things at the same rate as the one billion persons who presently live in economically developed nations.

There is also growing recognition that when the goal of life is 'happiness' there will always be frustration. Once the materialist philosophy seemed sunny and optimistic; but experience in the twentieth century and the prevailing sense of frustration has made for pessimism, and today any self-respecting "man of the world" has to sound sceptical if not cynical. We now see humanity as essentially selfish, greedy and violent; hardly a view that will encourage the building of a new world. Furthermore, there is an inexorable logic in the materialistic view that drives it towards a short-term perspective: 'for tomorrow we die'. And yet vision has always been about the long-term perspective. I do not mean to exaggerate or imply that all democracies are exactly the same. But I suggest there is an underlying trend that can be clearly seen, for instance, in the United States, the most powerful democracy and the one that is increasingly a model for the rest of the world.

The New World

Let me list a few characteristics of modern American society that are common knowledge. First, in politics it is obvious that the horizon of vision is essentially limited by the next congressional or presidential election. President Bush speaks disparagingly about 'this vision thing'. It is the Senate of this nation that voted against ratification of the League of Nations Covenant, and for forty years refused to approve the International Genocide Convention. Though there is apparently free public discussion, the reality is that voting and decision-making are largely responsive to rhetoric and TV 'sound-bites'. Wealth, both corporate and private, has an immense influence that it uses for its own perceived vested interest, and this frequently does not coincide with the general public good. The advice of Edmund Burke to representatives of the people, that they put the nation first, is largely ignored, and parochialism is what counts. Thus political favoritism dominates the Federal Budget. The economy is likewise preoccupied with short-term considerations, as epitomized by obsession with the price/earnings ratio in quarterly corporation reports. Takeover merchants buy and sell large corporations with borrowed money and show little concern for either employees or customers, whilst more people are obliged to live on the streets. Saving rates in this, the richest country in the world, are at an all time low; conversely debt, private, commercial and public, continues to rise for the financing of consumer goods and services rather than for investment in productive resources. Maintenance of the basic infrastructure of education, health, housing and communications is neglected. There is powerful inertia resisting attempts to protect natural resources and a healthy environment, as symbolized by the absurdly low tax on gasoline. In the social sphere there is the devastation of the family, routine divorce for all and abandonment of children; the result is good money for the psychiatrist and a culture of alcohol, drugs, guns, violence, racism and crime. My purpose in recounting this tale of woe is not to put down the country where I live or democratic capitalism in general, but rather to show that we need more lofty standards if we are to start to build a true world order for succeeding generations. Robert Browning identified the challenge:

Ah, but a man's reach should exceed his grasp,
Or what's a heaven for.[6]

If indeed the materialistic dreams of socialism and
democratic capitalism are inadequate, the logical
question to ask is whether we should take another
look at the religious experience, the main source of
vision and ethical values down the ages. Many
thinkers of modern times, as diverse as Toynbee,
Koestler and Campbell have come to this conclusion.
An intuitive sense of the correctness of this view is
supported by popular feeling in Eastern Europe where
there has been a new reaching out for the spiritual
dimension despite decades of state-directed
suppression of religion. Similarly there is a reaction
in the Islamic world against the corruption of Western
materialism. It is perhaps not irrelevant to observe
that about eighty per cent of the world's population
still claims religious affiliation[7].

What seems to be needed is a focus on the essence
of the vision: relevant universal themes that are
common to all the great religions. I wish to stress my
view that such a focus on the inspirational essence
of religion is very different from conventional
ecumenicalism, which so often ends in the dreary
lowest common denominator.

The Spiritual Dimension

I would suggest there are at least five universal
religious themes relevant to this discussion. The first
is an awareness of a spiritual dimension to life and
existence as well as a material dimension. A
consequence of such an awareness is that material
things become less important and are viewed as of
temporary interest. This does not mean indifference
or asceticism but rather a balance, a golden mean -
an enjoyment of the material creation but a
detachment and a willingness to let go when the time

comes.

This leads to a second key theme, namely a sense of the sacredness, interdependence and harmony of life. Hubris, which the Greeks so feared, can hardly exist when there is such an awareness. At the same time, balancing this humility, is a self-esteem that comes from the belief that man is the highest form of life, not simply because of his superior intelligence, but because he has a consciousness of the transcendental, and a spiritual side to his nature. He is, in essence, made in the image of God. From this privilege comes an acknowledgment of responsibility, including accountability for the stewardship of the earth. Linked to this perspective is a fourth theme, which is recognition that the purpose of life is to nurture and develop the spiritual side of our nature; to cultivate the noble qualities: truthfulness, honesty, courage, reliability, compassion, courtesy, and so on. This purpose is different from the utilitarian idea of 'happiness', because, though it can indeed bring in its wake intense happiness and a sense of fulfillment, the path to it is often through pain and sacrifice.

"Man is, so to speak, unripe; the heat of the fire of suffering will mature him. Look back to the times of the past and you will find that the greatest men have suffered the most."

'Abdu'l-Bahá[8]

A fifth theme of religion, closely linked to the other four, is an insistence on the fact that we are all Children of God - the human family. This theme is relevant at every level of society, from humanity as a whole down to its basic building block: the family.

When such themes are taken seriously, the consequences for a new world order are potentially immense. A feeling of human solidarity is the most powerful base for international co-operation and ultimately for a world government. That same solidarity makes it impossible to be indifferent to poverty among our brothers and sisters of the same race, whether living within one's own country or elsewhere. A focus on our spiritual development as the highest priority, a detached and balanced attitude towards material goods, and a feeling of respect for nature, are all factors that lead humanity towards a vastly enhanced concern for the protection of natural resources and the environment. There is a basis here for a new-style global economy which benefits all by putting emphasis on basic material needs and on high-quality services designed to enrich the general intellectual and spiritual experience. An emphasis on development of noble qualities also has implications for a higher level of honesty and efficiency in both the public and the private sectors. We in the west are perhaps conscious of this issue because of our experience, over several decades, of a decline in ethical standards simultaneously with a decline in religion. It is suggested that in the long term these goals, together with support for the family as one of the most vital institutions of society, represent the most effective way to reverse the devastating trend towards drugs, crime, and other symptoms of social breakdown.

A New Vision

The potential value of focusing on the essence of the religious experience suggests the need for radical change if we are to achieve a solid base from which to move forward to a new world order. First, there is a need for the leaders of religions to join together for the common good, an action that can only strengthen rather than undermine the religious tradition they love.

"The challenge facing the religious leaders of mankind is to...submerge their theological differences

in a great spirit of mutual forbearance that will enable
them to work together for the advancement of human
understanding and peace."

The Universal House of Justice[9]

Second, there is a need for global action on the
part of government and education authorities to
incorporate into the education system the basic
spiritual insights of religion. This should surely be
given the same order of priority as the elimination of
illiteracy. In the United States such an idea may
sound shocking, because the public education
authorities, particularly in recent decades, have made
almost a fetish out of excluding any mention of
religion from the syllabus. There is fear that otherwise
they could be accused of acting in contravention of a
constitutional requirement for separation of church
and state. However, there is a need to look at the
motives behind the requirement. It is clear that the
Founders were generally religious in outlook and did
not intend to make the new nation atheistic; their
concern was to make sure that a particular
denomination did not use the state to force its views
on a multicultural society whose peoples had in many
instances fled Europe on account of an unholy
authoritarian alliance of Church and state. The
proposal made here would not contradict that
objective and at the same time would avoid the terrible
price that American society has had to pay as a result
of present policies.

But the religious experience offers more than a
basic foundation for a new vision and a related system
of values, important as that undoubtedly is. In its
modern manifestation, religion also presents a
framework or superstructure around which humanity
can build a new global society of peace and justice.
This framework is a logical development of the basic
universal themes, adapted to the special needs of a

world maturing towards a global society.

A major element of this vision is a new system for management of public affairs, based on participatory local community government, and culminating, through national bodies, in a federal world government. The approach is to go beyond the democratic system of election by confidential universal suffrage, public accountability, free public discussion, and the rule of law, to a system incorporating several new principles of which perhaps the two most important are a spiritual dimension, and a process of consultation rather than democratic debate.

The spiritual dimension includes a requirement that those casting a vote in an election take account of spiritual or noble qualities as well as administrative capacity. It also means that elected government is responsible first to God rather than to the electorate. In practice, this means a holistic viewpoint, embracing not only the interests of the present but of the future, and of the environment as well as humanity. It means a focus on creating conditions that maximize opportunity for every man, woman and child on the planet to develop his or her full potential, physical, intellectual, and above all, spiritual. One aspect of this process is a style of government that is collective rather than dependent on the individual leader; a change designed to avoid the corruption that the latter role inevitably entails.

The process of consultation differs from democratic debate insofar as it aims to arrive at the truth through unity and a scientific process rather than through conflict and appeal to self-interest. This process involves both detachment and universal participation. It is akin in many ways to current ideas on conflict resolution.

This vision of a new way of managing public affairs is intimately related to a refined and heightened awareness of the basic universal religious themes. Thus, in promoting the idea of the human family there is an emphasis on conscious abolition of prejudice and appreciation of the diversity of culture as a means for enriching the common heritage. These are critical nuances in a world where migration, international trade and tourism bring us into contact more and more with peoples who are very different from ourselves. This theme of the oneness of humanity is reinforced by practicing the equality of men and women within the family and in society in general. Many see the latter process as vital to the establishment of peace because of the special perspective that women generally have on the priorities of society. This theme of oneness is further strengthened, as is a sense of responsibility and accountability, by the viewpoint that the highest form of worship is work in the service of humanity. Finally, the universal religious theme of detachment, which counters the materialistic drive towards conflict, is sharpened by the encouragement of intellectual integrity and independent investigation of truth and by the view that science and religion, dealing respectively with the material and the spiritual dimensions of existence, are in harmony, not conflict.

Getting from Here to There

A vision, to have reality, must surely incorporate some indication of how we get from here to there. This too can be found in the vision of religion in its modern form. It starts at the grassroots level with the individual and the local community gradually creating an alternative working model, initially on a small scale, of a diverse society with a global perspective. It continues with a reaching out to other groups and organizations that have goals fitting into the global vision, all with a view to mutual co-operation for the common good. A global perspective means avoidance of entanglements with partisan and parochial interests, and this, when combined with the principle of loyalty to established government, creates a sense of trust, a key factor in building a new world society. One of the most important stages on the way to the establishment of a world commonwealth, based on justice and spiritual values, is the abolition of war between nations, a stage that should be achieved by the end of this century.

To summarize, finding a new vision and an associated new system of values is a vital component of the process of evolving towards a peaceful global society. It is suggested that in searching for such a vision, there should be an objective analysis of what is offered by religious experience: the source of the great visions of the past.

NOTES

1. *Proverbs* 29:18.
2. *Isaiah* 2:4.
3. *The Penguin Dictionary of Quotations,* 1960, p. 29.
4. Though the failure has been most dramatic in the Communist countries, it should not be forgotten that in the West the welfare state, even in model Sweden, has been under siege for a decade on such issues as efficiency, dependency culture, and so on.
5. *The Penguin Dictionary of Quotations,* 1960, p. 1.
5. *Andrea del Sarto,* by Robert Browning.
7. See Religion: World Religious Statistics, *Britannica Book of the Year,* 1988.
8. *Paris Talks,* London: UK Bahá'í Publishing Trust, 1969.
9. *The Promise of World Peace,* London: One World Publications, 1985.

SOME OBSERVATIONS CONCERNING THE BAHÁ'Í CHAIR FOR WORLD PEACE

A presentation at the Third Annual Conference of the Association of Bahá'í Studies (Japan), Tokyo, Japan, 1994

I should like to thank the Association for inviting me to make a presentation on the Bahá'í Chair for World Peace, which I have the honor to represent on this short trip to Japan. There is much that should be said about this important and newly established institution. However, as time is short, I propose to limit myself to a few highlights and brief discussion of some of the more obvious subjects that might be of interest to the present gathering. The points I will touch on are: the significance of the Chair, it's functions and work program, and it's relationship to the Bahá'í community, including most especially, Bahá'í scholars.

It seems to me there are at least three observations that should be made with regard to the significance of the Chair in the context of the evolution of the Bahá'í community. The first, of course, is that it represents an early step in the process of obtaining academic recognition of the Bahá'í Faith as a worthy subject for study, one of the main goals of this Association. What is especially noteworthy, is that in this case, Bahá'í studies are not limited to what is sometimes referred to as the "religious ghetto", but are seen as immediately relevant to the great practical questions concerning the achievement of world peace. There can be little doubt that a major contributing factor to this process has been the prestige that the Bahá'í Faith has won as a great moral and intellectual force in the world as a consequence of the immense courage and spiritual strength of those suffering persecution in Irán after the revolution of 1978.

My second observation concerning the significance of the Chair as it relates to it's location and the timing of it's establishment. It's location is the capital city of the most powerful and influential nation on earth, the United States, which according to the Bahá'í Writings has a very special destiny in leading the nations of the world to both the Lesser Peace and the Most Great Peace. Opportunity to consult with those with influence in the government of this nation is clearly greatly enhanced by this special location. The timing of it's establishment is equally remarkable. It happened at the end of the Cold War, the third of the great global conflicts of the Twentieth Century, which for more than forty years had prevented humanity from taking proper advantage of the United Nations agreement which concluded the Second World War. It's establishment was also only a few years before the end of the second Christian millennium, which, Abdu'l-Bahá said, would see the end of war between nations.

A third significant aspect of the Chair is the fact that the initiative for it's establishment came from outside the Faith. This clearly adds to the respect with which the Chair is seen by the rest of the world, ie. it is not likely to be seen as simply a self serving instrument of a particular religion. The original initiative came from Professor Edward Azar, a Lebanese Christian and a distinguished scholar in the field of peace studies, who had recently, on invitation, established the Center for International Development and Conflict Management (CIDCM) at the University of Maryland, a leading center of higher learning in the United States. Laboring to help restore peace in his own war-torn land, he had met, in the early eighties, Professor Bushrui, who at that time was Head of the Department of English at the American University at the American University of Beirut as well as Cultural Advisor to President Gemayel. As a result of their friendship, Professor Azar became familiar with ***The Promise of World Peace***, which, as you will recall, was released by the Universal House of Justice in 1985, the UN Year of Peace --- just a few months after Mikhail Gorbachev became Secretary-General of the Communist Party of the Soviet Union. Professor Azar was so inspired by this statement that he wrote to the Universal House of Justice in 1988, proposing the establishment of a Bahá'í Chair for World Peace at the CIDCM. He had the full support of the University which is known for it's progressive and innovative approaches to education, and for its access to generous sources of funding.

Eventually the Chair was established in 1993 on the basis of an agreement between the University and the US National Spiritual Assembly, acting on behalf of the Universal House of Justice. The agreement provided for a seven member board, five nominated by the National Spiritual Assembly and two by the University, which would advise the latter on policy and administration of the Chair. The Assembly was also given responsibility for preparing a list of candidates for the Chair, with appropriate academic qualifications and with good standing in the Bahá'í community. The latter provision, which was suggested by the University, gives safeguard against the Chair being occupied by someone who might be hostile to the Faith.

I should now like to say a few words about the Chair's functions and it's work program. The Chair has been given three broad functions. First, it is to provide inter disciplinary research, courses and seminars on Bahá'í texts with regard to causes of conflict and peaceful resolution of such conflicts. Second, it is to organize a public forum for discussion of the issues raised in *The Promise of World Peace*. Third, it is to establish links with other institutions working on academic peace studies, including provision of technical assistance to help set up such studies. With regard to fund raising, it was agreed that the Bahá'í Community would be responsible for raising an endowment of $1.5 million, which would be matched equally by the University. The University would also provide facilities, such as the building and various support services.

Since inauguration in April 1993, the Chair has undertaken a heavy program of activities made possible by the drive and energy of Professor Bushrui who had been selected for the post by the University. In the first academic year (1993-94) an honors course on "The Spiritual Heritage of the Human Race" was presented and attended by some 22 students. It is planned to publish the text of the course in book form in the near future. The course has been so well received that the University is considering a proposal to make it a basic requirement for all undergraduate students --- a response to the widely perceived need to strengthen the spiritual dimension of public education in the USA. A second course on "The Religious Approaches to Peace" is in the planning stage. In April, 1994 the Chair cooperated with the History Department and the Meyerhoff Center for Jewish Studies in sponsoring a peace forum entitled "When Empires Fall", with participation by scholars from all around the world, Bahá'í and non-Bahá'í alike. Academic contacts, including technical assistance, have been established with the Bahá'í Academy at Landegg, Switzerland, which inter-alia provides a certificate program in World Order Studies, with the University of Indhore, where there is a newly established Chair for Bahá'í Studies, with the University of Nur at Santa Cruz, Bolivia, with the College of Micronesia, and with Makere University in Uganda.

A crucial factor in these early days of the Chair is to reach the endowment goal as soon as possible. The Bahá'í Chair itself has raised nearly $1 million towards the goal of $1.5 million. Non Bahá'ís may and do contribute to this fund raising activity because it is in support of an University of Maryland facility, not a Bahá'í institution as such --- obviously an important factor at this time when the highest priority for Bahá'í fund raising is in support of the Arc. The University, itself severely constrained by the present general crisis in public finances in the United States, has not been able, so far, to match the endowment directly, but is paying services in kind. In addition the Chair has been allocated a high proportion of special funds provided by the State of Maryland to encourage private financial support for the University. A separate financial issue is the establishment of a scholarship fund of $50,000 for less well off students, for which so far some $20,000 has been raised. Clearly during these early days, before the endowment is fully funded, the Chair is obliged to operate on a shoe string, with a few underpaid staff having to work unreasonably hard, and with the possibility that opportunities for desirable projects will be lost.

I should like now to say a few words about how the Chair relates to the Bahá'í Community, and in particular to Bahá'í scholars and such bodies as the Association for Bahá'í Studies. Clearly there is an opportunity for a great deal of cooperation in terms of mutual support in research and provision of intellectual resources. However, there is a need for great care in such activity to respect the independence of the Chair and to remember that the Chair reports to, and is managed by, the University, and that failure to observe this convention, even when the intent is well meaning, could be most damaging. The main point to stress is that Bahá'í scholars, including, of course, members of the Japanese branch of ABS are warmly encouraged to offer their services, and to be in contact directly with the Chair to that purpose.

Whilst on this subject of scholarship, I should like to finish, with your permission, on a note of caution, because as we all know we are venturing into risky if exciting and rewarding territory. As Bahá'ís we have to constantly remember what it is to be a Bahá'í scholar --- we are to be different from the academic world around us in certain important respects, as was so clearly spelt out in the statement on scholarship of the Universal House of Justice in 1979. We have to deal with the particular problem of ego associated with academia, with excessive and negative competition, and with narrowness of perspective. We need to focus on the purpose of Bahá'í scholarship which is to promote the well-being of humanity by illuminating the spiritual principles of the Faith. Past experience, especially in the field of Bahá'í history, suggests the need to carefully review our motivations, to take a broad view of the facts, and to avoid like the plague a conviction that we are the experts -- the authority. The latter hubris is something that is more difficult to avoid when there is excessive praise and adulation by other Bahá'ís. Moderation in all things!

THE BAHÁ'Í PLAN FOR WORLD PEACE

A presentation at "Once Empires Fade", an International Conference at the University of Maryland, U.S.A., 1994

The Bahá'í Peace Program was first set forth by Bahá'u'lláh (1817-1892), the Prophet-Founder of the Bahá'í Faith, in a series of letters addressed to the rulers of the world, which were written in the period 1867 and 1868. Since then there have been many authorized commentaries on the program, including, most notably, by 'Abdu'l-Bahá (1844-1921), Bahá'u'lláh's Son and Successor as leader of the Bahá'í community, in a letter to the Shah of Persia called *The Secret of Divine Civilization;* by Shoghi Effendi (1896-1957), 'Abdúl-Baha's grandson and Guardian of the Faith, in a letter to the Bahá'í community entitled *The World Order of Bahá'u'lláh;* and by the Universal House of Justice, the elected supreme world body of the community, in a statement to the peoples of the world, called *The Promise of World Peace*, which was issued in 1985, the UN Year of Peace.

The Bahá'í Peace Program is presented in the context of the history and evolution of civilization. Humanity has passed through "childhood", and in the age of science and the industrial revolution it has experienced the turbulence of "adolescence", when its physical capacities have exceeded its wisdom to handle such new found strength to best advantage. We are now at the point of emerging into "maturity" when humanity learns to manage its affairs on the basis of peace and justice. This process has two aspects. First, humanity is simply pushed in the right direction by the tide of history: modern communications have in effect made the world one; modern weapons threaten the destruction of civilization if a permanent peace is not established. Initially this "force majeure" is the main driving factor. Gradually, however, it is supplemented and eventually supplanted by the power of moral principle -- acknowledgment that justice and an awareness of the spiritual dimension is the only long term basis for civilization. The basis for this power has been laid by the great world religions which have all taught the brotherhood of man and peace as the essence of true religion.

In this time of advancement into the state of "maturity", humanity has the choice of achieving peace "by an act of consultative will" or after experiencing "unimaginable horrors". It is the highest priority of the Bahá'í community to persuade humanity to follow the first option rather than drift into the second. This task involves making the world aware of Bahá'u'lláh's Plan, and showing that it is practical and comprehensive, that it builds on established religious principles from the past, and is adapted to the very special conditions of the modern world.

Bahá'u'lláh presents a vision to humanity of a future "Golden Age" when all peoples will accept the oneness of religion and will be united by a basic understanding of the purpose of life, which is to grow towards God, or to acquire the qualities of nobility; when the affairs of society will be directed by a democratically elected federal world government; and when the natural and intellectual resources of the world will be used to create an "ever advancing civilization" . This vision He called "The Most Great Peace". The present state of the world precludes early achievement of such a vision. Accordingly, Bahá'u'lláh set forth an interim plan to cover the period between then and now, a plan with several stages, which together He called "The Lesser Peace".

In the first phase of the Lesser Peace, Bahá'u'lláh called upon the nations of the world to agree on fixing their borders and establishing international law, to reduce their armaments, and to establish a system of collective security by means of a confederation of all nations. Together these principles amounted to a call for the end of war between nations, a goal which 'Abdu'l-Bahá later promised could be achieved by the end of the twentieth century. In modern times humanity has indeed moved towards this goal, though with a great deal of anguish along the way. Thus after the wars of the French Revolution and the Napoleonic Empire, the Great Powers of Europe established the Congress System to try and maintain peace by consulting in advance to accommodate the status quo to changing situations; at the end of the 19th century nations met at the Hague, in response to the growing threat of modern weaponry, to establish a peaceful way to settle disputes between nations and to limit use of certain types of weapons; at the end of the First World War there came into being the League of Nations, a first attempt at world confederation with some ambition to provide for collective security; and after the Second World War, the League was replaced by the United Nations, an improved institution, not least because it made provisions for addressing some of the most fundamental causes of international conflict e.g. helping poorer nations to increase the standard of living of their citizens and the setting forth of an Universal Declaration of Human Rights.

Nevertheless, much remains to be done to achieve the basic goals set by Bahá'u'lláh more than a century ago. The end of the Cold War, the third of the great world conflicts of the twentieth century, clearly represents an opportunity to make a further major advance. It is in this context that the Universal House of Justice in *The Promise of World Peace* called upon the peoples of the world to hold a "mighty convocation" to decide on measures to finally establish a permanent peace between nations. Parallels might be drawn with international conferences in 1918 and 1945, and with the environmental Rio Conference of 1992.

In the Bahá'í view the time has now come to collectively eliminate the main causes of conflict in the world, such as racism, "the inordinate disparity between rich and poor", "unbridled nationalism" and "religious strife". A Federal World Government should be established with a Legislature whose members would be elected by the peoples of each nation and confirmed by their respective governments; a Supreme Tribunal with members chosen from amongst candidates selected by the legislatures of the constituent nations, whose decisions would be compulsory and final, and an International Executive, which would have sufficient force to carry out the decisions of the Legislature and the Tribunal. The World Federal Government should establish an international legal system and a true global economy for efficient development of all the world's resources for the benefit of all humanity. Such a global economy should, inter alia, include provision for a system of universal compulsory education, an auxiliary world language, and the total emancipation of women.

The Bahá'í role in this process is clear. First, there is the duty to promote such a vision in the world at large, to stress moral principle, as well as immediate self-interest, in management of global affairs, eg. through the Bahá'í office, with NGO status, at the UN and through the Bahá'í Chair for World Peace at this University. Second, it is to offer the Bahá'í community as a working model of a true world community: to show that the vision is achievable. There are at least three significant aspects to the Bahá'í community model.

● The first is at the individual level: demonstration of ability to become more noble, a key issue as history has shown that just societies require just citizens; they cannot be built by edict alone. We are all aware that this is now a major public concern in nearly all nations as extreme materialism and excessive individualism undermine a sense of civic responsibility. As individuals, Bahá'ís strive not only for the universal qualities taught by all the great religions: truthfulness, honesty, humility, compassion etc, but, most especially in relation to the needs of this time, the conscious abolition of prejudice, appreciation of the benefit of diversity of culture, and the principle that the highest form of worship of God is service for the benefit of others.

● The second is the creation of a new family structure based on the equality of men and women, in which all members of the family have a sense of responsibility for the spiritual and material well-being of all the others. It is in such an environment that a child can best learn to have a positive and loving view of others, a key factor in establishing a peaceful society.

● The third is a new approach to the conduct of community affairs. This includes a hierarchical federal structure, with elected governing bodies at the local community level, the national level, and the global level --- the latter being the Universal House of

Justice, first elected in 1963 and with its seat in Haifa, Israel. It also includes a method of election which precludes electioneering and stresses the need to elect representatives who are distinguished for spiritual principle as well as for administrative skill. Perhaps most important of all is a new approach to community discussion called "consultation". This differs from "democratic debate", in that the emphasis is on universal participation (not just the forceful and powerful), detachment from ego considerations, and a scientific approach to decision making with focus on identifying the objective facts and the spiritual principles that should apply.

An important footnote to the Bahá'í Peace Plan (which may come as a surprise to those preoccupied with the ugly side of America's affairs, domestic and overseas) is the "spiritual destiny" that North America will have in bringing about both the Lesser Peace and the Most Great Peace. Clearly the role has more to do with spiritual inheritance than material strength, important as that may be, and it is interesting to speculate on precisely what it is in the American inheritance that qualifies it for this glorious destiny. One clue may be the statements of 'Abdu'l-Bahá concerning the spiritual insights that will be associated with the Afro-Americans and the Native-Americans. The United States played a leading role in creating the League and the United Nations, and its responsibility now is to give the lead in moving forward from the present semi-confederation of the nations towards a new world federal union.

I should like to finish this very brief review of the Bahá'í Plan for World Peace by mentioning some general considerations which I suggest are worthy of note.

●First, it should be stressed that the Plan is an integral part of the basic teachings of a world religion, not the product of some committee, or political party, or university, or even religious sect. History suggests that this will give it a special power, because religion touches the hearts of people in a way more lasting and more profoundly than other sources of influence.

● Second, its positive but realistic approach gives reason for hope. This is of great practical importance because the prevailing fashion for cynicism, especially amongst educated Westerners, is one of the most formidable barriers standing in the way of progress towards peace. If man is essentially greedy and violent there is no point in trying to make improvements because they are doomed to failure. For example, it has long been fashionable for "experts" to sneer at the concept of a world federal government and even a world police force. If such a force, with direct recruitment and independent financing, were to exist today, we could have avoided the problem of "our boys being killed in other people's wars" and the disgrace of unaccountable national units, supposedly under UN command, abusing the people they were to protect. Events in Bosnia, Somalia, and Haiti for instance could have been very different indeed. In short, experts too often have ridden behind the wave of history, where they are safe but useless, instead of in front where they are needed.

● Third, the Plan offers a vision of where we should and can go. Such a vision is essential for our spiritual well-being:

● Where there is no vision, the people perish"
Proverbs 29:18

It is also necessary for giving a sense of direction and consistency of action. A need for such a long term plan was stressed, for instance, by former Secretary of State, Henry Kissinger, when reviewing the bilateral disarmament negotiations between the United States and the Soviet Union a few years ago. One important aspect of this need for a sense of direction is to accept that ultimately we have to treat all peoples equally (consider, for example, the way we handle the question of nuclear proliferation) if we are to have a society perceived to be just by all, and that it is the only basis for a lasting peace.

These three thoughts are best summarized by the closing sentence of **The Promise of World Peace**, which is a quotation from Bahá'u'lláh:

"Theses fruitless strifes, these ruinous wars shall pass away, and the 'Most Great Peace' shall come".

THE ROLE OF RELIGION IN CREATING A JUST SOCIETY

A presentation at the 10th National Seminar of the Institute of Orissan Culture on "Mahimadharma & Minor Religious Cults", Bhubaneswar, India, 1995

I should like to express my appreciation for the invitation to attend and address this seminar. This is a highlight of my visit with the Bahá'í community of Orissa. I have certainly been impressed by the quality of the discussion this morning and it is most clear that the Institute is providing a valuable service not just for India but for humanity as a whole.

In addressing the subject I have been given, I believe there are two comments that should be made about the issue of "a just society". The first is to do with definition. Historically there have been many dimensions to what people mean by justice, ranging, for instance, from the theme of reward and punishment to modern ideas about minimizing extremes of wealth and poverty. Ultimately, however, I would suggest that all these themes come down to one fundamental idea which is that a just society is one which facilitates and encourages all persons to achieve their full potential, physical, intellectual, and above all, spiritual. The second point is that "justice has always been a major concern in nearly all cultures. Put another way, when there is a perception of extreme injustice, ordinary people are likely to take great risks to express their dissatisfaction to the point of overriding the most basic drive of all life: simple survival. In short, whilst there is evident injustice in society there is likely to be turmoil and therefore it has to be an important issue for all members of society.

In modern times, there has been a strong tendency to see the political system as the main means for reducing the level of injustice in society. Some saw no role for religion and indeed characterized it as part of the problem: "the opium of the people" as Karl Marx put it. Many others, though less extreme, nevertheless saw it's role as been at best marginal: necessary perhaps to provide social stability through long established traditions which people could cling to. Most recently, these assumptions have come under question because of the evident failure of established political systems to meet popular expectations, and in particular the dramatic global collapse of the Marxist model of communism, the most explicitly materialistic and anti-religious political philosophy. Here was a system that promised to deliver a just society and in fact by all accounts ended up creating more injustice than justice.

In taking a second and more open minded position on the possible contribution of religion to the creation of a more just society, thinking people can look to the experience of history. There are at least two aspects to that experience that seem to be relevant to the question at hand. The first is that all of the world's great religions in their different ways, have taught basic universal principles that are conducive, indeed, necessary for a just society eg. the theme of brotherhood, ethical standards around the idea of doing to others as one would want them to do to you, and a motivating vision that someday things will be better: there will be justice and harmony. The second is that religion, far more than politics or philosophy or any other source, has an enormous power to affect peoples behavior, because it speaks with the authority of God rather than mere human beings, and because thereby it reaches the human heart as well as the mind. This is particularly true when religions are young and vibrant, as can be seen by the great civilizations that arose as a response to Hinduism, Buddhism, Zoroastrianism, Judaism, Christianity and Islám. Civilization by definition is about humanity stretching it's collective capacity and thereby moving in the direction of a more just society.

The problem has been that as religious institutions age they lose the pure spirit that came from their Founders, Messengers of God, and they become sources of disunity instead of unity, hatred and violence rather than love and peace, superstition rather than truth ennobling inspiration. The world is divided between several major religions that show little respect for the others and each of these is divided in turn into a multitude of conflicting sects. No wonder that many of the educated leaders of society turned away from religion for so many years. Seen in this perspective, the most that might be hoped of the traditional great religions in contributing to the creation of a just society is marginal: another "constituency" concerned about peace, poverty, human rights, the environment, etc.

What I should like to suggest to you today is another alternative to this tired, world weary point of view, and that is the promise that is held out by a new and vibrant Faith -- that of the Bahá'ís. Before I go any further I should observe, as we are at a seminar on religious cults, that the Bahá'í Faith is not a cult ie. a sect of some established religion, but an independent world religion, founded by Bahá'u'lláh, Who claimed to be a Messenger of God, in the same way as did Jesus and Muhammad, for instance, which has indigent followers from just about every land on earth and from every religious, ethnic and class background. The **Encyclopedia Britannica** has identified it as the second most widely spread world religion -- after Christianity. The reason I make this suggestion, is that the Bahá'í Faith is apparently free of the decadent characteristics of old religions and has certain key qualities that suggest that it can play a major role in taking humanity to a just society. I should like to complete my presentation by briefly mentioning a few of these qualities.

The first is it's credibility from the point of view of a thinking person. For instance, it puts great emphasis on intellectual integrity, seeking for the truth for ourselves, asking questions (a quality of God) especially about conventional wisdom coming from sources with a vested interest in it, e.g. priests or a political party. It recognizes explicitly that religion and science are two wings of the truth of existence and that when they are out of balance humanity suffers superstition (when science is weak) or immorality (when religion is weak). When they are in conflict it is probable that it is religion that is in the wrong. Finally, Bahá'u'lláh taught that the Founders of the Great Religions are all from God and should be equally revered, that they all teach the same universal verities, and that differences are to do with (i) temporary teachings to meet needs at particular times in history, and (ii) the corruption that comes when religions age and lose their original spirit. These themes clearly are relevant in terms of the struggle to achieve the just society because that ultimately must be based on truth and spiritual unity.

The second quality that is relevant to our subject is a restatement of universal ethical principles which are explicit on key aspects of a global society. Thus the Bahá'í Faith puts great emphasis on such principles as conscious abolition of prejudice and appreciation of the diversity of cultures, both refinements of the universal principle of love they neighbor, common to all religions, which are necessary in an increasingly close knit society, and on the equality of man and women, an absolute necessity if women are to be able to achieve their full potential. Service and care for our fellows is greatly encouraged as being the highest form of worship of God: what counts is good deeds not simply praying in the temple.

The third aspect of the Bahá'í Teachings I should like to draw to your attention are those to do with managing community affairs in a just manner. Though the democratic national state is generally more just than authoritarian empire it clearly has many deficiencies even in the most mature examples. There are at least three major differences between Bahá'í practice and democracy that are relevant to our theme. The first is the community structure which consists of democratically elected assemblies at the local, national and world levels. In short, the interest of all humanity has priority over parochial interest, and decisions are made collectively, not by the individual leader (in the case of the world body, known as the Universal House of Justice, the chair, which basically is limited to a coordinating function, is rotated regularly so as to avoid any suggestion of individual leadership). In electing members of these ruling bodies Bahá'ís are enjoined to take account of such spiritual qualities as service and detachment, as well as administrative skills. Electioneering and formation of parties or cliques is strictly forbidden. Community affairs are conducted on the basis of consultation rather than democratic debate with its emphasis on adversary discussion, winners and losers, rhetoric and demagoguery. Consultation differs from debate in three vital ways. First, the emphasis is on universal participation including those who are so often not heard from in democracy: the poor, minorities, and women. This is not simply a matter of fairness, it is essential for arriving at the truth by hearing from the experience of all, including those who are not shielded from the harsh realities of life. Second, Bahá'ís are taught the spiritual quality of detachment so that an issue can be discussed objectively without individuals feeling a need to defend at all costs their suggestion as a matter of ego and self worth. Third, there is emphasis on an orderly, scientific procedure: identifying in sequence the problem, the principle that is relevant, consideration of alternatives, decision, and means for review of action after it has been implemented. How rarely this procedure alone happens in debate!

A fourth aspect of the Bahá'í teachings which seems to be relevant is a very clear vision of where humanity has come from, where we are, and where we are going. History is about humanity's spiritual evolution: about the struggle as individuals to become noble beings, and collectively to create an ever advancing civilization -- the twin purposes of life. Like an individual, humanity has grown from infancy, through childhood, and at present is in the process of moving from adolescence, a turbulent time when we have typically great physical strength but little experience and wisdom, into maturity when the latter qualities are acquired. Adolescence might be considered to be modern times when humanity has acquire great physical prowess from science and the Industrial Revolution, and maturity is when we learn to live, globally, in peace and harmony, as a matter of survival as well further advancement. In the early stages of peace (the Lesser Peace in Bahá'í terminology), the main issue is to end the practice of war, the most terrible instrument of injustice, but gradually the objective will be to achieve full spiritual unity and peace based on justice. The process involves the maturation of international organizations into a world federal democracy, the unification of the peoples of the world by such means as an auxiliary world language, and the establishment of a just economic system which combines the best of the socialist idea of equality with the best of the capitalist idea of freedom by infusion of the spiritual dimension. Such a vision helps humanity understand present turmoils and at the same time provides the hope that gives strength to commitment in working with others to create the just society. That this is not simply an idle dream is shown by the model of the global Bahá'í community which for more than a hundred year's has been working to show that these things are possible if we follow those key exhortations of Bahá'u'lláh:

"The Earth is But One Country"[1].

"The Best Beloved Thing in My Sight is Justice"[2].

NOTES

1. *Gleanings,* p 249.
2. *Hidden Words*, (Arabic), No. 2.

RENEWING SOCIETY'S BASIC BUILDING BLOC : MARRIAGE

Presentation at the Bahá'í School, McLean, Virginia, U.S.A. 1994

I. THE GLOBAL EXPERIENCE

1. Marriage is one of the oldest and most essential institutions of civilization. For most individuals it is the most important life relationship. At the animal or material level, social scientists say, marriage represents a pact between male and female with regard to propagation of the species, a physical drive second only to the will to survive—indeed, in a sense it is an extension of the survival imperative. This explains the immense power of sex in our lives. Historically, for a woman marriage is an institution which ties to her a man who will provide protection for her and her child particularly during the time when she carries extraordinary burdens e.g. during pregnancy and nursing. Her side of the pact has always been that marriage would assure the male that his seed is carried into the next generation by her children[1].

2. The best guarantee of the interest of both parties is monogamy as shown in the behaviour of many animals and in traditional folk stories, which often portray step-parents as less willing to play a fully protective role for children that are not their own[2]. Nevertheless, in history monogamy is only one of

several models of marriage which also include variations on polygamy, concubinage, temporary marriage, etc. These alternatives usually arise when there are unequal relationships between men and women, ie. typically where the male manages to have his "cake and eat it too". Of course, there are other factors as well, such as a significantly shorter average life expectancy for men during times of constant warfare, which leads to an imbalance in the population between males and females and a situation where it may well be in the interest of all to have male centered polygamy. Concubinage and temporary marriage are justified on the grounds that they help to regulate the male sex drive and reduce the social risks associated with free-for-all promiscuity.

3. A major aspect of the propagation instinct, of course, is the common desire to mate with a strong partner, physically and intellectually, so as to increase the chances of survival of the resulting offspring. One clear indicator of such strength and capacity is wealth. Another is physical beauty which is often associated with a balanced physique, absence of disease, and cultural refinement and "education". It is not surprising therefore that physical beauty is such a major element in sexual attraction, sometimes at the cost of other qualities that rationally would seem to be of equal or greater importance in ensuring the wellbeing of the future child and the marriage partnership e.g. such qualities as loyalty and kindness.

4. Because the marriage bond creates a long term relationship between the individual male and female, and between parents and children, it has implications of stability, and associated prosperity and advancement for society as a whole. As a result, in addition to the male and female immediately involved, other "constituencies" have a major interest in

supporting the marriage institution.

5. Thus the parents and family of the two parties have an interest, partly because of the propagation drive, once removed, and partly because of its relationship to disposal of accumulated wealth between generations. The family, with its different perspective will typically tend to play down the "physical" attraction factor and put greater emphasis on other aspects such as family background and alliances, as well as perhaps a more objective assessment of other vital qualities of character.

6. The state, representing society as a whole, also has a major interest in protecting the marriage institution because of its role in ensuring the physical safety of the next generation while still young and defenceless, as well as its role in bringing up children in a caring environment so that they in turn have a cooperative attitude towards others when they grow up. Hence the state traditionally has provided laws that uphold and support the marriage bond. This perspective is also reflected in the very common high social value given to protection of women and children as in Western codes of chivalry and the "Titanic" principle at sea of "women and children first".

7. Finally, and most important, religious institutions in all cultures typically give strong support for the marriage bond because of its relationship to the act of creation, the birth of a new human being, and its strong interest in the moral education of the new being. As such, religion adds a vital spiritual dimension to the institution and lifts it to a higher level of civilization than a simple business contract. This partly accounts for the phenomenon, in our own time, of non religious people often wanting to have a religious marriage ceremony. Religion usually makes at least two contributions to the strengthening of the marriage institution. First, is a solemn wedding

ceremony giving public blessing and a sense of holiness to the particular marriage. Secondly, there are normally teachings that uphold the institution especially against the temptations of the flesh—sexual promiscuity and such related activities as prostitution, masturbation, homosexuality, pedophilia, bestiality and so on.

8. Such supportive factors have helped to make marriage a basic and lasting institution of civilization and have kept within bounds human drives and failings which tend to weaken it. Society has long been familiar with such causes of conflict in marriage as the "wandering eye" of the male, a tendency to want promiscuous sex and to spread his seed even when he has the apparent security of the marriage bond; male violence when frustrated by a woman's traditional superiority, and sometimes devious skills, in verbal battle and in marshalling women allies to her point of view; the argument between advocates of thrift and free spending; differences over how to raise the children, with the father generally standing for discipline and the mother for compassion; and excessive and disruptive intervention by relations, including, of course, the "music hall" mother-in-law. Statistics in the United States show consistency over the years in the leading causes of divorce: first, money, second, absence of affection and sexual problems, third, raising of children, and fourth the family-in-law. In about one third of divorces, such factors are aggravated by alcohol which in turn is associated with much domestic violence.

9. The general stability of the institution has, of course, varied over time and between cultures. In recent times, it is generally recognised that there has been quite a significant world wide decline in the institution particularly in the West. There has been a massive increase in the number of divorces with a rate

of some 50 percent of all marriages in some countries. At the same time there has been an upsurge in the practice of casual sexual relationships leading to vast numbers of illegitimate children who, in effect, never have a father[3]. Whilst religious bodies have generally expressed dismay at this trend, and there have been cries of outrage from social conservatives[4], many who considered themselves progressive and rational, including the women's movement, argued that it represented liberation for women[5] and a more natural and less hypocritical approach to sexual relations. The coming of more effective contraceptives made the latter position more practical for a much broader range of society.

10. However, most recently the general breakdown in respect for all institutions and the resulting weakening of public law and order has prompted some rethinking of this and related issues[6]. There now seems to be a convergence of opinion in the direction of a need to revitalise the marriage institution. It is recognized that too often divorce and single parenthood leads to poverty for women and children, that casual sex leads to the spread of dangerous sexual diseases, and that children of such arrangements tend to be less successful in life and to have an increased tendency to deliquency. In extreme cases, children survive from an early age in social anarchy where there are few models of ethical standards: no father figure and a mother who is young and untrained and who sees a baby as her one chance for self esteem and achievement. Such children quickly come to have a view of life where there is low expectation of survival and no remorse in hurting others if that in anyway is required to gain even temporary or minor material advantage[7]. The cycle of instability becomes a self perpetuating process. Even the father, apparently getting a free pass and with little

responsibility for his own action, ends up lonely and, as studies have shown, experiencing reduced quality of health and shorter life expectancy[8].

11. Solutions proposed to deal with the problem and make marriages more stable and lasting include (i) the state reforming the welfare system so as to reduce the climate of social dependency and lack of responsibility with regard to sexual relations and procreation; (ii) voluntary organizations providing role models such as a "big brother"; and (iii) religious institutions encouraging young girls to take pride in "chastity", young people to take pre-marital classes, engaged couples to sign pre nuptial contracts of fidelity, and married couples in conflict to take counselling.

12. These ideas are clearly useful, but experience shows that they are not enough and that some more fundamental solutions are needed: a new model of marriage that responds to the needs and challenges of modern society. There is evidence, it is submitted, that this is provided most systematically and effectively in the teachings of the Bahá'í Faith. Accordingly, the remainder of this presentation is to be focussed on (i) a brief overview of the Bahá'í model; (ii) what this means in terms of finding a marriage partner; and (iii) what it means in terms of preserving and nurturing marriage.

II. THE BAHÁ'Í MODEL

Introduction

13. *Authority.* In making this presentation reference is made to authorative statements on the Bahá'í teachings by (i) Baha'u'lláh (1817-1892), the Founder of the Bahá'í Faith; (ii) 'Abdu'l-Bahá (1844-1921), Bahá'u'lláh's eldest son who was his successor

as leader of the Bahá'í Community and who was designated by his father the Bahá'ís' "Exemplar", (iii) Shoghi Effendi Rabbani (1896-1957), 'Abdu'l-Bahá's grandson and Guardian (leader) of the community after the latter's passing; and (iv) the Universal House of Justice, since 1963 the supreme body of the Bahá'í World Community, which is elected every five years.

14. ***Impact of Materialism.*** The Bahá'í approach to marriage should be seen in the context of the view that a critical problem for society today is the decline of religion and a growing obsession with material things:

"If carried to excess, civilization will prove as prolific a source of evil as it had been of goodness when kept within the restraints of moderation."

Bahá'u'lláh[9]

"A world dimmed by the steadily dying light of religion...enervated by a rampant and brutal materialism; disintergrating through the corrosive influence of mortal and spiritual decadence."

Shoghi Effendi[10]

With such a culture, there is a tendency for the short term perspective of "to live today, for tomorrow we die', and a diminished willingness to make sacrifice for the greater good and for moral principle. Put another way, it produces a growing selfishness, especially when materialism is combined with excessive individualism. This process is seen as a key element in the marriage crisis[11].

15. ***Basic Themes.*** Perhaps one of the most useful ways of discussing the Bahá'í marriage model is to make an analysis around three basic themes: (i) its purpose; (ii) its distinctive character; and (iii) its requirements...

Purpose of Marriage

16. ***Fortress of Wellbeing.*** The Bahá'í teachings

and laws on marriage, like all its other teachings and laws, are to promote the wellbing of humanity and provide for its protection. As such they are rational and consistent.

"He established the Law of Marriage, made it a Fortress for wellbeing and Salvation...

Bahá'u'lláh[12]

Within this general concept, it is possible to identify four specific purposes: two with regard to the material aspects of marriage and two with regard to the spiritual.

17. **Material Purposes of Marriage.** The Bahá'í Teachings reaffirm the importance of the material aspect of marriage. Its basic purpose is to provide an orderly framework (i) for the creation and raising of *children* and (ii) for *accommodation of the natural sex drive* of both men and women[13].

"Thou hast enjoined marriage upon the peoples, that generations of men may succeed one another in this contingent world..."

'Abdu'l-Bahá[14]

"The proper use of the sex instinct is the natural right of every individual, and it is precisely for this very purpose that the institution of marriage has been established."

Shoghi Effendi[15]

18. **Spiritual Purposes of Marriage.** However, the Bahá'í Faith, like other religions, teaches that marriage has a spiritual dimension and it is this that ultimately gives it lasting strength and significance.

"The union must be a true relationship, a spiritual coming together as well as a physical one, so that through out every phase of life, and in all the worlds of God, their union will endure."

'Abdu'l Bahá[16]

The Bahá'í view is that marriage has two broad spiritual purposes which, in turn, link with the general purposes of life. Bahá'u'lláh, like all the F ounders of the world's great religions, said that our first purpose in life is to develop the spiritual side of our nature, to become noble beings, to grow toward God. In other words, our short time on earth is to prepare for our spiritual life after the physical death, just as the embryo in the womb acquires the physical faculties that it will need when it is born into the world.

"The purpose of God in creating man hath been, and will ever be, to enable him to know his Creator and to attain His presence."

Bahá'u'lláh[17]

"...one must remember that the purpose of life is to prepare the soul for the next."

Universal House of Justice[18]

Following this theme in the marriage context, each marriage partner has responsibility not only to develop his/her own spiritual qualities but to support his/her partner in doing the same, and most important in nurturing the spiritual development of their children.

"Husband and wife should be united both physically and spiritually that they may ever improve the spiritual life of each other."

'Abdu'l-Bahá[19]

"Marry, O People, that from you may appear he who will remember Me amongst My servants".

Bahá'u'lláh[20]

"A Bahá'í child must be trained according to the moral precepts of Bahá'u'lláh"

'Abdu'l-Bahá[21]

The Bahá'í Faith teaches that the second purpose in life for every human being is to contribute to the spiritual well being of society as a whole and the advancement of civilization[22]:

"All men have been created to carry forward an ever advancing civilization."

Bahá'u'lláh[23]

In pursuit of this second purpose of life, marriage partners have a unique contribution, which is to make their home a center of unity and enlightenment:

"My home is the home of peace. My home is the home of joy and delight. My home is the home of laughter and exaltation. . .This is the home of light; whoever enters here must be illumined"

'Abdu'l-Bahá[24]

Bahá'í literature stresses that such a goal embraces most particularly such matters as raising children to be free of all prejudice and the creation of unity in the extended family.

"If love and agreement are manifest in a single family, that family will advance, become illuminated and spiritual... when love is realized... the whole human race will be uplifted, the world will continually grow more spiritual and radiant and the happiness and tranquility of mankind be immeasurbly increased".

'Abdu'l-Bahá[25]

Distinctive Characteristics

19. *Sacredness and Equality.* With such purposes a marriage acquires two distinctive characteristics: (i) it is eternal and sacred, and (ii) it is based on the equality of men and women.

20. *Marriage Eternal and Sacred.* As spiritual development is a preparation for the spiritual life after the end of the physical life, marriage becomes in effect an eternal relationship.

"Know thou that the commnand of marriage is eternal... this is a Divine Institution."

'Abdu'l-Bahá[26]

"Their purpose must be this: To become loving companions and comrades and at one with each other for time and eternity"

'Abdu'l-Bahá[27]

It also follows from its role in promoting advancement towards God, that it is a *holy* or *sacred institution,* worthy of the utmost commitment and sacrifice.

"Marriage is in the the Aqdas set forth as a most sacred and binding tie.

Bahá'u'lláh[28]

21. **Marriage based on Gender Equality.** The equality of men and women is one of the fundamental principles of the Bahá'í Faith and is one aspect of the theme that humanity has now reached the stage in its spiritual evolution of moving from adolescence to maturity.

"The world of humanity is posssessed of two wings-the male and the female. So long as these two wings are not equivalent in strength the bird will not fly. Until womankind reaches the same degree as men, until she enjoys the same arena of activity, extraordinary attainments for humanity will not be realised, humanity cannot wing its way to heights of real attainment... happiness of mankind will be realised when women and men coordinate and advance equally, for each is the complement and helpmate to the other."

'Abdu'l-Bahá[29]

"The denial of such equality perpetuates an injustice against half of the world's population and promotes in men harmful attitudes and habits that are carried from the family to the work place, to political life, and ultimately to international relations. There are no grounds, moral, practical or biological, upon which such denial can be justified."

Universal House of Justice[30]

This principle clearly has major implications for the marriage institution. It also means that the Bahá'í marriage is a new and distinctive model, not a return to the old authoritarian and male dominated model which has prevailed throughout most of history and which has been failing, especially since the middle of the twentieth century[31].

22. ***Complementary Roles of Marriage Partners.*** It is important to add that equality of the sexes does not necessarily mean that they should both have the same, totally interchangeable functions. Marriage is a partnership, not a competition, and should be flexible enough to allow for some complementary as well as some identical contributions to the wellbeing of the family. Clearly, the wife has special responsibilities with regard to carrying and nursing of a new child, and in the Bahá'í Writings the mother is recognised as having a special role in the early moral education of an infant.

"The mother is the first teacher of the child...it is she who establisheth the character and conduct of the child"

'Abdu'l-Bahá[32]

It is for this reason that Bahá'í teachings give priority to the education of a girl over a boy, if a choice has to be made.

"Furthermore, the education of woman is more necessary and important than that of man, for woman is the trainer of the child in its infancy."

Universal House of Justice[33]

At the same time, the father has responsibilty for providing for the later education of the child.

"Unto every father hath been enjoined the instruction of his son and daughter in the arts of reading and writing and in all that hath been laid down in the Holy Tablet"

Bahá'u'lláh[34]

This has bearing on financial responsibilites in the family. The Bahá'í teachings make it clear that women should have equal opportunity to contribute to the material prosperity of the family:

"In the Tablet of the World, Bahá'u'lláh Himself has

envisaged that women as well as men would be breadwinners... a very important element in the attainment of such equality is Bahá'u'lláh's provision that boys and girls must follow essentially the same curriculum in schools"

Universal House of Justice[35]

Nevertheless, if choices have to be made because of family circumstances, it is clear that the ultimate responsibility for providing necessary income is that of the husband[36]:

"This principle of the husband's responsibilty to provide for the family can be seen applied also in the law of interstacy which provides that the family's dwelling passes, on the father's death, not to his widow, but to his eldest son; the son at the same time has responsibility to care for his mother."

Universal House of Justice[37]

The Requirements of Bahá'í Marriage

23. *Five Requirements.* As mentioned earlier, Bahá'í Writings identify this time as one when humanity, simply in order to survive and carry forward civilization, is growing from adolescence to maturity, a process that includes achieving unity in peace and justice at the global level. This has implications for the institution of marriage, in particular, because it is the basic building bloc of civilization, the place where young children most naturally acquire attitudes of love and compassion towards others, attitudes that are essential for the unity of humanity. Bahá'í Writings identify at least *five requirements* for a marriage model so that it may carry out its mission effectively: monogamy; a minimum age; parental consent; a marriage vow; and appointed witnesses to the ceremony. Some of these requirements may seem self evident in modern society, but it should be remembered, that these principles are

for all humanity, including less advanced societies which have different practices. Accordingly, it is appropriate to have a quite explicit statement of all requirements without omission on account of assumptions on the part of some.

24. ***Monogamy.*** First, marriage is between one man and one woman, as this is the most equitable model and other models can no longer be justified in the modern world.

"Bigamy is conditioned on justice, and justice is impossible, it follows that bigamy is not permissable, and monogamy alone should be practiced."

'Abdu'l-Bahá[38]

It should be added, in passing that if a Bahá'í already has more than one spouse, prior to becoming a Bahá'í, then he/she may continue this arrangement as a Bahá'í, but, not of course, add to the number thereafter! It might be further added that the Bahá'í Faith is the first religion to specify monogamy in its basic marriage teaching, though, of course, this is now the general practice in many parts of the world.

25. ***Minimum Age for Marriage.*** Second, the partners must be adult, ie. age 15 or over, both as a matter of physical well being and so that they are mature enough to understand the commitment they are making. The main purpose of this law is to prohibit child marriages, still the practice in some cultures.

"Marriage is conditioned upon both parties having attained the age of maturity which is fixed at fifteen."

Bahá'u'lláh[39]

Westerners used to a minimum age of 16 to 18 and a general practice of actually marrying at about 25 to 30, may find a minimum age of 15 to be on the young side. However, the Bahá'í view is that this will become increasingly feasible in the future as a more civil society facilitates closer synchronization of spiritual

and physical maturity in young people. Bahá'í
teachings put great emphasis on early spiritual
education when peoples' characters are still adaptable
and before they become more rigid and resistant to
new influences. Early marriage is seen as a protection
for society, in principle, because it gives a legitimate
outlet for the sex drive when it is at a peak of
intensity.

"...the Bahá'í youth...should be advised, nay
encouraged, to consider marriage while still young and
in full possession of their physical vigour. Economic
factors, no doubt are often a serious hindrance to
early marriage, but in most cases only an excuse, and
as such should not be overstressed."

Shoghi Effendi[40]

This theme is closely linked to chastity, both before
and after marriage which is discussed later in
connection with the topic of finding the right partner.

"Chastity implies both before and after marriage
an unsullied, chaste sex life. Before marriage
absolutely chaste, after marriage absolutely faithful
to one's chosen companion. Faithful in all sexual acts,
faithful in word and deed."

Shoghi Effendi[41]

Early marriage also has the advantage that the
characters of the two partners would have had less
time to have become rigid in their habits and thereby
more difficult to adjust to the circumstance of living
in close harmony with the other.

26. **Parental Consent.** Thirdly, though the
marriage should be based on the wishes of the couple
involved, it should also have the consent of all
biological parents. This principle combines the
practice of modern romantic courtship, on the one
hand, and the widespread tradition in many cultures
of the parents choosing the marriage partners, on the
other hand. It serves to create family unity and to

reinforce assurance that the proposed marriage has characteristics that will help it last.

"...first thou must choose one who is pleasing to thee, and then this matter is subject to the consent of the father and mother. Before your selection they have no right of interference."

'Abdu'l-Bahá[42]

"Bahá'u'lláh has clearly stated the consent of all living parents is required for Bahá'í marriage. This applies whether parents are Bahá'ís or non-Bahá'ís, divorced for years or not."

Shoghi Effendi[43]

"Bahá'u'lláh has stated that the consent of the parents of both parties is required in order to promote unity and avoid friction..."

Shoghi Effendi[44]

Thus giving consent is seen as a weighty parental responsibilty:

"When parents are Bahá'ís they should, of course, act objectively in withholding or granting their approval. They cannot evade this responsibility by merely acquiesing in their child's wishes."

Shoghi Effendi[45]

Sometimes this principle will cause heartache for a couple if consent is withheld unjustly, but if they are genuinely committed to each other and demonstrate this in a loving manner over time and through thick and thin, parents will normally be impressed and give their consent. The chances are that the marriage will be that much stronger after the partners have survived such a test.

27. ***Marriage Vow.*** Fourth, the key point in the Bahá'í marriage ceremony[46] - the marriage vow-emphasises that a marriage has a third, reinforcing, dimension, the relationship of the couple to God; a relationship which means obedience to His Will—His laws for this Age as revealed by Bahá'u'lláh.

"It is incumbent upon both parties to recite a specifically revealed verse... "We will all, verily, abide by the will of God."

Bahá'u'lláh[47]

28. ***Appointed Witnesses to the Marriage.*** Fifth, in recognition of the fact that a marriage is a matter of concern for society as a whole, as well as for the couple and their families, the Bahá'í teachings require that there be authorized witnesses to the ceremony who are charged with making sure that all the conditions of Bahá'í marriage, as just described, have been properly observed.

"These two witnesses may be chosen by the couple or by the Spiritual Assembly, but must in any case be acceptable to the Assembly."

Universal House of Justice[48]

The Model: Impact and Implementation

29. ***Impact on Marriage Partners.*** The significance of these Bahá'í concepts of marriage (its purposes, distinctive character, and requirements) is that they strongly encourage marriage partners to view their relationship as something that has to be preserved and nourished as a matter of the first priority. For those who accept such values, terminating a marriage when tests and difficulties come is simply out of the question. The only issue is how best to work together to triumph over them. Nevertheless, it is important to add that the Bahá'í Faith with its emphasis on realism and compassion for the human condition, does recognize that there will be occasions, especially in this age of turbulence and if the Bahá'í teachings have not been followed, when a marriage will become irredeemably broken. In such cases provision is made for divorce as described at the end of section IV.

30. ***Implementation of the Model.*** I should now

like to address briefly two broad issues about making the Bahá'í model a reality. The first issue, which is discussed in Section III is the process of choosing a marriage partner, the single most important aspect of placing a marriage on a sound footing. The second is the issue of how best to preserve and nourish marriage once it is consummated, and this is discussed in Section IV.

III. CHOOSING A MARRIAGE PARTNER

31. ***An Alternative to Choice on the Basis of Romance or Family Decision.*** The importance for the well being of a marriage of choosing the right partner is self evident. The question is how does one set about making such a choice? In the modern romantic culture of the West, it is largely based on physical beauty, admiration for some capacity, such as intelligence or education, or simply charm and social gregariousness. Whilst immediate attraction of this sort may well be useful for a marriage, it can also be deceptive, either because it is based on temporary factors, such as physical beauty, or because it blinds or distracts from the deeper flaws of character which can undermine the long term sexual and parenting relationship of marriage. In the East and in agricultural societies, on the otherhand, it has been the practice for marriage to be based on choice by families, sometimes without the two persons primarily involved seeing each other before the marriage ceremony. Though sometimes comparatively successful[49], this practice has obvious dangers, and in anycase it is not likely to last as living standards and education levels rise, and young people insist on making their own decisions. The Bahá'í model represents a third approach.

32. ***Four Aspects to the Bahá'í Approach.*** There

are at least four important aspects to the Bahá'í
approach to the task of finding a suitable marriage
partner. The first is to take time to get to know the
character of the prospective partner. The second is to
identify characteristics which are generally conducive
to a long lasting and successful marriage. The third,
closely linked to the second, is to focus on
compatibility of the potential marriage partners. The
fourth is the role of love. All these issues are relevent
to Bahá'ís and non Bahá'ís alike.

**Thoroughly Knowing, before Marriage, the
Character of Yourself and Your Partner.**

33. *The Goal.* Partners getting to know each other
thoroughly before marriage may seem an obvious
thing to do for a rational person, but it has not been
the normal procedure in either Western "Romantic"
practice or in the Eastern practice of choice by family.
Hence this point, together with the related advice of
not "rushing to judgement", is given strong emphasis
in the Bahá'í community:

"a couple should study each other's character and
spend time getting to know each other before they
decide to marry, and when they do marry it should
be with the intention of establishing an eternal bond."

Universal House of Justice[50]

"...but concerning thy marriage with the maid
servant of God...do not be in a hurry"

'Abdu'l-Bahá[51]

The task of getting to know the character of the
prospective partner has to be linked to knowing
oneself. This is necessary both so as to help learn
what would be needed from a partner and so as to
find what changes oneself needs to make in order to
become a successful marriage partner.

"....man should know his own self, and recognize
that which leadeth unto loftiness, glory or abasement,

wealth or poverty."

Bahá'u'lláh[52]

34. ***How to Achieve that Goal.*** One effective way to get to know the character of a prospective marriage partner is through consultation as discussed later. Another important way, which is often overlooked, is to observe him or her in a wide variety of situations involving many other people.

"Ways of learning about these qualities of character include working together on Bahá'í or other projects, evaluating his/her job record, observing how he/she relates to family and friends, noticing how he/she behaves around children, and examining attitudes about money."

National Spiritual Assembly of Canada[53]

Courtship in the open and the company of others also has the virtue that it reduces the pressure to give way to sexual passion which occurs so often when a couple conducts a romantic courtship in isolation.

35. ***The Families.*** Experience suggests the particular wisdom of getting to know all about the family of the prospective partner, simply because the family has such an impact on the experience and development of any person. It is common, for instance, for a woman to be heavily influenced by her mother because of the intimate relationship that they typically have, whilst for men there is often either a rivalry or near worship on the part of the son. A prospective partner who comes from a broken or dysfunctional home may well have suffered and had his or her character deeply affected, for better or for worse, by this experience. Studies show that the vast majority of criminals come from dysfunctional homes. A history of violence in a family should be a particular cause for caution especially for a women considering a partner from such a backgound. Care should also be taken when considering marriage into a family of an

entirely different culture to have a clear understanding
of the expectations and likely consequences. A good
example of what can happen when this is overlooked
was shown in the movie *Not without my Daughter*
about an American woman of liberal "Christian"
background marrying an apparently Westernized
Iranian and then having to live with him in a very
traditional Muslim family in Irán[54]. As noted earlier,
problems with the extended family is one of the four
leading causes of divorce in the United States.

36. *Friends.* Of great wisdom too is the advice in
the above quotation, with regard to getting to know a
prospective marriage partner, of the importance of
finding out who are his/her friends. In the Bahá'í
Writings we are enjoined to associate with people of
all backgrounds:

"Wherefore, O my loving friends! Consort with the
all the peoples, kindreds and religions of the world
with the utmost truthfulness, faithfulness, kindliness,
goodwill and friendliness"

'Abdu'l-Bahá[55]

At the same time, we are advised to avoid those who
are of bad character who can drag us down. If a
potential marriage partner keeps bad company,
common sense suggests much caution:

"The company of the ungodly increaseth sorrow,
whilst fellowship with the righteous cleanseth the rust
from the heart"

Bahá'u'lláh[56]

Characteristics Conducive to a Successful Marriage
37. *Six Qualities.* There are some broad character
qualities that are universally conducive to creation of
a good marriage, and that a wise person would try to
cultivate in him/her self and to find in the prospective
partner. These qualities are essentially about being
mature: emotionally, intellectually, and spiritually.

There are at least six groups of qualities that fall into this category: (i) loyalty and sexual fidelity; (ii) trustworthiness; (iii) reliability and ability to handle tests and difficulties; (iv) kindness and compassion; (v) being just and fairminded; and (vi) willingness to consult as a way of conducting family life.

38. ***Loyalty and Sexual Fidelity.*** Loyalty is fundamental to a life long relationship; a person who is not mature enough to value loyalty as a necessary qualification for marriage is going to put immense stress on a partnership and hold it back from achieving its full potential.

"The bond that unites hearts most perfectly is *loyalty*. True lovers once united must show forth the utmost faithfulness one to another."

'Abdu'l-Bahá[57]

As marriage is, at the most basic level, a sexual relationship and a parenting partnership the most elementary aspect of marital loyalty is sexual fidelity or chastity within the marriage. Throughout history marriages have coexisted with spouses resorting to prostitutes and mistresses on the side, and in recent times social liberals have promoted the benefits of "open marriage". However, such activity is not in accord with the Bahá'í concept of the basic material and spiritual purposes of marriage.

"A *chaste* and holy life must be the controlling principle in the behaviour and conduct of all Bahá'ís, both in their social relations with the members of their own community and in their contact with the world at large."

Shoghi Effendi[58]

"Bahá'u'lláh says adultery retards the progress of the soul in the after life"

Shoghi Effendi[59]

39. ***Trustworthiness.*** This quality is close to loyalty but a separate and absolutely necessary

support of it. Not to be trustworthy will undermine
any relationship no matter how loyal the person
concerned may be:

"The most precious of all things in the estimation
of Him Who is the Sovereign of Truth is
trustworthiness"

Bahá'u'lláh[60]

When there is absence of trust in marriage, there are
likely to be one or two dehilibating consequences: a
self defence hard shell of indifference to the marriage
partner, or when lack of trust pertains to relationships
with others, seen as rivals for the partner's affections,
deep feelings of jealousy, one of the most distructive
of all emotions:

"*Jealousy* consumeth the body and *anger* doth
burn the liver; avoid these two as you would a lion"

Bahá'u'lláh[61]

Trustworthiness embraces at least four related
qualities: *truthfulness, honesty, sincerity and integrity*.

"*Truthfulness* is the foundation of all the virtues
of humanity; without truthfulness progress and
success in all the worlds of God are impossible for
the soul"

'Abdu'l-Bahá[62]

"..enjoineth on you *honesty* and piety. Blessed the
city that shineth by their light. Through them man is
exalted"

'Abdu'l-Bahá[63]

"...*sincerity* is the foundation-stone of faith"

'Abdu'l-Bahá[64]

"You must demonstrate, by your high moral
standards, your courtesy, your *integrity* and nobility
that our Faith is not one of words but truly changes
the hearts and conduct of its adherents."

Shoghi Effendi[65]

An important quality that straddles truthfulness and
honesty is straightforwardness and openess: no

dissimulation, deviousness, and secretiveness, character defects which are, unfortunately only too common in many cultures. Integrity implies most importantly standing up for what is right and ethical and the courage to resist pressure to yield on such matters.

40. ***Reliability and Ability to Handle Tests and Difficulties.*** This issue of strength of character leads on to the third desirable, not to say essential, quality in a life time marital partner, and that is reliability. This term can cover a whole range of behaviour from relatively minor matters, like been timely, to the more important issue of keeping promises or one's word. Most important of all is the ability to handle the inevitable tests that any marriage and family will encounter in the normal course of life.

"Anyone can be happy in the state of comfort, ease, health, success, pleasure and joy; but if one will be happy in the time of trouble, hardship and prevailing disease, it is proof of nobility"

'Abdu'l-Bahá[66]

One important aspect of reliability is attitude to *money.* A partner who is a spendthrift is not going to be reliable and will cause a lot of anxiety. On the otherhand, meanness can also be a major cause of unhappiness and conflict in a marriage, and may result in lack of financial support in time of need. Reliability with regard to money is to follow the golden mean: to combine responsibility with generosity.

"We are asked to give what we have, not what we do not possess, especially if such act causes suffering to others".

'Abdu'l-Bahá[67]

Closely linked to the money issue with regard to reliability is whether or not the potential partner is a *hardworking* person, who, particularly in the case of the husband, can be relied upon to make every effort to meet his responsibility as the ultimate breadwinner[68]. Extreme caution should be observed, as a matter of commonsense, if the potential spouse is lazy:

"Waste not your time in idleness and indolence, and occupy yourself with that which will profit yourself and others"

Bahá'u'lláh[69]

Another indicator of likely future reliability as a marriage partner is whether or not he/she uses *alcohol and drugs*. As noted earlier, alcohol alone is a contributing factor in one third of all divorces in the United States. It is often associated with waste of family income, promiscuity, and violence. The Bahá'í teachings are very clear on the dangers that are involved with alcohol and drugs.

"Alcohol consumeth the mind and causeth man to commit acts of absurdity, but..this wicked hashish extinguisheth the mind, freeth the spirit, petrifieth the soul, wasteth the body and leaveth man frustrated and lost"

'Abdu'l-Bahá[70]

"...the use of alcohol drinks and drugs have been explicitly forbidden in the Kitáb-i-Aqdas (The Book of Laws)"

Shoghi Effendi[71]

41. **Kindness and Compassion.** Perhaps as important as loyalty and reliability in contributing to the well-being of a marriage are the qualities of kindness and compassion.

"My first counsel is this: possess a pure, *kindly* and radiant heart, that thine may be a sovereignty ancient, imperishable and everlasting."

Bahá'u'lláh[72]

"Beware, beware lest ye deal unkindly towards any person."

'Abdu'l-Bahá[73]

These qualities subsume other qualities such as the ability to easily *forgive* and *to be courteous.*

"Among the teachings of Bahá'u'lláh is one requiring man, under all conditions and circumstances, to be *forgiving,* to love his enemy and to consider an ill wisher a well wisher."

'Abdu'l-Bahá[74]

"Blessed is he who is illumined with the light of *courtesy*...he who is endowed with courtesy is endowed with a great station."

'Abdu'l-Bahá[75]

Without question courtesy is an indicator of the quality and refinement of civilization. An important aspect of this quality is being *even tempered.* If a potential partner is prone to anger and bad temper, especially if associated with violence, verbal and physical, then caution is a matter of common sense and self protection. Violence and abuse in the family is much more common than once thought, and is a terrible threat to the future well being not only of the spouse but also of children[76].

"Defile not the tongue with cursing or execrating anyone"

Bahá'u'lláh[77]

"No husband should subject his wife to abuse of any kind, whether emotional, mental or physical"

Universal House of Justice[78]

42. **Being Just and Fairminded.** A fifth quality of immense importance in creating a successful marriage is the core issue of justice and fairness, concerns which are at the heart of Bahá'í teachings.

"The best beloved thing in My sight is *justice*"

Bahá'u'lláh[79]

"Now speak forth with *fairness,* do not misrepresent this matter neither to thyself nor to the people"

'Abdu'l Bahá[80]

One aspect of fairness is to acknowledge the *rights* of

all members of the family[81].

"The rights of the son, the father, the mother, none of them must be transgressed, none of them must be arbitrary...The injury of one shall be considered the injury of all; the comfort of each, the comfort of all"

'Abdu'l-Bahá[82]

Another aspect of fairness is to have *mutual respect.* In any relationship, it is not fair to have lack of respect for another, a failure to recognize the potential spark of the Divine spirit in all humans. Sometimes in marriage, even when there is mutual romantic love, respect is limited from the beginning, especially, for instance, if the man has a better education than the woman, historically a common situation because of unequal social practices. Another common cause of disrespect in the past has arisen when the characters of the two partners have moved away from one another because one has had experiences which are more stimulating to growth, especially intellectual, than the other, e.g. in the traditional setting of the husband working in a competitive profession whilst the wife has been confined to the home looking after infant children and as a result has had limited contact with other adults. Too often in such cases the husband comes to see his wife as an increasingly dull companion (i) compared with the bright young women he meets at work, or (ii) as a partner at social events when he wishes to create a favourable impression that will help forward his ambitions.

Yet another fundamental aspect of fairness is *absence of prejudice.* Put another way, prejudice is by definition unfair because it is based on broad negative assumptions concerning a whole category of humanity (according to race, sex, nationality, class, etc) without allowing for balancing positive characteristics, or for the actual qualities of each individual.

"As long as these prejudices prevail, the world of

humanity will not have rest...war was due to either religious *prejudice,* racial prejudice, political prejudice or patriotic prejudice. It has therefore been ascertained and proved that all prejudices are destructive of the human edifice".

'Abdu'l-Bahá[83]

43. ***Ability to Consult.*** A most practical aspect of being just and fair minded is the ability of both partners to *consult* together on all issues in the marriage and on a regular basis. This is true today more than ever before. The old authoritarian patriarchal model clearly will not work in an age of democracy and equality of the sexes [see article on consultation for further development of this theme].

"The atmosphere within a Bahá'í family as within the community as a whole...is not dictatorial authority, but humble fellowship, not arbitrary power, but the spirit of frank and loving consultation."

Universal House of Justice[84]

As noted in the article on consultation, a key requirement in the process is to be detached, to judge the quality of a suggestion on its own intrinsic merit, rather than on who proposed it. This is about controlling one's own ego and not wanting to be always right.

"There are, therefore, times when a wife should defer to her husband, and times when a husband should defer to his wife. But neither should ever unjustly dominate over the other... [but rather] cause them to become the signs of harmony and unity till the end of time."

Universal House of Justice[85]

44. ***Absence of Qualities Conducive to a Successful Marriage.*** Of course, not all people are strong in these six qualities that are conducive to a lasting marriage. What should they do? In the Bahá'í Faith marriage is recommended as a desirable state

for the majority as already observed. Accordingly, it would seem reasonable to suggest that those who are weak in such qualities should strive to strengthen them, a task which is much easier for the young than it is for the older who are likely to be more resistant to changing their ways. A person not able or willing to do this should consider not marrying at all as a matter of fairness to a potential partner and future children. The Faith does recognize that there will *always be some who will not marry* for one reason or another.

"Under normal circumstances every person should consider it his moral duty to marry, but marriage is *by no means an obligation*"

Shoghi Effendi[86]

"Although to be married is highly desirable...it is *not the central purpose of life*"

Universal House of Justice[87]

At a minimum, such a person should only consider marriage after being absolutely open about such deficiencies with the intended partner, with a view to realistically assessing together whether both will be able to handle them over an extended period of time.

Compatibility

45. *Similarities and Differences.* Though such qualities conducive to a successful marriage are a vital consideration for marriage partners, it is important to recognize that they should be seen in the broader picture of overall compatibility of the prospective partners. Sometimes people of the highest qualities and character are simply not able to live together in a harmonious and successful marriage because of incompatibilities. This is not to say that a successful marriage can only be achieved if the two partners are similar in their characters and ways, rather that where there are differences they are complementary, or at

least can be tolerated, and result in mutual constructiveness and growth, not frustration and paralysis. Knowing one another thoroughly is as important in this context as having the qualities conducive to a lasting marriage. There are two broad aspects to the problem: (i) how the couple would handle important specific issues in the marriage, and (ii) simple personality or temperamental similarities and differences.

46. **Life Goals.** It seems reasonable to assume that a marriage based on shared goals is likely to be stronger than one where there are differences, other things been equal. A useful broad indicator of whether a couple will have common goals is whether or not they have the same religion or the same social, economic and political philosophy. Nevertheless, the Bahá'í teachings emphasise that such consideration should, in broad terms, be secondary to high moral standards and the qualities conducive to marriage just mentioned. A marriage can be successful even when there are differences of religion or philosophy if there is mutual tolerance, nobility of character and love.

"There is a difference between character and Faith, it is often very hard to accept this fact and put up with it, but the fact remains that a person may believe in and love the Cause—even to be ready to die for it— and yet not have a good personal character, or possess traits at variance with the Teachigs."

Universal House of Justice[88]

"...the House of Justice points out that unity of your family should take priority over any other consideration...for example, service to the Cause should not produce neglect of the family. It is important for you to arrange your time so that your family life is harmonious and your household receives the attention it requires."

Universal House of Justice[89]

"...when dealing with your non Bahá'í relatives; they cannot be expected to feel the way we do on questions of racial amity, and we must not force our views on them, but rather lovingly and wisely seek to educate them."

Shoghi Effendi[90]

"Under no circumstances should you try to dictate and impose upon him by force your personal religious convictions. Neither should you allow his opposition to the Cause to seriously hinder your activities."

Shoghi Effendi[91]

47. **Cultural Diversity.** The subject of life goals and toleration of differences leads on to the question of opportunities and diffculties that might arise in a marriage to someone from a different culture: in addition to religion/philosophy, this embraces differences in race, nationality, language, tribe, class, caste, etc. This is a subject already touched on when discussing the family of a potential marriage partner. An intercultural marriage can bring enormous richness and growth for the whole family, and the Faith puts particular emphasis on the benefits to humanity of an *interracial marriage:*

"If it be possible, gather together these two races, black and white, into one assembly, and put such love into their hearts that they shall not only unite but even intermarry. Be sure that the result of this will abolish differences and disputes between black and white."

'Abdu'l-Bahá[92]

Nevertheless, potential partners should be conscious of the extra stress, as well as the extra enrichment, that may come from an intercultural marriage, and that success will only come with deep understanding and tolerance as well as strength of character. Such stress can be internal to the marriage, e.g. an ability to tolerate and love cultural practices that are new or strange, or quite opposite one's own e.g. with regard to cleanliness, tidiness[93], noise, food, music, dress, socializing, etc. They can also be external, e.g. criticism and hostility to the couple and their children from family and friends and from society in general.

48. ***Raising Children.*** The creation and raising of children is one of the prime purposes of marriage and one which can be the cause of both great joy, especially when there is unity, and great anguish when there is disunity. As already noted clashes over children are a prime cause of divorce, and studies have shown that because such clashes are frequent marriages are usually at their most happy state before children come and after they have left home[94]. In many ways the coming of children represents a bigger change in the lives of couples than their marriage itself. For many this is when they really become adult as a result of the responsibility that is thrust upon them. Couples planning to marry are well advised therefore to thoroughly explore together their feelings about children: how many they would like to have, the roles of mother and father, discipline and education. Of particular importance for Bahá'ís is the question of the spiritual education of the children.

"When a Bahá'í marries a non Bahá'í, he (or she) can in no wise surrender his right to teach his children the Bahá'í Faith; the non Bahá'í partner enjoys the same right and should not be prevented from teaching the children what he (or she) believes"

Universal House of Justice[95]

49. ***Money.*** a third issue in the conduct of marriage is money. This is of critical importance and when handled badly is a leading cause of divorce. In discussing qualities conducive to a successful marriage, mention has already been made of the desirability of the golden mean in the handling of the

money question: that neither partner be a spendthrift or miserly in their ways. Other points already discussed relevent to this matter include gender equality and the spiritual nature of marriage. A couple planning to marry should thoroughly discuss and agree on how they will handle money matters. Such agreement should be based on the principles mentioned in this paragraph[96].

50. ***Personal Temperaments.*** Similarities and differences in temperaments are both likely to be, on a daily basis, to be either sources of joy or of intense annoyance. Thus if both partners have volatile emotions frequent clashes are likely. On the otherhand, if one is shy and the other happy go lucky there may be potential for each to benefit and grow from the influence of the other. A couple planning to marry should review such similarities and differences between them and make a realistic assessment of how they would manage them together over an extended period of time in the intimacy of a common home.

51. ***Humour.*** One aspect of temperament compatibility that is sometimes understimated is humour. To be able to laugh together is a most wonderful physical and spiritual medicine, and a source of strength and unity during times of tests and difficulty. Most healthy is a sense of humour which is selfdeprecating, as for instance in much Jewish humour. Most destructive is sarcasm and humour at the expense of others, especially the spouse in a marital relationship who is sensitive on matters of self esteem. More broadly, unnecessary stress can be created when one partner puts a great deal of value on humour and the other one does not.

52. ***Three Test Questions of Compatibilty.*** As a basic test of compatibility, the following questions, for each partner to consider alone, can some times be illuminating:

1. Are you proud or embarrassed when in public with your potential marriage partner?
2. Would you be happy to have your proposed marriage partner as parent of your child?
3. Do you see each of you contributing to the spiritual wellbeing and growth of the other?

Role of Love

   53. ***Bahá'í Definition of Love.*** As noted, modern Western culture gives the highest priority to romantic love as a basis for marriage as captured in the expression: "all is fair in love and war". Anthropologists now say that it has been important in most other cultures as well though often suppressed by society[97]. The Bahá'í Writings also put great emphasis on love, but as a universal phenonomen broader than the romantic concept.

   "Love is the most great law that ruleth His mighty and heavenly cycle, the unique power that bindeth together the diverse elements of this material world, the supreme magnetic force that directs the movements of the spheres and the celestial realms."

'Abdu'l-Bahá[98]

   "There are four kinds of love. The first is love that flows from God to man...The second is the love that flows from man to God...The third is the love of God toward the Self of Identity of God...through one ray of this love all other love exists...The fourth is the love of man for man...each sees in others the beauty of God reflected in the soul, and finding this point of similarity, they are attracted to one another in love... This love will bring the realization of true accord, and the foundation of real unity".

'Abdu'l-Bahá[99]

   A Bahá'í Study Guide, makes the following distinctions between "true love" and "romantic love".

True Love	Romantic Love
* Attained through the knowledge God	* Based on of physical attraction
* Characterized by continuing growth	* Fluctuates with changing/waning physical attraction
* Accepting of another's limitations	* Relatively short in duration
* Demands discipline, work, overcoming of self	* Thinking only of self in relation to partner
* Is a conscious decision	* Just happens; seems accidental

National Spiritual Assembly of Canada[100]

A succinct definition of real love is: "a condition when the satisfaction of another becomes as significant or more significant than one's own satisfaction."[101]

54. **Solid Foundations.** Love between man and woman is one of the most wondrous experiences known to humanity and it has inspired some of the greatest art of civilization. It is clearly a vital element in marriage, but it should be based on solid foundations. There should be mutual attraction before marriage, but a successful marriage does not depend on that attraction being a burning passion. Love is a feeling that will often blossom and come to full fruition only after years of marriage. In otherwords, it is not necessarily a prerequisite for a successful marriage that there be a burning passion between a couple before they get married.

"(that) the two people should live their lives in love and harmony is of far greater importance than that they should be consumed with passion for each other. The one is a great rock of strength on which to lean in time of need; the other is a purely temporary thing which may at anytime die out.

Shoghi Effendi[102]

55. **Habit.** Ruhíyyih Khánum, the widow of Shoghi Effendi, has pointed out that even if love in marriage begins to weaken with time, its unifying role can be reinforced by habit acquired when love was young and strong.

"To the influence of love in marriage is gradually added another powerful catalyst: habit. The common home, the daily association, produces a common framework, and habit, one of the most powerful forces in life, begins to knit husband and wife together. It acts as a wonderful stabilizer; if loves is allowed to fail, habit itself may be strong enough to preserve the union."[103]

IV. PRESERVATION OF MARRIAGE

56. *Growth through Tests and Difficulties.* Relations between marriage partners are, of course, as varied as human beings. Some partners undoubtedly experience marriage with little or no conflict because of similarity of outlook and calm emotions, or because of complementary natures, e.g. one taking a leadership role and the other a more supportive position. However, for the majority, some stresses and strains of varying degrees of intensity naturally arise, perhaps as a result of clashing personalities, emotional volatility, changing phases in the life cycle, differences of culture etc. Such strains may be manifested by minor irritations over an extended period of time, or come about as a result of differences when major crises have to be faced. Such stresses and strains are not necessarily a negative experience; after all it is through tests and difficulties that we grow as spiritual beings. The challenge is to be able to successfully manage such stresses.

"The mind and spirit of man advance when he is tried by suffering. The more the ground is ploughed,

the better the seed will grow, the better the harvest
will be. Just as the plough furrows the earth deeply,
purifying it of weeds and thistles, so suffering and
tribulation free man from the petty affairs of this
worldly life until he arrives at a state of complete
detachment...Look back to the times past and you will
find that the greatest men have suffered the most."

'Abdu'l-Bahá[104]

Marriages are living institutions and require constant
nourishment in order to flourish and grow, even those
that are based on firm foundations, and where there
is little conflict.

"Do not expect too much of marriage or too little.
Water cannot rise above its own level. Your union
cannot produce more than you two contribute to it.
If you are full of imperfections, intolerant, impatient,
exacting, dictatorial, suspicious, short tempered,
selfish, do not imagine that these characteristics are
going to make your marriage happy or that by
changing your partner a new union will be successful:
marriage, like all our other relationships in life, is a
process which, among other things, serves to grind
the sharp edges off us. The grinding often hurts. The
adjustment to another person's character is difficult
at first, that is why love is needed. Here more than
in any other relationship, love, being essentially a
Divine force, binds; it leaps like a spark the gap
between people's thoughts and conflicting desires,
between perhaps widely different temperaments or in
moments of rage, jealousy or spite."

Ruhiyyih Khanum[105]

57. ***Nine Good Habits for Nurturing Marriage.***
Abundant wise advice on preserving marriage is
available to the general public, e.g. Ann Landers'
Twelve Rules for a Happy Marriage[106], and in Bahá'í
literature e.g. Eric Blumenthal's fourteen points
Everyone Can Learn[107], and it is not the purpose of

this review to mention or summarize all such advice. Rather this section will be confined to noting some nine practices or habits or skills which are of universal value in reducing conflict in marriage and in helping it grow and flourish. The nine useful habits are as follows.

58. ***The First Good Habit is to Keep Things in Perspective,*** especially when life is most stressful, because this in itself is conducive to successful response to tests and difficulties. It prompts understanding, reflection and detachment.

"Should prosperity befall thee, rejoice not, and should abasement come upon thee, grieve not, for both shall pass away and be no more."

Bahá'u'lláh[108]

Three matters in particular need to be kept in perspective. First, there is the Bahá'í view of the nature of marriage and its exalted purposes, and that accordingly *maintenance of the marriage,* no matter how great are the difficulties, must be *the highest priority.* Second is the fact that marriage today is subject to abnormal stresses, as earlier described, on account of materialism, instability and breakdown of social structures, and problems of transition as society moves towards gender equality and, more broadly, a global society. Third, it important to be conscious of the main causes of marital breakdown in modern society e.g.:

General Causes
  * Character clash e.g. spouse crushed by dominant partner;
  * Cultural clash e.g. from differing social classes, races, religions, nations etc
  * Emotional clashes e.g. one or both tired, angry, depressed, stressed, unmotivated, etc, on a continuing basis;

* Drifting apart on account of differing speeds of spiritual, emotional and intellectual growth.

Typical Specific issues
* Sexual relations, e.g. differing and changing needs of the two partners;
* Lack of care and attention, ie partners are no longer courting one another;
* Raising of children, e.g. the traditional clash between the discipline style of the father and the compassion style of the mother;
* Money and property—as noted already one of the leading causes of divorce, along with differences with regard to raising children and sexual/ affection needs;
* Functions in the home and family, ie differing views on sexual equality[109];
* Lack of communication, e.g. failure of husband to talk about large and small issues;
* Extended family relations, e.g. clumsy, unsolicited interference by in laws and other family members;
* Differences about social life, e.g. tired husband not wanting to go out in the evening;
* The Faith, e.g. one spouse inadvertently neglecting the family because of involvement in community affairs, prompting resentment in the children and jealousy of non Bahá'í spouse.

Awareness of the issues and that they are not unique to a particular marital situation makes it easier to handle them.

59. ***The Second Good Habit is to Focus on the Positive*** and not the negative in the marital relationship:

"*To look always at the good and not at the bad. If a man has ten good qualities and one bad one, to look at the ten and forget the one; and if a man has ten bad qualities and one good one, to look at the one* and forget the ten."

'Abdu'l-Bahá[110]

This means looking at the good qualities of the marital partner, remembering the joyous times of the past together, including the reasons why you chose your partner and the love of that time, and focussing on common goals for the future.

"...when a person is without plans and goals, he becomes disheartened, depressed, and disinterested in life and all that it entails..."

Hossein Danesh[111]

60. **The Third Good Habit is not to be Judgemental or Complaining,** but rather to be *patient and forgiving:*

"*Do not complain* of others. Refrain from reprimanding them and if you wish to give admonition or advice let it be offered in such a way that it will not burden the hearer."

'Abdu'l-Bahá[112]

The American Indians have a saying that before you criticize someone, you need to walk in his mocassins for two weeks.

"We must be *patient* with others, infinitely patient! But also with our own poor selves. Remember that even the Prophets of God sometimes got tired and cried in dispair."

Shoghi Effendi[113]

If you have a grievance, give your partner time to deal with it at his/her own initiative, rather than in resentful compliance with your complaints or in fear of your bad temper.

61. **The Fourth Good Habit is to Review Ones Own Behaviour and Deficiencies** : to be emotionally mature and to be conciliatory by trying to eliminate or reduce those habits or practices which distress or irritate your partner.

"Be calm, be strong, be grateful and become a

lamp full of light, that darkness of sorrows be annihilated and that the sun of everlasting joy arise"

'Abdu'l-Bahá[114]

"...it is incumbent upon thee to treat him with great kindness, to consider his wishes and be *conciliatory* with him at all times."

'Abdu'l-Bahá[115]

"How shall I overcome seeing the faults of others...? ....Whenever you recognize the fault of another, think of yourself: What are my imperfections ...and try to remove them"

'Abdu'l-Bahá[116]

In most situations the irritants are minor and can be easily handled at little cost in relation to the benefit gained. To achieve this goal it is most advisable to bring ones self to account each day:

"Bring thyself to account each day ere thou art summoned to a reckoning."

Bahá'u'lláh[117]

62. **The Fifth Good Habit is to Continue Courtship** of your spouse throughout your married life, and to be *attentive* to small matters of courtesy, respect, and love which can mean a great deal to the recipient. At the same time be *gracious* in receiving such attention yourself. Do not be like the boorish woman who screams at the man who offers her his seat on the bus! One important aspect of this habit is to *keep yourself attractive* and not let your appearances and manners decline because you have "captured" your spouse. At the same time, especially when newly wed, have the wisdom to know the right balance between attractiveness for your spouse and provoking unnecessary jealousy through flamboyance in front of others. Cultivate those areas of relaxation, e.g. music, dance, food, sport, literature, the arts, nature, hobbies, which you both can enjoy together:

"I will be a happy and joyful being"

'Abdu'l-Bahá[118]

63. ***The Sixth Good Habit is to Provide 'Space'
for One Another.*** In many marriages today, especially
when both partners may be well educated and have
their own special interests, it is important to find a
mutually agreed balance between time spent doing
things together, and giving time and *"space" for each
partner* to pursue their own interests and growth:

"Love one another but make not a bond of love;
let it rather be a moving sea between the shores of
your souls."

Khalil Gilbran[119]

"...and stand together, yet not too near together:
for the pillars of the temple stand apart and the oak
tree and the cypress grow not in each other's shadow."

Khalil Gilbran[120]

"...there must be opportunities in the context of
marriage for both husband and wife to pursue plans
and goals both individually and as a couple."

Hossein Danesh[121]

64. ***The Seventh Good Habit is to Focus on
Serving Each Other*** and to put less emphasis on
being constantly preoccupied with your "rights" which
so easily leads to confrontation and selfishness.
Certainly rights in the family must be upheld, as
previously noted, but it is surely best to achieve this
goal by giving to the partner and looking to his/her
wellbeing in such a generous way that he/she will
never think about rights. For Bahá'ís this is to follow
our Exemplar, 'Abdu'l-Bahá, whose name in Arabic
means "the Servant of God".

"Service in love for mankind is unity with God. He
who serves has already entered the kingdom and is
seated at the right hand of his Lord."

'Abdu'l-Bahá[122]

"They are two helpmates, two intimate friends who

should be concerned about the welfare of each other."

'Abdu'l-Bahá[123]

65. ***The Eigth Good Habit is to Consult Together on a Regular Basis*** on matters both great and small. Under no circumstances should either partner seek to dictate to the other, even if one is apparently willing to be submissive—that would be exploitation.

"Family consultation employing full and frank discussion, and animated by awareness of the need for moderation and balance, can be the panacea for domestic conflict."

Universal House of Justice[124]

"Settle all things, both great and small, by consultation. Without prior consultation, take no important step in your personal affairs. Concern yourself with one another."

'Abdu'l-Bahá[125]

66. ***Main Features of Bahá'í Family consultation.*** There are at least four essential requirements of Bahá'í style consultation. First, as discussed in more detail in the article on consultation, it is important to begin any consultation of consequence with ***prayers*** so as help put both partners in the right spirit. Indeed praying together on a daily basis is one of the most effective practices for nourishing family unity.

"Prayer and fasting is the cause of awakening and mindfulness and is conducive to protection and preservation from tests."

'Abdu'l-Bahá[126]

Second, both parties should be given ***equal opportunity to present their point of view,*** each should be treated with respect, and, if at all possible, no decision should be made without the sincere consent of both. Third, each partner should try to be as ***detached*** and objective as possible: in short each should consider the cases presented according to their intrinsic merit, and not on the basis of who suggested them.

"This faculty of meditation frees man from the animal nature, discerns the reality of things, puts man in touch with God."

'Abdu'l-Bahá[127]

Finally, as much as possible, the consultation should **take account of the agreed basic goals of the family,** for instance with regard to raising of the children, management of financial assets, jobs, location of home etc.

67. ***The Ninth Good Habit is to be Willing to Seek Outside Help if Necessary.*** Generally, Bahá'ís are advised not to share their marital problems with others but to try and resolve them together within the family. However, if the level of stress and conflict simply becomes unmanageable, then a couple should have the courage and commitment to seek professional advice and/or ask for the help of the Bahá'í Local Spiritual Assembly:

"He feels, in regard to your family problems, that you should take these matters up with your Assembly, if you desire advice; one of the duties of these Assemblies is to advise and aid the friends, and it is your privileged to turn to the Assembly."

Shoghi Effendi[128]

It should be added that such Assemblies stand ready to provide assistance in such matters to any couple that should ask: both Bahá'ís, only one Bahá'í, or neither Bahá'í.

68. ***Aversion between Marital Partners.*** The Bahá'í teachings on marriage recognize that when disunity in a marriage is very profound, the partners may come to have a deep aversion for each other. In such circumstances, the Bahá'í stance against divorce

is waivered:

"They must strictly refrain from divorce unless something ariseth which compelleth them to separate because of their aversion for each other..."

'Abdu'l-Bahá[129]

"...a number of other terms are used in describing the situations that can lead to divorce in Bahá'í laws, such as 'antipathy', 'resentment', 'estrangement', 'impossibility of establishing harmony', and 'irreconcilibility'. The texts, however, point out that divorce is strongly condemned, should be viewed as a 'last resort' when rare and urgent circumstances exist, and that the partner who is the 'cause of divorce' will unquestionably become the victim of formidable calmities."

Universal House of Justice[130]

"Irreconcilable antipathy arising between the parties to a marriage is not merely a lack of love for one's spouse but an antipathy which cannot be dissolved."

Universal House of Justice[131]

"The presence of children, as a factor in divorce, cannot be ignored for surely it places an even greater weight of moral responsibility on the man and woman in considering such a step. Divorce under such circumstances no longer just concerns them and their desires and feelings but also concerns the children's entire future and their attitude towards marriage."

Shoghi Effendi[132]

69. **Year of Patience.** Even when Bahá'í divorce proceedings start, the whole emphasis is on creating conditions that might even at this late stage promote reconciliation. To obtain a Bahá'í divorce a couple will take their case to the Local Spiritual Assembly, which will wait a full year, significantly called the *Year of Patience,* before granting a divorce. During that year,

both the couple and the Assembly are to try every means to find a reconciliation:

"When a Spiritual Aseembly receives an application for Bahá'í divorce its first duty is to try to reconcile the couple. If this is not possible, and the couple seperates, further efforts at reconciliation should be made during the ensuing year."

Universal House of Justice[133]

"During the year (of patience) the couple have the responsibility of attempting to reconcile their differences."

Universal House of Justice[134]

The couple are to live seperately so as to have time for reflection away from the normal arena of conflict. If they should live together temporily during this period, and then separate again, then the *Year of Patience* would begin again from the date of the new seperation. During the *Year of Patience* both parties should strictly refrain from "dating" third parties.

V. CONCLUSIONS

70. To conclude, the theme of this presentation has been that the institution of marriage is one of the most important pillars of civil society and, accordingly, it is in the general interest that each individual marriage be strong and long lasting. The Bahá'í Faith has a major contribution to make in achieving such a goal because it offers a new model adapted to meet the challenges of today and the needs of an emerging global society, based on self governance, gender equality, and, above all, clear moral and spiritual principle.[135]

NOTES

1. See for instance *Hot Monogamy,* by Patricia Love, Penguin, 1995

2. See, for instance, "The Bad News about Step parents"
   section in *Dan Quayle was Right*, by Barbara Defoe
   Whitehead, Atlantic Monthy, April 1993. This is, of course,
   a different situation to that of couples, unable to have their
   own biological children, who gladly accept adopted children
   as a substitute. Presumably, a Darwinist would argue that
   in this case there is a, perhaps unconscious, material
   motivation of providing for security in old age.

3. In the USA, 30 percent of children are now born out of
   wedlock, including 70 percent of Afro American children.
   (*The Demoralization of Soceity*, by Gertrude Himmelfarb,
   Knof, 1995). In Scandinavia the figure hovers around 50
   percent (*Economist*, February 21, 1998).

4. See for instance *The Index of Leading Cultural Indicators*,
   by William J. Bennett, Empower America, The Heritage
   Foundation, and the Free Congress Foundation, 1993, *The
   Abolition of Marriage: How We Destroy Lasting Love*, by
   Maggie Gallagher, Regnery Publishing, Inc., Washington
   D.C., 1996, *The Demoralization of Society*, by Gertrude
   Himmelfarb, 1995, and *Dan Quayle was Right*, by Ba rbara
   Defoe Whitehead, 1993. The latter article, in particular,
   stirred up considerable opposition from social liberals who
   feared that these themes would divert society from economic
   issues including, most importantly, job creation for those
   in the ghettoes (see for instance: *Dan Quayle is Still Wrong*
   by Stephanie Coontz, *Washington Post*, May 9, 1993.)
   (Stephanie Coontz is the author of *The Way We Never Were:
   American Families and the Nostalgia Trap*). It is interesting
   that, in America, one of the first to raise these issues, in
   the late sixties, was Daniel Moynihan, a Democratic senator
   representing New York.

5. Seventy percent of divorces are initiated by women (The
   Marriage Doctor, *Financial Times*, July 21, 1991).

6. The relationship between public morality and the
   functioning of civil society was clearly spelt out two hundred
   years ago by Edmund Burke in a January 19, 1791 letter
   to the (French) National Assembly:
   "Men are qualified for civil liberty in exact proportion to their
   disposition to put moral chains upon their own appetites...
   society cannot exist unless a controlling power upon will and
   appetite be placed somewhere and the less there is within,
   the more there must be without."

7. As pointed out by William Raspberry, a distinguished Afro-
   American journalist, a child born out of wedlock is deprived

of much of the formal but very real network of family support that occurs when a child is the result of a marriage (*Washington Post,* April 11, 1994).

8. See "Family Values", the *Economist,* December 26, 1992, and "Why Men Need Family Values" by Robert Samuelson, *Washington Post,* April 3, 1996.

9. *Gleanings,* p.242.

10. *Advent of Divine Justice,* p.39.

11. "Fewer than half of all adult Americans today regard the idea of sacrifice for others as a positive moral virtue" (*Dan Quayle was Right*). In *Divided Families: What Happens to Children When Parents Part,* the authors, Frank Furstenberg and Andrew Cherlin, say that strengthening of values to reduce divorce "would have to swim against the flood tide of individualism that has unindated the West."

12. *Bahá'í Marriage and Family Life,* p.1.

13. Like other great religions, the Bahá'í Faith does not recognize so called "same sex" marriages. Homosexuals are loved and welcomed, like any human being into the community, but they are urged not to practice homosexuality which is seen as a sickness and not in accord with the natural purposes of the sex impulse.

14. *Bahá'í Prayers,* pp.105-106

15. *Bahá'í Marriage and Family Life.*

16. *Lights Of Guidance,* p.277

17. *Fortress of Wellbeing,* p.4

18. *Bahá'í Marriage and Family Life,* p,25

19. Ibid, p.3

20. Ibid, p.13

21. *The Earth is but One Country,* p.109

22. A UN pamphlet issued for the 1994 *International Year of the Family,* echoed this sentiment with the subheading: *Building the Smallest Democracy at the Heart of Society,* UN Office at Vienna, 1991. Two other illuminating references on this theme are as follows: "The family is the nurture ground of love. If you generate alienated people, then your capacity for loving, which is one of the keys to civilized society suffers" Jack Dominian, marriage psychiatrist, *Financial Times,* July 21, 1991. "The family is responsible for teaching lessons of independence, self restraint, responsibility, and right conduct, which are essential to a free democratic society. If the family fails these tasks, then the entire experiment in democratic self rule is jeopardised"

Dan Quayle is Right.
23. *Fortress of Wellbeing,* p.5
24. *Family Repairs and Maintenance Manual,* p.41.
25. *Bahá'í Marriage and Family Life,* p.31.
26. Ibid, p.2
27. Ibid, p.3
28. *Preserving Bahá'í Marriage,* p.22.
29. *Bahá'í Revelation,* p.212.
30. See *What Men Gain from Equality,* by Janet Higgins, *Herald of the South,* Oct/Dec 1993.
31. "What makes for a strong marriage? There are two key components. One is fidelity—a faithfulness and loyalty between man and wife. The other is mutuality—*being equal, not using one another"* Krister Stendahl, Professor of Christian Studies, Brandeis University, as quoted in *Parade Magazine,* November 22, 1992.
32. *Bahá'í Education,* (UK) p.48.
33. *Lights of Guidance,* p.501.
34. *Bahá'í Marriage and Family Life,* p.46.
35. *Lights of Guidance,* p.527.
36. One reason given for the prevalence of single parents in the black ghettos of America is that men are perceived to be "a poor source of economic support", William Raspberry, *Washington Post,* January 3, 1992.
37. Ibid, p.525
38. *Aqdas Synopsis,* p.59.
39. Ibid, p.39
40. *Lights of Guidance,* p.268.
41. *Bahá'í Marriage and Family Life,* p.14.
42. *Bahá'í Marriage and Married Life,* p.17.
43. Ibid, p.23
44. *Lights of Guidance,* p.279.
45. *Fortress of Wellbeing,* p.43.
46. "Persons wishing to marry after they become Bahá'ís must have a Bahá'í ceremony" Universal House of Justice (*Bahá'í Marriage and Family Life,* p.5)
47. *Bahá'í Marriage and Family Life,* p.4
48. *Lights of Guidance.* p.286
49. See, for instance, "Marriage of Minds not Hearts" by Yasmin Alibhai Roberts, *New Statesmen,* February 12, 1993.
50. *Bahá'í Marriage and Family Life,* p.20
51. *Tablets of 'Abdu'l-Bahá,* p.455.

52. *Bahá'í Marriage and Family Life*, p.16
53. *Bahá'í Marriage Study Guide*, p.25
54. Another potential problem to be wary of is one where the dowry is of great importance to the family into which one is marrying. In India's poorer families there have been many recorded instances of the wife being murdered if the promised dowry has not been delivered. In the Bahá'í Writings, Bahá'u'lláh has decreed that if a dowry is given its maximum value, expressed in gold, should be relatively small (no more than US$300 in today's terms) so that it is really symbolic rather than a real transfer of wealth between families.
55. *Bahá'í Revelation* (UK), p.313.
56. *Hidden Words (Persian)*, No. 56
57. *Bahá'í Prayers*, pp.47-50
58. *Pattern of Bahá'í Life*, p.10
59. *Living the Life*, p.30
60. *Trustworthiness* (UK), p.9
61. *Bahá'í Marriage and Family Life*, p.36
62. *Pattern of Bahá'í Life*, p.41
63. Ibid, p.31
64. *Secrets of Divine Civilization*, p.96
65. *Lights of Guidance*, p.25
66. *Bahá'í World Faith*, p.363
67. *Bahá'í Marriage and Family Life*, p.66
68. See earlier section on the distinctive character of Bahá'í marriage.
69. *Bahá'í World Faith*, p.195
70. *The Earth is but One Country*, p.61
71. *Lights of Guidance*, p.225
72. *Hidden Words (Arabic)*, No.1
73. *Bahá'u'lláh and the New Era*, p.68
74. *Bahá'í Marriage and Family Life*, p.17
75. Ibid, p.38
76. See *The Violence Free Family: The Building Bloc of Peaceful Civilization*, a presentation at an International Symposium, May 23-25, 1994, New York, by H.B. Danesh.
77. *Bahá'í World Faith*, p.169
78. *Fortress of Wellbeing*, p.71
79. *Hidden Words (Arabic)*, No.2
80. *Bahá'í Marriage and Family Life*, p.33

81. See *Rights and Responsibilities in the Bahá'í Family System*, by Hoda Mahmoudi and Richard DaBell, *Journal of Bahá'í Studies*, Volume 5, No.2.

82. *Lights of Guidance*, p.534.

83. *Bahá'í Revelation (U.K.)*, p.210

84. *Family Repairs and Maintenance Manual*, p.24

85. *Lights of Guidance*, p.526

86. *Bahá'í Marriage and Family Life*, p.2

87. Ibid, p.2

88. Ibid, p.20

89. Ibid, p.76

90. Ibid, p.41

91. Ibid, p.40

92. *Bahá'í Marriage and Family Life*, p.19

93. Bahá'í Teachings strongly encourage both cleanliness and tidiness:

    "External cleanliness, although it is but a physical thing, hath a great influence upon spirituality" 'Abdu'l-Bahá (*Bahá'í World Faith*, p.334)

    "The home should be orderly and well organized" 'Abdu'l Bahá (*Lights of Guidance*, p.535)

94. Survey for the American Sociological Association, Toronto, 1997 (*US ToDay*, August 13, 1997).

95. *Lights of Guidance*, p.286

96. For advice on how to handle money, from a Bahá'í perspective, see *Created Rich*, by Patrick Barker, Naturegraph Publishers, California, 1995.

97. A recent study has shown that 87 percent of 167 cultures reviewed "acknowledged romantic love in all its glory", *Anatomy of Love*, by Helen Fisher, Norton, 1992. See also the *New York Times*, November 24, 1992.

98. *Divine Art of Living*, p.108

99. *Fortress of Wellbeing*, p.13

100. *Bahá'í Marriage Study Guide*, p.26

101. Notes on Marriage Curriculum Development meeting, February 18-20, 1994, Wilmette, U.S.A.

102. *Lights of Guidance*, p.277.

103. *Prescription for Living*, p.87.

104. *Paris Talks* (U.K.), p.178

105. *Prescription for Living*, p.87. With regard to the observation about remarriage in this quotation, the divorce rate for such marriages in the U.S.A. is about 60 percent, i.e. significantly

higher than for first marriages (*Washington Post*, February 14, 1992).

106. *Twelve Rules for a Happy Marriage:*
   1. Never be angry at once.
   2. Never yell at each other unless the house is on fire.
   3. Yield to the wishes of the other as an exercise in self discipline if you can't think of a better reason.
   4. If you have a choice between making yourself or your mate look good, choose your mate.
   5. If you feel you must criticize, do so lovingly.
   6. Never bring up a mistake of the past. Your silence will be greatly appreciated.
   7. Neglect the whole world rather than each other.
   8. Never let the day end without saying at least one complimentary thing to your life's partner.
   9. Never meet without an affectionate greeting.
   10. When you've said or done something hurtful, acknowledge it and ask for forgiveness.
   11. Remember, it takes two to get an argument going. Invariably the one who is wrong is the one who will be doing most of the talking.
   12. Never go to bed mad.

107. *Everyone Can Learn:*
   to believe that people can change
   to accept the social equality of man and woman
   to make decisions consciously and responsibly
   to recognize the power of belief
   to allow themselves to be led by the word of God
   to have a positive attitude to life
   to choose a direction for their lives, and follow it
   to choose a partner more consciously
   to stop wanting to be right all the time
   to recognize the importance of discussion
   to become less emotional and more loving
   to act, rather than simply react
   to become less self-centered and more spiritual
   to believe more in themselves and in their partners...and
   to believe in lasting happiness rather than fleeting moments of pleasure

108. *Hidden Words (Arabic)*, No.52

109. That this is a serious issue is illustrated by a 1998 law in Austria which requires husbands "to do at least half of the

household chores".

110. *Bahá'í Marriage and Family Life*, p.35
111. *The Development and Dimensions of Love and Marriage*, ABS Notebook III, nos 1 & 2, p.32
112. *Fortress of Wellbeing*, p.69
113. *Bahá'u'lláh and the New Era*, p.79
114. *Fortress of Wellbeing*, p.37
115. *Bahá'í Marriage and Family Life*, p.38
116. Ibid, p.42
117. *Hidden Words (Persian)*, No.2
118. *Bahá'í Prayers* (USA), 1967, p.64
119. *The Prophet*
120. Ibid
121. *The Development and Dimensions of Love*
122. *Pattern for Bahá'í Life*, p.39
123. *Bahá'í Marriage and Family Life*, p.3
124. Ibid, p.36
125. Ibid, p.34
126. *Divine Art of Living*, p.27.
127. *Paris Talks*
128. *Bahá'í Marriage and Family Life*, p.71
129. *Preserving Bahá'í Marriage*, p.3
130. Ibid, p.30
131. Ibid, p.27
132. *Lights of Guidance*, p.296
133. *Guidelines for Spiritual Assemblies (USA)*, 17.8
134. Ibid, p.17.2
135. Some basic texts on the Bahá'í teachings on marriage are as follows:

Compilations:

Bahá'í Marriage and Family Life (includes study guide), Canada;

Kitáb-i-Aqdas: Synopsis and Codification (sections on marriage & divorce), Haifa;

Divorce, U.K.;

Family Life, U.K.;

Guidelines for Spiritual Assemblies (section on marriage & divorce), U.S.A.;

Lights of Guidance (sections on family, marriage, love, unity, etc), India;

Marriage: a Fortress of Wellbeing, U.S.A.;

Preserving Bahá'í Marriage, Canada.

Commentaries:

Danesh, Hossein, & others: *Divine Institution of Marriage*, Bahá'í Studies Notebook, Canada;

Furután, A.: *Mother, Fathers, Children*, George Ronald;

Ghaznavi, Agnes: *Family Repairs and Maintenance Manual*, George Ronald;

Hellaby, Madeline: *Education in the Bahá'í Family*, George Ronald;

Khavari, Khalil & Sue: *Creating a Successful Family*, One World;

Khavari, Khalil & Sue: *Together Forever*, One World;

Mahmoudi, Hoda & Dabell, Richard, *Rights and Responsibilities in the Bahá'í Family System*, Journal of Bahá' Studies, Volume 5, No.2.

Rabbani, Ruhiyyih Khanum: *Prescription for Living* (chapter 4), George Ronald;

Ruhe, Margaret: *Guidelines for Parents*, India;

Ruhe, Margaret: *Some Thoughts on Marriage*, Kalimat Press;

Wilcox, Patricia: *Bahá'í Families, Perspectives, Principles and Practice*, George Ronald;

Interracial Marriage: A Bahá'í View, U.S.A.

THE UNITY OF RELIGION: BAHÁ'Í COMMENTARIES ON THE GREAT RELIGIONS OF THE WORLD

Draft chapters of on unpublished book on the Bahá'í Faith, 1982

Introduction

In the Bahá'í view each of the great religions of the world is a stage in the revelation of God's word to man; in short all religions are one and their Founders are equally revered and loved along with the Founder of the Bahá'í Faith, Bahá'u'lláh (1817-1892). All religions have two sides to their teachings. First, there are universal principles, common to all religions, pertaining to man's relationship with God, his fellow humans, and the universe, God's creation. Second, there are also particular teachings developed from those universal principles which are applicable to the time of each religion and which become more advanced with each succeeding revelation, as man's capacity and understanding increases.

Another side to this theme of "Progressive Revelation" is that each religion goes through a seasonal cycle: a springtime of spiritual inspiration when the Founder of the religion appears; a summer of great achievement and civilization; an autumn when the original pure teachings become obscured by the interpretations and additional teachings of priests and other followers; and finally a winter when the original inspiration is almost totally lost and all that effectively remains is a hollow outward structure. It is then time for a new Teacher or Manifestation to arise, in accordance with spiritual laws that are as evident as the physical laws of the material world.

These themes are developed in the Bahá'í writings for the most part in rather general terms. However, in addition there are specific references to individual religions, usually in response to questions, especially with regard to Christianity and Islám, the two most recent and widespread of the world's religions. Most, but not all, of these references address two broad topics: first, distinctions between the original teachings of the Founders of the great religions and what was subsequently added by their followers; and second, the connections with the Bahá'í Faith, which normally means references to prophecies in the holy books of past religions which are interpreted as referring to this age and the coming of the Bahá'í Faith.

The purpose of this essay is to briefly review these references, religion by religion, beginning with Hinduism, Buddhism and Zoroastrianism, and then moving forward chronologically to Judaism, Christianity, Islám, and finally to the Bahá'í Faith itself.

Before starting this review, some preliminary comment should be made concerning other Great Educators, Manifestations or Messengers of God whose names have been lost in the mists of history, but traces of whose teachings can still be found in the indigenous religions of, for instance, Africa, Australasia and the Americas. Though heavily overlaid with superstition and ritual, as is true to a greater or lesser extent of all old religions, there is nevertheless still some of the original spirit, and the teachings of the Bahá'í Faith encourage the peoples of these regions to be proud of the essence of their religions and cultural heritage. Bahá'ís make it clear, for instance, that they do not subcribe to the teachings of many Christian missionaries that the ancestors of such peoples have been condemned to everlasting hellfire because they were not Christians. This is a cruel, irrational and narrow minded philosophy which overlooks basic justice: how could God condemn people for not being Christians when they never had such an opportunity because they never had heard of it. In the Bahá'í view, these peoples have a special role to play in the spiritual development of the world, because of the suffering which they have endured, and perhaps on account of the faint light of these ancient religions which still shines in their hearts. 'Abdu'l-Bahá (1844-1921), eldest son of Bahá'u'lláh and his successor as head of the Bahá'í Community, made the following comments on this theme with regard to African peoples and American Indians:

"Bahá'u'lláh once compared the coloured people to the black pupil of the eye surrounded by the white. In the black pupil is seen the reflection of that which is before it, and through it the light of the spirit shineth forth"

'Abdu'l-Bahá[1]

"Likewise should Indians be educated and properly guided, there can be no doubt that through the Divine teachings they will become so enlightened that the whole earthwill be illumined".

'Abdu'l-Bahá[2]

Hinduism, Buddhism and Zoroastrianism

Hinduism, that most ancient of today's religions is recognised in the Bahá'í writings as one of the lights of humanity.

"Blessed Souls - whether Moses, Jesus, Zoroaster, Krishna, Buddha, Confucius or Mohammed - were the cause of the illumination of the world of humanity"

'Abdu'l-Bahá[3]

Though this is so, the Bahá'í writings do not make many references to Hinduism for the following reason provided by Shoghi Effendi (1896-1957), grandson of 'Abdu'l-Bahá: and Guardian of the Faith from 1921 to 1957:

"The origins of this (Hindu) religion and many other religions that abound in India are not quite known to us, and even Orientalists and the students of religion are not in complete accord about the results of their investigations in that field. The Bahá'í Writings also do not refer specifically to any of these forms of religion current in India. So the Guardian feels it is impossible to give you any definite and detailed information on the subject"

Letter on the behalf of Shoghi Effendi[4]

Though Krishna is generally believed to have been the Founder of Hinduism and is occasionally mentioned in Bahá'í writings, as in the above quotation, there is virtually no historical record of such a person, and the more precise Bahá'í references to Hinduism make attributions to the Hindu Holy Book, the ***Bhagavid-Gita,*** rather than directly to Krishna himself, as in the following quotation concerning the Hindu prophecy of the coming of another Messenger of God:

"To Him, the Bhagavid-Gita of the Hindus had referred as the Most Great Spirit, the Tenth Avatar, the Immaculate Manifestation of Krishna"

Shoghi Effendi[5]

In this context, it is interesting to note the following passage from the ***Bhagavid-Gita*** which appears to contain a simple version of the idea of Progressive Revelation:

"Whenever there is decay of rightenousness, O Bharata, and there is exaltation of unrighteousness, then I myself, come forth for the protection of Good, for the destruction of the evil doers, for the sake of firmly establishing righteousness, I am born from age to age".[6]

The few references to Buddha in the Bahá'í Writings make it clear that he is recognised as one of the Manifestations of God. In consequence, it is the Bahá'í view, contrary to the general belief, that Buddha did teach the existence of God:

"The founder of Buddhism was a wonderful soul. He established the oness of God, but later the original principles of his doctrines gradually disappeared, and ignorant customs and ceremonials arose and increased, until they finally ended in the worship of statues and images."

'Abdu'l-Bahá [7]

This view, it might be added, is supported by Mahatma Gandhi who wrote in his book *The Way of Buddha* that:

"I have heard it contended...that the Buddha did not believe in God. In my humble opinion such a belief contradicts the very central fact of Buddha's teachings."

A contemporary Bahá'í scholar, Jamshid Fozdar, in his book, *The God of Buddha,* has put forward the theory that the early Buddhists feared that Hinduism would absorb their religion, as it had other cults and sects, and made a point of playing down the supernatural so as to distinguish Buddhism from Hinduism with its myriads of gods. He points out that if the Buddhist texts are reviewed carefully there is ample evidence that Buddha's teachings are predicated on the existance of a Supreme Being, e.g.

"There is, O Monks, an Unborn, Unoriginated, Uncreated, Unformed. Were there not, O monks, this

Unborn, Unoriginated, Uncreated, Unformed, there would be no escape from the world of the born, originated, created formed."[8]

Other Bahá'í authors, notably William Sears in his book ***Thief in the Night*** have drawn attention to prophecies in the Holy Books of Buddhism which make reference to future Manifestations:

"I am not the first Buddha who came upon the earth, nor shall I be the last. In due time another Buddha will arise in the world, a Holy One, a supremely enlightened one, endowed with wisdom, in conduct auspicious, knowing the universe, an incomparable leader of men, a master of angels and mortals. He will reveal to you the same eternal truths which I have taught you. He will preach his religion, glorious at the goal, in the spirit and in the letter. He will proclaim a religious life wholly perfect and pure such as I now proclaim."

Buddha[9]

Zoroaster, who probably lived at the end of the seventh century B.C.(10), brought new teachings to purify the ancient beliefs of the Aryans, and these teachings later became the religion of the Persian Empire, one of the most powerful states, indeed civilizations, from the end of the sixth century B.C. until its eventual overthrow by the Arabs in the middle of the seventh century A.D. Today adherents of Zoroastrianism are mainly limited to a few thousands in Persia and India (mostly in Bombay). The power of the religion can be gauged from the fact, that despite its age and decline in numbers of followers, its adherents are still known for their cleanliness, honesty and generally high ethical standards and personal purity - there is no such person, for instance, as a Zoroastrian prostitute. Zoroaster abolished blood sacrifice centuries before Western societies did, and, in place, substituted the sacrament of fire, symbol of the holy spirit. The advanced teachings of Zoroaster are believed to have been studied by both the Greeks and the Jews. In later years Zoroastrian priests began to refer to the existence of an evil God, co-equal with the God of good (Ahra Mazda), and so developed a duallist concept of the universe. Modern scholars, however, are in accord with the Bahá'í view that Zoroaster himself was a monotheist like the Founders of the other great religions.

Turning now to prophecies, Zoroaster is recorded, in the **Dinkird,** the Holy Book of the Zoroastrian Faith, as having made the following statement which is quite remarkable from the Bahá'í view:

"When a thousand two hundred and some years have past from the inception of the religion of the Arabian and the overthrow of the Kingdom of Iran and the degradation of the followers of My Religion, a descendant of the Iranian Kings will be raised up as a Prophet."

The Persian monarchy was overthrown shortly after the inception of Islám which was born in Arabia. The Bahá'í Faith began in the year 1260 of the Muslim calendar and Bahá'u'lláh, its Founder, was descended from the Sassanian kings of Iran. Zoroaster is also recorded as having said that the saviour foretold, by name Shah Bahram, would come from the Land of Nur, a province near the Caspian Sea which was the home of the family of Bahá'u'lláh. The **Dinkird** contains some highly specific passages regarding the time when the saviour would appear which 'Abdu'l-Bahá explained as follows:

"Thou hast written that in the sacred books of the followers of Zoroaster it is written that in the latter days, in three separate Dispensations, the sun must needs be brought to a standstill. In the first Dispensation, it is predicted, the sun will remain motionless for ten days; in the second twice that time;

in the third for no less than one whole month. The interpretation of the prophecy is this: the first Dispensation to which it refers is the Muhammadan Dispensation during which the Sun of Truth stood still for ten days. Each day is reckoned as one century. The Muhammadan Dispensation must have, therefore, lasted no less than one thousand years, which is precisely the period that has elapsed from the setting of the Star of the Imámate to the advent of the Dispensation proclaimed by the Báb. The second Dispensation referred to in this prophecy is the one inaugurated by the Báb Himself, which began in the year 1260 A.H. and was brought to a close in the year 1280 A.H. As to the third Dispensation - the Revelation proclaimed by Bahá'u'lláh - inasmuch as the Sun of Truth when attaining that station shineth in the plenitude of its meridian splendour its duration has been fixed for a period of one whole month, which is the maximum time taken by the sun to pass through a sign of the Zodiac. From this thou canst imagine the magnitude of the Bahá'í cycle - a cycle that must extend over a period of at least five hundred thousand years."

'Abdu'l-Bahá[11]

Judaism

As mentioned earlier, it is the Bahá'í view that there have been numerous Educators who have come to lead mankind to the spiritual path but that knowledge of the teachings and personalities of many of them have been lost in the mists of history. Probably the earliest Manifestation of which we have record is Adam. 'Abdu'l-Bahá said that there were many spiritual meanings to the story of the Fall in Genesis, one of which is that the followers of Adam had deviated from the spiritual path by becoming too attached to the material things of the world. Another interpretation is that when Adam brought religion and standards of right and wrong, man's spiritual evolution was taken a step further and the innocence of ignorance was gone forever.

Both Noah and Abraham are recognized in the Bahá'í writings as Messengers of God:

"...among the Prophets was Noah. When He was invested with the role of Prophethood and was moved by the spirit of God to arise and proclaim His Cause, whoever believed in Him acknowledged His Faith, was endowed with the grace of a new life. Of Him it could truly be said that He was reborn and revived."

Bahá'u'lláh[12]

Abraham like many other Messengers of God was persecuted for his views, being driven from his homeland for teaching the oneness of God. The story of Ishmael signifies the immense suffering which every Manifestation has to undergo to carry out his mission:

"...Abraham stood fast and showed forth supernatural firmness; and God made His exile to be to His eternal honour, because He established the Unity of God, in the midst of a polytheistic generation."

' Abdu'l-Bahá[13]

It is interesting that the founders of Judaism, Zoroastrianism, Christianity, Islám (and the Bahá'í Faith) all claimed to be descended from the line of Abraham, which perhaps says something of the importance of his station. 'Abdu'l-Bahá said that Abraham prophecized the coming of Moses and his Dispensation.

"His Holiness Abraham, on Him be peace, made a covenant concerning His Holiness Moses and gave the glad tidings of His Coming."[14]

Bahá'ís deeply revere Moses, the fourth great Messenger (after Adam, Noah and Abraham) of the **Torah,** as the Founder of Judaism. Bahá'u'lláh spoke of him as being:

"Armed with the rod of celestial dominion, adorned with the white hand of Divine knowledge, and proceeding from the Paran of the love of God, and wielding the serpent of power and everlasting majesty. He shone forth from the Sinai of light upon the world."[15]

'Abdu'l-Bahá drew attention to the greatness of Moses in achieving his mission despite tremendous odds. Thus (i) he had a reputation of being a murderer because he had killed a man in defending someone who was being persecuted, (ii) he stuttered, and (iii) he was opposed by the Pharoah of Egypt, the most powerful monarch in the world of that day.

"This people from the depths of degradation were lifted up to the height of glory. They were captive, they became free; they were the most ignorant of peoples, they became the most wise. As the result of the institutions that Moses gave them, they attained a position which entitled them to honour among nations, and their fame spread to all lands; to such a degree indeed that among surrounding nations if one wished to praise a man one said, 'surely he is an Israelite'. Moses established the religious law and the civil law, these gave life to the people of Israel and led them to the highest possible degree of civilization at that period. To such a development did they attain that the sages of Greece came to regard the illustrious men of Israel as models of perfection."[16]

The **Torah** (or Old Testament) abounds with prophecies of future Messengers of God. Bahá'í writings say that some of these referred to the coming of Jesus, some to Muḥammad, and some to the Bab and Bahá'u'lláh. 'Abdu'l-Bahá mentions, in particular, that Moses announce the coming of Jesus. He went on to say that the Jewish people failed to recognize Jesus as the Christ because they interpreted prophecies in too literal a fashion:

"When Christ came they denounced and slew Him,

saying: 'This is not the One for whom we wait. Behold when the Messiah shall come, signs and wonders shall testify that He is in truth the Christ. We know the signs and conditions, and they have not appeared. The Messiah will arise out of an unknown city. He shall sit upon the throne of David, and behold, He shall come with a sword of steel, and with a sceptre of iron shall He rule! He shall fulfil the law of the Prophets, He shall conquer the East and the West, and shall glorify His chosen people the Jews. He shall bring with Him a reign of peace, during which even the animals shall cease to be at enmity with man. For behold the wolf and the lamb shall drink from the same spring, and the lion and the doe shall lie down in the same pasture, the serpent and the mouse shall share the same nest, and all God's creatures shall be at rest'

"According to the Jews, Jesus the Christ fulfilled none of these conditions, for their eyes were holden and they could not see. He came from Nazareth, no unknown place. He carried no sword in His hand, nor even a stick. He did not sit upon the throne of David, He was a poor man. He reformed the Laws of Moses, and broke the Sabbath Day. He did not conquer the East and the West, but was Himself subject to the Roman Law. He did not exalt the Jews, but taught equality and brotherhood, and rebuked the Scribes and Pharissees. He brought in no reign of peace, for during His lifetime injustice and cruelty reached such height that even He Himself fell victim to it, and died a shameful death upon the Cross.

"Thus the Jews thought and spoke, for they did not understand the Scriptures nor the glorious truths that were contained in them. The letter they knew, but of the life-giving Spirit they understood not a word."[17]

'Abdu'l-Bahá explained what the Jewish priests failed to see as follows:

"Hearken, and I will show you the meaning thereof.

Although He came from Nazareth, which was a known place, He also came from Heaven. The sword He carried was the sword of His tongue, with which He divided the good from the evil, the true from the false, the faithful from the unfaithful, and the light from the darkness. His word was indeed a sharp sword! The Throne upon which He sat is the Eternal from God from which Christ reigns forever, a heavenly throne, not an earthly one, for the things of earth pass away but heavenly things pass not away. He reinterpreted and completed the law of Moses and fulfilled the Law of the Prophets. His word conquered the East and the West. His Kingdom is everlasting. He exalted those Jews who recognised Him. They were men and women of humble birth, but contact with Him made them great and gave them everlasting dignity. The animals who were to live with one another signified the different sects and races, who, once having been at war, were now to dwell in love and charity, drinking together the water of life from Christ the eternal Spring.

"Thus, all the spiritual prophecies concerning the coming of Christ were fulfilled, but the Jews shut their eyes that they should not see, and their ears that they should not hear, and the Divine Reality of Christ passed through their midst unheard, unlived and unrecognized".[18]

In the Bahá'í view it was the failure of the Jewish people to recognize Jesus that has caused the tribulations which they have suffered in the last two thousand years. Certainly it might be argued that if they had followed Jesus they would have been less concerned with national pride which led to the initial disasterous clash with the Roman Empire in the first century after the Crucifixion. This view, it should be stressed, is quite different from the abhorrent traditions that the Jewish people are "Christ killers",

a slander which goes back to the fourth century
A.D.,when Christianity first became a state religion.
The Jewish people have certainly not been the only
ones to fail to recognize a new Manifestation of God
and to have suffered accordingly. Bahá'u'lláh pointed
out that the Muslims who are given to chastising the
Jews for their tradition that:

"The Hand of God is chained up"[19]
are themselves guilty of the same attitude with regard
to the Bahá'í Dispensation.

'Abdu'l-Bahá added that though it was true that
Jesus had changed some of the laws concerning
divorce and food, had abrogated the practice of
circumcision and had put a liberal interpretation on
the law of the Sabbath, nevertheless he had upheld
the station of Moses and the main structure of his
laws, particularly the Ten Commandments. He also
said that as a result of the spread of Christianity the
Torah had been translated into over 600 languages,
whereas previously it had been only available in
Hebrew and Greek. In view of all this, he issued an
invitation to the Jewish people, when speaking in
synagogues during his tour of North America, to drop
old prejudices and look upon Jesus in an objective
light - just as when he spoke in churches he asked
Christians to understand the status of Muhammad.
Could they not take pride in the fact that Jesus was
a Jew? In a synagogue in Washington D.C. he said:

"What harm could come from a statement by the
Jews that Jesus was also a Manifestation of the Word
of God"[20]

Earlier in a synagogue in San Francisco he had
said:

"Why do the Hebrews refuse to praise and accept
the other great Messengers who have appeared in the
world? What harm could there be in this? What
rightful objection? None whatever. You would lose

nothing by such action and statement, on the contrary you would contribute to the welfare of mankind."[21]

Of course, it would be up to Christians to make such an act easier by eliminating their own prejudices against the Jews.

There are many prophecies in the **Torah,** which Bahá'ís claim refer to the coming of the Bahá'í Faith, most notably in the Books of Daniel, Micah and Isaiah. Some of the most significant are as follows:

(i) "Then I heard one saint speaking and another saint said unto that certain saint which spoke; How long shall be the vision concerning the daily sacrifice, and the transgression of desolation, to give both sanctuary and the lost to be trodden under foot? And he said unto me, Unto two thousand and three hundred days; then shall the sanctuary be cleansed."[22]

'Abdu'l-Bahá explained that this passage referred to the coming of a Messenger of God two thousand three hundred years (in Biblical terminology a day equals one year[23]) after an edict for the rebuilding of the Temple of Jerusalem. Four such edicts were issued: by Cyrus in 536 B.C., by Darius in 519 B.C., by Artanersces in 457 B.C., and again by Artanersces in 444 B.C.. 'Abdu'l-Bahá said Daniel was referring to the third edict. Two thousand three hundred years from 457 B.C.is 1844 A.D., the year of the Báb's Declaration (there is no year zero A.D.) The same calculation had been made by the Millerites and other Christians who confidently were awaiting the Second Coming of Christ in the early 1840s. 'Abdu'l-Bahá remarked also that in Chapter 9, verse 34, Daniel makes reference to another event occurring 490 years after the same edict - this would be 32 A.D., the probable year of the Crucifixion of Jesus.

(ii) "And one said to the man clothed in linen, which was born upon the waters of the river, How long shall it be to the end of these wonders? And I heard the man clothed in linen, which was upon the waters of the river, when he held up his right hand and his left hand unto heaven, and swore by him that liveth for ever that it shall be for a time, times, and a half; and that when he shall have accomplished to scatter the power of the holy people, all these things shall be finished."[24]

'Abdu'l-Bahá said that this passage was a reference to the 1,260 years during which Islám was the latest religion of God, i.e. until the Declaration of the Báb in 1260 A.H. (Muslim calendar), 1844 A.D. (Christian calendar). A time, times and a half signified three and a half years which is equal to forty-two months or twelve hundred and sixty days, or years in Biblical terminology.

(iii) "And from the time that the daily sacrifice shall be taken away, and the abominations that maketh desolation to be set up, there shall be a thousand two hundred and ninety days"[25]

'Abdu'l-Bahá explained that the reference was to the 1,290 years from the Proclamation of Muhammad, which occurred ten years before the Hejira (year one A.H.) to the Declaration of Bahá'u'lláh which was made in 1280 A.H., (1863 A.D.).

The following four quotations are taken by Bahá'ís as referring to the coming of Bahá'u'lláh, a Persian nobleman, whose title means "The Glory of God' in Arabic, (i) who was exiled from the fortified city of Constantinople to the fortified city of Akká, (ii) who when released went to an island in the river Namayn, (iii) who prepared for his mission in the mountains of Kurdistan and willed that the center of his cause should be located on Mount Carmel, and (iv) who during the course of his exile travelled from the Black Sea to the Mediterranean. Since the arrival of Bahá'u'lláh in Akká in 1868, the area which was then a desert has become a prosperous agricultural area.

(i) "and I will set my throne in Elam (Persia) ... saith the Lord"[26]

(ii) "In that day also he shall come even to thee from Assyria and from the fortified cities, and from the fortress even to the river, and from the sea and from mountain to mountain"[27]

(iii) "and behold, the Glory of God of Israel came from the way of the East"[28]

(iv) "The wilderness and the solitary place shall be glad for them; and the desert shall rejoice, and blossom as the rose. It shall blossom abundantly, and rejoice even with joy and singing: the glory of Lebanon shall be given unto it, the excellency of Carmel and Sharon, they shall see the glory of the Lord, and the excellency of our God"[29]

Finally, there is the well known passage from Isaiah which is sometimes understood to refer to the coming of Jesus but which 'Abdu'l-Bahá said referred in fact to the present age:

"And there shall come forth a rod out of the stem of Jesse, and a Branch shall grow out of his roots: And the spirit of the Lord shall rest upon him, the spirit of wisdom and understanding, the spirit of counsel and might, the spirit of knowledge and of fear of the Lord: and he shall not judge after the sight of his eyes, neither reprove after the hearing of his ears: But with righteousness shall he judge the poor, and reprove with equity for the meek of the earth: and he shall smite the earth with the rod of his mouth, and with the breath of his lips shall he slay the wicked. And righteousness shall be the girdle of his loins, and faithfulness the firdle of his reins. The wolf also shall dwell with the lamb, and the leopard shall lie down with the kid; and the calf and the young lion and the fatling together; and a little child shall lead them. And the cow and the bear shall feed; their young ones shall lie down together: and the lion shall eat straw like the ox. And the sucking child shall play on the hole of the asp, and the weaned child shall put his hand on the cockatrice' den. They shall not hurt nor destroy in all my holy mountain: for the earth shall be full of the knowledge of the Lord, as the waters cover the sea. And in that day there shall be a root of Jesse, which shall stand for an ensign of the people: to it shall the Gentiles seek: and his rest shall be glorious"[30]

'Abdu'l-Bahá explained that Jesus led mankind along the road to peace but it was not achieved during the period of his Revelation, and he never claimed that it would be. It is Bahá'u'lláh who has brought teachings for the establishment of universal peace and justice between nations. Joseph was descended from Jesse, the third wife of Abraham, but, as Christians are the first to assent, he was not the putative father of Jesus. Bahá'ís claim that Bahá'u'lláh was descended from Jesse.

Christianity

When a growing number of persons from the Christian West heard of the Bahá'í Faith from the 1890s onwards, they naturally asked a large number of questions about Bahá'í views on Christianity. They respected and did not question the high ethical teachings of the Bahá'í Faith, which were similar in broad principles to those of Christianity. Their main concern was frequently to do with the more controversial aspects of Christian belief which asserted its claim to be superior to other religions; in extreme form this attitude denied any validity to other religions. The first part of this section summarizes the answers which were given to this type of question.

The exclusiveness of Christianity begins with the belief that Jesus was God, that part of the Trinity called the Son of God. In Bahá'í writings Jesus, like the other Messengers of God, is described as a Mirror reflecting the "The Sun of Reality, the essence of Divinity". The Messengers are such perfect channels for God's message that many of them, including Jesus, would sometimes speak as if they were God Himself, whereas at other times, they, the Messengers, would address God as if they were completely separate entities. In this sense it is reasonable in the Bahá'í view to say "The Father is in the Son". The title "Son of God" is used with reference to Jesus in the Bahá'í writings, as indeed it was used by Jesus himself. It should be observed, however, that this title need not imply uniqueness as the term was used to refer to others as well as Jesus by his contemporaries[31]. Thus John the Baptist said of his desciples that they:

"Were born, not of blood, nor of the will of the flesh, nor of the will of man; but of God"

The Bahá'í view is that the theory of the Trinity, the idea of God being split into three, and that part of God actually walked on earth, is not reasonable:

"God is pure perfection, and creatures are but imperfections. For God to descend into the conditions of existence would be the greatest of imperfections;

... the Sun did not descend to dwell and abide in the mirror. No, it continues to subsist in its exaltation and sublimity, while appearing and becoming manifest in the mirror in beauty and perfection.

Anything else would be illogical"[32]

A similar view has been expressed by a group of modern Christian theologians in a recent book entitled **The Myth of God Incarnate** which states that there is nothing in the early Christian texts which indicates that Jesus said or believed that he was God. It goes on to argue that Jesus was elevated to the status of God by early followers influenced by pagan and other Mediterranean beliefs (several Roman emperors, for instance, claimed to be gods). The view became frozen into dogma in the Nicean Creed.

A second matter which is of great significance to many Christians is the belief in the Virgin Birth and the special status of Mary as the "Mother of God". In the Bahá'í writings the immaculacy, i.e. spiritual purity, of Mary is constantly stressed and she is always spoken of with the utmost reverence. However, Bahá'ís believe that the station of Jesus does not depend in anyway on belief in the Virgin Birth, but rather on the qualities of God which he reflected in his character, and on the greatness of his teachings. 'Abdu'l-Bahá, with the gentle humour which was so typical of him, pointed out that if having no human father was so important, then Adam would be the greater because he was recorded as having had neither a human father nor a human mother!

Two important Christian rites are baptism and holy communion. As noted earlier, it is not a Bahá'í belief that man is innately sinful and that baptism is a necessary act to wash away that sin. Bahá'ís believe that Jesus was sinless and that he only underwent baptism at the hands of John the Baptist as a symbolic statement to his followers to strive for purity. 'Abdu'l-Bahá also said that the holy communion is a purely symbolic act:

"To eat is to draw near to him and to drink is to believe in him.

"It is thought by some that the Eucharist is the reality of Christ, and that the Divinity and the Holy Spirit descend into and exist in it. Now when one, the Eucharist is taken after a few moments it is simply disintergrated, and entirely transformed. Therefore how can such a thought be conceived? God forbid! Certainly it is an absolute fantasy" (33).

Of supreme importance in the story of Jesus is the climax of the Crucifixion. Bahá'í literature refers at some length to two aspects of this event. The first point which is made is that Jesus was persecuted because Jewish religious leaders thought him an imposter because he did not literally fulfill their prophecies, as previously discussed, a lesson for all religious leaders to learn. The second aspect of the Crucifixion which is stressed in Bahá'í writings is that Jesus sacrificed himself so that his teachings might spread. It is a spiritual law that Messengers of God will undergo great suffering whilst carrying out their mission, simply because they and their teachings are a challenge to prevailing practices. This is a quite different concept, however, from the idea that Jesus had to make a bloody atonement to God for the "sin" of Adam:

"Christ's intention was to represent and promote a cause which was to educate the human world, to quicken the children of Adam, and to enlighten all mankind; and since to represent such a great cause - a cause which was antagonistic to all the people of the world and all the nations and kingdoms - meant that he would be killed and sacrificed, so Christ in proclaiming His mission sacrificed His life ... Christ was like a seed, and this seed sacrificed its own form so that the tree might grow and develop. Although the form of the seed was destroyed, its reality became apparent in perfect majesty and beauty in the form of a tree".[34]

The amazing physical events which the gospels record as having taken place at the time of the Crucifixion are understood to underline the spiritual significance of this remarkable event in the history of humanity and should not be taken literally:

"...in the Gospel it is written that at the martyrdom of Christ darkness prevailed, and the earth quaked, and the veil of the Temple was rent in twain from the top to the bottom, and the dead came forth from their graves. If these events had happened they would indeed have been wonderful, and would certainly have been recorded in the history of the times. They would have become the cause of much troubling of heart. The soldiers would either have taken down Christ from the cross or they would have fled. These events are not related in any history, therefore it is evident they ought not to be taken literally, but as having an inner significance".[35]

Bahá'ís also see the story of the Resurrection in spiritual terms rather than physical":

"And as it has become evident that Christ came from the spiritual heaven of the Divine Kingdom, therefore his disappearance under the earth for three days has an inner signification, and is not an outward fact. In the same way his resurrection from the interior of the earth is also symbolical; it is a spiritual and divine fact, and not a material one ... the ascension of Christ with an elemental body to the visible heaven is contrary to the science of mathematics".[36]

'Abdu'l-Bahá explained the Bahá'í view of the Resurrection as follows:

"...the desciples were troubled and agitated after the martydom of Christ. The reality of Christ, which signifies his teachings, his bounties, his perfections, and his spiritual power, was hidden and concealed for two or three days after his martyrdom, and was not resplendent and manifest. No rather it was lost; for the believers were few in number and were troubled and agitated. The Cause of Christ was like a lifeless body; and when after three days the desciples became assured and steadfast, and began to serve the Cause of Christ, and resolved to spread the divine teachings, putting his counsels into practice, and arising to serve him, the Reality of Christ became resplendent and his bounty appeared ... In other words the Cause of Christ was like a lifeless body, until the life and the bounty of the Holy Spirit surrounded it".[37]

A summary of the Bahá'í position on Christianity as a whole is given in the following passage from Shoghi Effendi:

"As to the position of Christianity, let it be stated without any hesitation or equivocation that its divine origin is unconditionally acknowledged, that the Sonship and Divinity of Jesus Christ are fearlessly asserted, that the divine inspiration of the Gospel is fully recognised, that the reality of the mystery of the Immaculacy of the Virgin Mary is conferred, and the primacy of Peter, the Prince of the Apostles, is upheld and defended".[38]

Before closing this section on Christianity, reference should be made to the most significant subject of all: the "Second Coming". Jesus spoke of this matter to his desciples just before the Feast of the Passover and his words are recorded in all four gospels. The following passages from **St Matthew** relating to that event are of particular interest for Bahá'ís:

"For many shall come in my name, saying I am Christ; and shall deceive many and this gospel of the kingdom shall be preached in all the world for a witness into all the nations; and then shall the end come.

"When ye shall see the abomination of desolation, spoken of by Daniel the prophet stand in the holy place (whoso readeth, let him understand)"

"For as the lightening cometh out of the east, and shineth even unto the west; so shall also the coming of the Son of Man be.

"Immediately after the tribulation of those days shall the sun be darkened, and the moon shall not give her light, and the stars shall fall from heaven and the powers of the heaven shall be shaken.

"... and they shall see the Son of Man coming in the clouds of heaven with power and great glory"[39]

Bahá'ís make the following observations
concerning these passages. First, Christ warned
against those who would claim to be the physical
return; Bahá'u'lláh, however, claimed that he was the
return in the spirit, not the flesh. Second, in the first
half of the nineteenth century, just before Bahá'u'lláh
made his declaration, there was a great surge in
missionary activity by Christians and as a result the
written gospel finally reached all parts of the earth for
the first time in history. Third, as mentioned already,
the verses in **Daniel** referred to by Jesus, prophecied
the great turning point in the spiritual history of
mankind would happen in 1844. Jesus would return
in the spirit when established religion is in decline and
he would sweep aside accumulated rituals and
superstitions which had suffocated the spirit of true
religion.Fourth, in fulfillment of prophesy, Bahá'u'lláh
came from the land to the east of the "Holy Land" and
his name means "The Glory of God".

Additional details concerning Jesus's discourses
on the "Second Coming" are noted by Bahá'ís in
St Luke and **St John.** The following verse in St Luke,
for instance, is understood to refer to the Edict of Toleration issued by the Sultan of the Ottoman Empire
in 1844, which allowed Jews for the first time in centuries to return to Jerusalem:

"...and Jerusalem shall be trodden down by the
Gentiles, until the times of the Gentiles be fulfilled".[40]

Verse 2, Chapter 10 of **St John** states:

"But he that entereth in by the door is the
shepherd of the sheep"

Bahá'ís see this as a prophesy that at the "time
of the end" the main mission, that of Bahá'u'lláh,
would be preceded or led in by the short mission of
the Bab, the "Door or Gate". Other passages in
St John, as quoted below, are interpreted as saying
that the coming Manifestation of God will uphold the

station and teachings of Jesus, as has been the case with Bahá'u'lláh, but that he will also bring new teachings which were not appropriate at the time of Jesus, because society had not developed to the point where they were either practicable or understandable.

"But when the Comforter is come, whom I will send unto you from the Father, he shall testify of me.

"I have yet many things to say unto you, but ye cannot bear them now. Howbeit when he, the Spirit of truth is come, he will guide you unto all truth;

"These things have I spoken unto you in proverbs: but the time cometh, when I shall no more speak unto you in proverbs, but shall show you plainly of the Father".[41]

A second group of prophecies in the **New Testament** concerning the "time of the end" occur in the **Revelation of St John.** 'Abdu'l-Bahá gave extended commentaries on the meaning of passages in Chapters 11 and 12, including the following verses of particular interest:

"And the holy city shall they tread under foot forty and two months;

"And I will give power unto my two witnesses, and they shall prophecy a thousand two hundred and three score days clothed in sackcloth".[42]

'Abdu'l-Bahá said that these verses prophecied the number of years between the beginning of the mission of Muhammad and that of of the Báb - both quote 1,260 days which, as already mentioned means in Biblical terms 1,260 years: the Báb's Declaration occurred in the year 1260 of the Islámic calendar. The two witnesses were Muhammad and Ali, his most stalwart follower, and the first Imám (see the following section on Islám). Other passages of interest in Chapter 11 are;

"And when they shall have finished their testimony, the beast that ascendeth out of the bottomless pit shall make war aginst them, and shall overcome them and kill them.

"The second woe is past; and behold the third woe cometh quickly"[43]

The beast, 'Abdu'l-Bahá said, is the Ummayyad clan who murdered Ali and his family, the true successors of Muhammad, in the view of both the Bahá'í Faith and the Shia sect of Islám, and so caused a terrible corruption of Islám. Woes are the days of the Lord when mankind is called to account. The first woe occurred when Muhammad announced his Mission, the second was at the time of the Báb, and the third was when Bahá'u'lláh announced his Revelation, which occurred only a short time after the Báb. Similar themes are to be found in Chapter 12. The opening verses of that chapter read as follows:

"And I saw a new heaven and a new earth: for the first heaven and the first earth were passed away: and there was no more sea. And I, John, saw the holy city, new Jerusalem, coming down from God out of heaven"[44]

'Abdu'l-Bahá said that in this passage heaven and earth represent the laws of religion and that it is a prophecy of a coming new dispensation of God, a new Jerusalem, which will cover the whole earth.

Islám

Islám is of special interest to Bahá'ís because, as pointed out by Shoghi Effendi, it is the source and background of the Bahá'í Faith. It is also the most recent and most accurately documented of all the other religions. Thus Shoghi Effendi made the following observation regarding the **Qurán**:

"...the Quran, which book is more authentic than the Bible, including both the New and Old Testaments. The Bible is not wholly authentic, and in this respect not to be compared with the Quran"[45]

Two of the most important Bahá'í principles are independent investigation and the abolition of uninformed prejudice, including religious prejudice. In accord with these principles, Bahá'ís are urged, amongst other activities, to make fair presentations of all other religions when there is prejudice against them. Mention has been made earlier of 'Abdu'l-Bahá speaking in defense of Christianity in Jewish synagogues during his visit to the West. More important, because of the scope of the prejudice involved, has been the Bahá'í effort to defend and justify Islám in the West. 'Abdu'l-Bahá, himself, spoke often on Islám in Christian churches in North America and Europe, and there are several Bahá'í publications now available which develop this theme (46).

The long tradition of antagonism to Islám in the West goes back to the seventh century A.D. when a local bishop sent back to his fellow Christians prejudiced reports concerning the then infant religion. The prejudice reached its peak in the early Middle Ages during the Crusades, when it is now recognised by most objective historians that the standard of conduct of the Christians was far below that of the so called "infidel". The prejudice was so strong that Dante, for instance, placed Muḥammad and the Imám Ali in the eigth circle, ninth pouch of the Inferno. His name was insulted by changing it to "Mahound" as in "hound". He was always portrayed as being lecherous and violent. Over the years, especially after the Renaissance, more scholarly views began to prevail and gradually it was conceded that he had been a great warrior, philosopher and statesman. The prejudice,though reduced, nevertheless remained strong and was undoubtedly given a strong boost in the nieteenth and early twentieth centuries by Christian missionaries, frustrated by their almost universal failure to win converts in the Islámic countries. Thus Rodwell, in his introduction to the best known translation of the **Qurán,** writes:

"The shortcomings of the moral teachings contained in the Koran are striking enough if judged from the highest ethical standpoint with which we are acquainted"[47].

Certainly the writer has yet to come across a book published in the West, other than by Bahá'ís or Muslims, which treats Muhammad with the same respect and reverence as, for instance, Muslims treat Jesus.

In view of these circumstances, it is perhaps useful to devote the first part of this summary of the Bahá'í view concerning Islám to an analysis of the principle Christian criticisms of Islám.

One fundamental criticism often heard is that Muḥammad collected his teachings from other religions, notably Christianity and Judaism. In response Bahá'ís note: (i) that all religions have the same universal principles; (ii) that the only direct quotation in the **Qurán** from the **Bible** is Psalm 37:29 which occurs in Surih 21: 105; (iii) that there are a large number of teachings in Islám which are not specifically referred to in either Christianity or Judaism, e.g. ordinances against gambling, usury, and alcohol, the special emphasis on prayer, respect for non combatants (the basis of the code of chivalry later adapted by Christian Europe), and the requirement that Muslims give alms to the poor. It might be added that in Islám, all are considered responsible for their own actions and there is an absence of the Pauline theme of original sin. In addition, it is pointed out that the theory that Muhammad was not inspired but only a collector of existing ideas would not account for the tremendous power of his teachings nor does it allow appreciation for the **Qurán** as one of the world's greatest pieces of literature.

Another favourite canard against Islám is that Muḥammad was lecherous. It is gleefully noted that he had thirteen wives whereas Jesus had none. A detailed analysis of the actual circumstances of Muhammad's marriages is to be found in **Prescription for Living** (pages 132-133) by Ruhiyyih Rabbani, wife of Shoghi Effendi. That analysis might be summarized as follows. First, as to the question of marriage itself, it should be noted that Jesus died young and there is nothing to indicate that he intended celibacy to be the ideal state for his followers. Ambiguity regarding this question came about in the writings of St Paul. Second, it is pointed out that Muhammad was reported to be chaste until he first married at the age of 25 or 26. When he did marry, he chose a woman of 42 who was already twice widowed. This was hardly an act of lechery, especially when it is remembered that most marriages in the East at that time were when the bride was very young by present day Western standards. During the period of this marriage, which lasted for 23 years until she died, Muḥammad did not have any other wives. His twelve remaining wives were acquired in the last few years of his life, after the age of 50. Of the twelve later wives, nine were widows of companions and they were taken in by Muhammad as a form of protection for them; one of the nine had been offered first to his followers but she had been rejected as too hot tempered and only Muḥammad would take her! Of the remaining three, one was a divorced cousin, one was a seven year old child, an arranged marriage necessary to reduce tribal rivalries, and the last was a princess provided on a political basis by the Roman governor of Egypt.

A related criticism voiced in the West has been that Muḥammad has given a low place to women, especially in permitting men to have more than one wife

simultaneously. In response, it is pointed out that critics should remember that neither Jesus nor Moses
had spoken on the subject of number of wives
although polygamy was generally prevalent in nearly
all societies of the time. It might be added that early
Christians quite often had more than one wife. Islám
was the first religion to put a limit on numbers - not
more than four at one time. Furthermore it can be
argued, as do liberal Islámic thinkers, that
Muḥammad's injunction could be interpreted to mean
that in practice a man should restrict himself to one
wife. This intrepretation is based on Muhammad's
statement:

"Marry but two, or three or four: and if ye still fear
that ye shall not act equitably then one only".[48]

Quite apart from the issue of numbers of wives,
there is ample evidence that Muḥammad raised the
status of women considerably, probably as far as
contemporary society would go without rebelling
against the new religion. Women were to be treated
with new respect, the duties of husbands were defined
and it was confirmed that women had souls (a view
that, surprisingly, has been doubted by some Islámic
theologians). These principles were given to a people
which had.formerly condoned the practice of burying
alive newly born female children. Muhammad also
instituted new property rights for women including the
right to inherit and to dispose of property and various
rights of alimony.

Another criticism of Islám is that its picture of
Paradise is overly materialistic with its references to
gardens, fountains, and beautiful women. Again the
picture was symbolic and was well understood to be
so by listeners brought up with the colourful imagery
of the Arabic language.

Yet another criticism is that Islám condoned,if not
actually encouraged, slavery. Again, Christians who

make this observation should note that Jesus did not say anything specific about slavery although it was a condition of his day, and indeed large numbers of Christians have held slaves until modern times. Though Muḥammad did not specifically abolish slavery he did attempt to ameliorate its effect by improving the conditions of slavery and by encouraging manumission by his own example. In Islámic society slaves were able to rise to the highest ranks, as for instance those who became sultans in the Ottoman empire.

Perhaps the strongest and widest criticism of Islám is that it spread by the sword rather than by the merit of its philosophy and spiritual power. The tremendous expansion of the Islámic empire in the 7th and 8th centuries as a result of military conquest seems to support this contention, and was it not Muḥammad who preached the Jihad, or Holy War? But closer examination suggests that this criticism is too facile. Muḥammad said:

"Let there be no compulsion in religion".[49]

and he specifically said that his followers were to respect people of the Book (i.e. Christians and Jews). When the converted Arabs conquered other lands, native people were allowed to maintain their own religions. For centuries after the conquest, Muslims were a minority in Egypt, as was true also in Spain. During the Middle Ages, many Jews and Christian Protestants, persecuted in Catholic Europe, preferred to live in Muslim countries because of the much greater degree of toleration. Of course, with time the spirit of toleration began to weaken and as a result persecution of minority religious groups in Islámic countries has often been as savage, if not worse, than ever it was in Christian countries, a most notable example being the fierce repression of the Babis and Bahá'ís in modern times.

War itself, including Holy War against unbelievers, was permitted by Muhammad but only in self defence, and he forbade his followers from starting war. Muḥammad himself, fled from Mecca rather than fight, and in his subsequent career he always negotiated whenever he could, frequently to the disgust of some of his more militant followers and allies.When eventually he returned to Mecca from Medina he proclaimed an amnesty for his enemies who had harassed him for so long. The later conquests of the Arabs were the acts of soldiers and politicians, motivated largely by self interest and not in accordance with the teachings of Muḥammad, much as Christian soldiers and politicians in the West have engaged in regular warfare among themselves, little deterred by the teachings of Jesus.

No summary of Bahá'í teachings regarding Islám would be complete without mentioning the esteem and reverence Bahá'ís have for Muḥammad and his Holy Book, the **Quran.** Bahá'u'lláh spoke of Muḥammad as being "God's Beloved".[50] At another time he wrote:

"If ye cherish the desire to slay Muhammad, seize Me and put an end to My life, for I am He and Myself is His Self".[51]

Bahá'u'lláh recognized Muḥammad's title "Seal of the Prophets", although it is this title which is used to deny any successor religion (this view seems to contradict other Muslim beliefs in the Return of Christ (Sunnis) or the Imám Husayn (Shias)). Bahá'u'lláh responded that all Founders of the great religions are spiritually as one, therefore each may be described as the First or the Last, Alpha or Omega. He also said that the title signified that Muhammad was the last of the prophetic line before the Revelation of Fulfillment.

The **Qurán** was written down on palm leaves, leather, stone, the shoulder blades of sheep, in short any material to hand when Muḥammad had his Revelation. The writings were collected together after his death by his amuensis, Zaquil ibm Thabit and certified as correct by Ali, Muḥammad's son in law who had been with him almost from the beginning of his ministry. Shoghi Effendi said that the **Qurán**:

"Apart from the sacred scriptures of the Babi and Bahá'í Revelations, constitutes the only Book which can be regarded as an absolutely authenticated Repository of the Word of God".[52]

Bahá'í writings also have a clear position with regard to the split in Islám between the Shia (party of Ali) and the Sunni (followers of the Prophet's Way). The former sect predominates in Iran whereas the latter are the majority in virtually all other Islámic lands. The dispute between the two sects goes back to the succession after the death of Muḥammad in 632 A.D. The Shia version of events is that shortly before his death, when returning from a farewell pilgrimage to Mecca, Muḥammad had raised up Ali, his nephew, the husband of his eldest and favourite daughter, Fatimah,[53] and the earliest of his followers, and said:

"Whoever hath me as his Master hath Ali as his Master ... I have been summoned to the Gate of God, and I shall soon depart ... to be concealed from you". Then he added that he would leave two treasures:

"The greatest treasure is the Book of God ... Hold fast to it and do not lose and do not change it. The other treasure is the line of My descendents"[54]

When Muhammad was on his death bed he asked for pen and paper, presumably to record the succession, but these materials were not given to him because he was in such pain. In view of the closeness of Ali to Muhammad it would seem logical for him to be the successor. However, there is no record in the Quran of Ali's right and it is ignored by the Sunnis. For twenty four years following the death of

Muḥammad, the leadership of the new religion was denied to Ali and was held first by Abu Bakr (632-634), then by Omar (634-644),and then by Othman (644-656). All three, who had the title of Caliph (Successor) were selected by a small group of the most powerful tribes of Arabia. Apparently Ali did not press his claim on any of the three occasions, and, in fact, on the first occasion was not even present at the election as he was preparing the body for burial. As a reaction to corruption under the third Caliph, Ali, known for his high principles and learning, was elected by popular acclaim to be the fourth successor of Muhammad.

However, Ali was fiercely opposed by the Governor of Syria, Muawiya, and the most powerful of the Arab clans, the Ummayyads, who had consistently resisted Muḥammad himself in the early days of his ministry. In 680 Ali was finally overthrown and killed by the Ummayyads. Hasan, his eldest son, ruled for a few months, but then abdicated in face of the overwhelming military force of Muawiya, who succeeded him and ruled as Caliph until his death later that year.

There was then a movement, especially among those who took exception to the dominance of the Arab tribes, to restore the leadership of Islám to the family of Muḥammad, in the person of Husayn, the second son of Ali. However, in October 680, Husayn and most of his family were brutally killed as a result of treachery at Karbila in Iráq. This tragedy induced a deep sense of guilt among Husayn's followers who had failed to come to his rescue, and even today his martyrdom is remembered each year by the Shia sect in the month of Murraham with great public displays of anguish and contriteness. As a result of the incident at Karbila the Caliphate remained in the hands of the Ummayyads, who maintained their position for another seventy years.

The Shia sect does not recognize the Caliphate succession beginning with Abu Bakr, and claims that the divinely ordained successors of Muhammad were his descendents, beginning with Ali, then Hassan, then Husayn, who were all given the title of Imám (Spiritual Interpreter). In all, the main body of the Shia recognize twelve Imáms,[55] all of whom after Husayn lived under the shadow of the Caliphate. The fourth and later Imáms abstained from political activity and confined themselves to spiritual and moral example and learning; nevertheless they were seen as a potential threat by the Caliphs, and not one, with the possible exception of the last, died of natural causes. The twelfth Imám disappeared (or died) in 260 A.H. (880 A.D.) at the age of five, soon after the death of his father, the eleventh Imám. The Shia belief is:

"That when the fullness of time is come; when the earth is filled with injustice and the faithful are plunged in dispair, he will come forth heralded by Jesus Christ, overthrow the infidels, establish universal peace and justice and inaugurate a millenium of blessedness".[56]

Briefly, the Bahá'í view is that the Shia belief regarding the succession is correct, although it recognizes that over time Shia stories of the Imáms have been so elaborated that now they are hardly believable. Bahá'u'lláh referred to Ali as:

"Ali, He the exponent of the law of God".[57]

and to Husayn in the following terms;

"No warrior could be found on earth more excellent and nearer to God than Husayn, son of Ali, so peerless and incomparable was he. There was none to equal or match him in the world.

"Should we wish to impart unto thee a glimmer of the mysteries of Husayn's martyrdom, and reveal unto thee the fruits thereof these pages could never suffice, nor exhaust their meaning".[58]

Two other facts might be mentioned with regard to the Bahá'í relationship to the Shia position. The first is that one of the most profound works of Bahá'u'lláh, **The Hidden Words**, is described as the book of Fatimih, wife of Ali, which contains words of comfort for her upon the death of her father, Muḥammad. The second is the quite explicit statements of 'Abdu'l-Bahá, already referred to in the preceding section, to the effect that the "beast that ascendeth out of the bottomless pit (**Revelation of St John,** chapter 11) was the Ummayyad clan which undermined the spiritual legacy of Muḥammad and thereby prevented the new religion from reaching its full potential.

The final subject of this section, as with the preceding sections on the other religions, is prophecy. Bahá'ís see a close link between the Bahá'í Faith and many of the prophecies of Islám. Three of the most interesting Islámic prophecies in the Bahá'í view are as follows;

(i) "And there shall be a blast on the trumpet and all who are in the Heavens and all who are on the earth shall expire, save those whom God shall vouchsafe to live. Then shall there be another blast on it and low! arising they shall gaze around them: And the earth, shall shine with the light of her Lord, and the Book shall be set, and the prophets shall be brought up, and and the witnesses; and judgement shall be given between them with equity; and none shall be wronged: And every soul shall receive as it shall have wrought, for well knoweth He men's actions".[59]

(ii) "From the Heaven to the Earth He governeth all things: hereafter shall they come up to Him on a day whose length shall be a thousand of such years as ye reckon".[60]

(iii) "Verily in the year sixty, His cause shall be revealed and His name shall be noised abroad".[61]

The Bahá'í view is that the first quotation refers to the twin Revelations of the Bab and Bahá'u'lláh (the first and second trumpet blasts). Bahá'u'lláh (the Glory of God), a spiritual light, brought forth a new book (the Book of Laws: *Kitáb-i-Aqdas*) for the guidance of humanity. The second and third quotations refer to the timing of the coming of the new Revelation, one thousand years after the disappearance of the twelfth Imám (the last Interpreter of the word of Muhammad, Founder of the previous Dispensation) in 260A.H. (880 A.D.). One thousand years after the year 260 A.H. is 1260 A.H (1844 A.D.). The date is confirmed by the "short hand" statement of the sixth Imám: the year 60.

The Bahá'í Faith

Reference was made in the introduction to this article to the seasonal cycle of each Revelation of God. In the Bahá'í view the great religions of the past, including the most recent, Islám, have past the peak of their greatness and have gone into serious decline. Each one, to a greater or lesser degree, has lost its spiritual power and influence; each is divided within itself and in opposition to other religions; and each is dragged down by traditions, prejudices and superstitions which obscure the original glory of the teachings of their Founder, and cause conflict with science. As a result there is growing scepticism including even disbelief in the existence of God, and there is dispair in the air. It was in response to this situation and the universal need for a new Revelation from God that Bahá'u'lláh made his claim to be the Manifestation of God for this Age.

As observed in the last few sections, Bahá'u'lláh has claimed to be the One prophesied in all the other great religions, the return of Krishna in Hinduism, the fifth Buddha in Buddhism, the Shah Bahram in Zoroastrianism, the Lord of Hosts in Judaism, the Second Coming of Jesus in Christianity, the Spirit of God in Sunni Islám, and the return of the Imám Husayn or the Q'aim in Shia Islám.[62] Bahá'ís point out how remarkable is the fact that so many prophecies from all religions can be reasonably interpreted as referring to this day, a phenomenon which has been understood, at least in part, by others, quite unaware of the Bahá'í Faith, for example the Millerite movement in the United States, which in the the 1830s confidently predicted the return of Jesus Christ in about 1844, on the basis of prophecies. There were similar movements in Germany and in Shia Persia at the same time.

Like previous Manifestations, Bahá'u'lláh fulfills two purposes of God: to revive religion and the spiritual awareness of humanity, and to provide new principles and guidelines for living in the modern world. With regard to the latter purpose, Bahá'u'lláh's predominant theme is that man's next step in his spiritual evolution can only be achieved if man is united at the world level, and all his teachings are designed to help man fulfill this goal. The idea of the brotherhood of man under one God permeates the principles of the Faith with regard to attitudes and behaviour of the individual and the family. It is also basic to a new system of government, spiritual and democratic in form which is equally applicable at the local, national and world levels, and to principles for the equitable distribution of the world's resources for the benefit of all humanity.

In discussing Bahá'u'lláh's mission, Bahá'ís point out that it is only in modern times that the world has become one. Though the globe has been long since circumnavigated by pioneer sailors and explorers, it was not until the nineteenth century that regular

cheap and speedy communication between all parts
of the world became possible as a result of the fast
sailing ship, the railway engine, the steamship, the
telegraph and the telephone.

Not only is the world now effectively one society
for the first time in history, but also the major
problems which face humanity are world wide in their
scope, and they require solutions on a world scale. A
nuclear war between two nations would represent a
tremendous threat to the well being of every other
nation, and nations therefore cannot afford to be
disinterested in the disputes between other nations.
Damage to the natural environment as a result of rash
industrial and social policies by one nation will affect
many other countries. World trade is now so important
to the economy and social welfare of every nation that
any action by one nation to manipulate overseas trade
for short term parochial advantage will cause harm
to others. Fashions and ideas travel around the world
with great speed and the breakdown of respect for law,
for government, for the family, and slack views on
drugs and sexual promiscuity in one country soon
affect the social life of other countries. All this, Bahá'ís
will say, shows that a new religion for the whole of
humanity is now not only feasible for the first time in
history, but also absolutely essential.

The special importance of this day is conveyed by
the Bahá'í concept of universal spiritual cycles.
Bahá'u'lláh said that the Messengers of God have
appeared as part of the great universal spiritual
cycles, each of which has had a period of prophecy
and a period of fulfillment:

"Briefly, we say a universal cycle in the world of
existence signifies a long duration of time, and
innumerable and incalculable periods and epochs. In
such a cycle the Manifestations appear with splendour
in the realm of the visible, until a great and universal

Manifestation makes the world the centre of his radiance. His appearance causes the world to attain to maturity, and the extension of his cycle is very great. Afterwards other Manifestations will arise under his shadow, who according to the needs of the time will renew certain commandments relating to material questions and affairs while remaining under his shadow"

'Abdu'l-Bahá[63]

Past cycles have been lost in the mists of history. 'Abdu'l-Bahá explained that:

"... important events and great occurrences will take place which entirely efface every trace and record of the past; a new universal cycle begins in the world".[64]

In the present cycle, which began with Adam, the prophetic revelations have been completed and Bahá'u'lláh's revelation is that of fulfillment.

"We are in the cycle which began with Adam, and its universal Manifestation is Bahá'u'lláh"

'Abdu'l-Bahá[65]

Though Bahá'u'lláh's Revelation is the peak point in the universal cycle, Bahá'u'lláh's station as a Manifestation of God is not different from that of the other Founders of the great religions. Bahá'u'lláh prophecied that another Manifestation of God will appear in not less than one thousand years to continue the period of fulfillment which all told will last for some five hundred thousand years.

These may seem to be mighty claims for a religion which is as yet not well known. The Bahá'í response to such comment is that the Faith is young and might be compared with Christianity in say the first part of the second century A.D. It is believed that the tide of history is inexorably moving forward and that in a relatively short period the peoples of the world will come to understand that there is no alternative to the

Bahá'í Faith if civilization is to progress, indeed if it is to survive.

NOTES

1. *Advent of Divine Justice,* p. 31.
2. ibid, p. 46.
3. *Promulgation of Universal Peace,* p.346. It will be noted that this quotation refers to Confucius. Nevertheless, it is clear from the following quotation that in the Bahá'í view he was not a Messenger of God, but rather the founder of an ethical system and a great reformer: "Confucius was not a prophet. It is quite correct to say he is a founder of a moral system and a great reformer" *Letters from the Guardian to Australia and New Zealand,* 1923-1937, p. 41.
4. *Dawn of a New Day,* p. 198.
5. *God Passes By,* p. 95.
6. 4th Discourse, verses 7 & 8.
7. *Some Answered Questions,* p. 189.
8. *Udana,* pp. 80-81.
9. Gospel of Buddha, by P. Carus, p. 245.
10. There is a Zoroastrian tradition that he lived one thousand years earlier.
11. *World Order of Bahá'u'lláh,* pp. 101-102.
12. *Kitab-i-Iqan* (Book of Certitude), p. 154.
13. *Some Answered Questions,* p. 14.
14. *Bahá'í World Faith,* p. 358.
15. ibid, p. 13.
16. *Paris Talks,* pp. 54-56
17. ibid.
18. ibid.
19. *Bahá'í World Faith,* pp. 16-17.
20. *Promulgation of Universal Peace,* p. 409.
21. ibid, p. 369.
22. *Daniel,* Chapter 8, verses 13-14.
23. *Numbers,* Chapter 8, verse 34.
24. *Daniel,* Chapter 12, verses 6-7.
25. ibid, Chapter 8, verses 11-12.
26. *Jeremiah,* Chapter19, verse 18.
27. *Micah,* Chapter 7, verse 12.
28. *Ezekiel,* Chapter 42, verse2.
39. *Isaiah,* Chapter 35, verse 1-2.
30. ibid, Chapter 11, verses 1-10.
31. Jesus also said 'I am the Path' which at first seems to also

imply uniqueness. The Bahá'í view is that what Jesus meant was that he was the Messenger of God for that age and that all living at that time should follow him.

32. *Some Answered Questions,* pp. 129-130.
33. ibid, pp113-114.
34. *Some Answered Questions,* p. 137.
35. ibid, p. 45.
36. ibid, p. 45.
37. ibid, p. 124.
38. *The Promised Day is Come,* p. 113.
39. *St Matthew,* Chapter 24, verses 5, 14, 15, 27, 29 & 30.
40. *St Luke,* Chapter 21, verse 24.
41. *St John,* Chapter 15, verse 26; Chapter 16, verses 12, 13 & 25.
42. *Revelation of St John,* Chapter 11, verses 2 & 3.
43. ibid, Chapter 11,, verses 7 & 14.
44. ibid, Chapter 12, verses 1-2.
45. *US Bahá'í News,* October 1936, p. 1.
46. Most notably *Six Lessons in Islám,* by Marzieh Gail, Wilmette: Bahá'í Publishing Trust, 1957; *Islámic Contributions to Civilization,* by Stanwood Cobb, Washington D.C.:Avalon Press, 1963; and *Muhammad and the Course of Islám,* by H.M. Baluzi, Oxford: George Ronald, 1976.
47. *The Koran,* Everyman Paperback, 1971, introduction p. viii.
48. 4th Surih, verse 3.
49. 2nd Surih, verse 257.
50. *World Order of Bahá'u'lláh,* p. 106.
51. *Gleanings,* p. 101.
52. Advent of Divine Justice, p. 41.
53. Fatimah is revered by Bahá'ís as the most distinguished woman of the Islámic Dispensation.
54. *Six Lessons in Islám.*
55. Some sub groups of Shia Islám do not accept all twelve Imáms. The Ismailis (followers of the Aga Khan), for instance, only recognize seven.
56. *Dawnbreakers,* Introduction, p.11.
57. *Kitab-i-Iqan* (Book of Certitude), p. 119.
58. ibid p. 129.
59. 39th Surih, verses 67-71.
60. 32nd Surih, verse 4.
61. *Dawnbreakers,* p. 49.
62. Prophecies in several religions refer to twin Revelations. The other Messenger is named Ushioku Mah in Zoroastrianism, Elijah in Judaism, John the Baptist in Christianity, the Mahdi in Sunni Islám, and the Quaim in Shia Islám. Bahá'ís

believe these prophecies were fulfilled in the person of the Báb.

63. *Some Answered Questions,* p. 184.
64. ibid, p. 184.
65. ibid, p. 184.

INDEX

Y

Year of Patience (see Bahá'í
    Year of Patience)
Yugoslavia, 77, 223

Z

Zaire, 47
Zaqu'ilibm Thabit, 396
Zoroaster and Zoroastrian-
    ism, 8, 25, 84, 252,
    310, 364, 365, 368,
    370, 401, 405, 407